Origin of Christian

CHURCH ART

Earls Barton Tower, Northamptonshire.
See p. 234.

Origin of Christian
CHURCH ART

New Facts and Principles

of Research

BY

JOSEF STRZYGOWSKI

*Eight Lectures delivered for the Olaus-Petri
Foundation at Upsala, to which is added
a chapter on Christian Art in Britain*

TRANSLATED FROM THE GERMAN

BY

O. M. DALTON, M.A., AND H. J. BRAUNHOLTZ, M.A.

HACKER ART BOOKS
NEW YORK 1973

Originally published 1923
by Oxford University
at the Clarendon Press
Reissued 1973 by
Hacker Art Books
New York, New York 10019

Library of Congress Catalogue Card Number 72-95118
ISBN 0-87817-127-4

Printed in the United States of America

TO
MY FRIENDS
IN
OXFORD

PREFACE

THERE may be not a few who would care to know how the problem of the origin of Christian art (I purposely exclude sepulchral art from the discussion) presents itself to-day to an investigator with more than thirty years of unremitting labour in the East behind him. That no claim to finality can be made will be readily understood by all who reject easy movement along the ruts prepared by some chosen School, preferring to break their own way through obstacles to the truth. The aim of the present book is merely to summarize conclusions reached after the personal research and individual struggle of decades. Many gulfs are yet unbridged ; the gaps often seem broader than the firm ground, but it is worth while to survey the achievement as a whole, to bring isolated facts into their true relation to guiding ideas, and to point out the paths which the next generations will probably have to tread. Each of my eight chapters is concerned with such a path.

The first chapter establishes a new horizon extending from Europe, the Mediterranean and the ancient East, as far as Persia. The Iranian people, the second great source of Aryan energy, joined forces with the inhabitants of the North and the pastoral nomadic tribes to develop the 'mediaeval' spirit in Christian art, and in the South had already made it prevail before Northern Europe laid hand to the work.

The second chapter follows the successive changes in social order in the early stages of Christian art. It traces the development from Founder and primitive community to State and Church ; it shows the artist drawn into the service of autocracy ; and finally asks how much was now left for the initiative born of artistic freedom.

The third chapter seeks to show how in the fourth century East-Aryan Christianity advanced by way of Armenia, bringing with it the centralized domical plan. It further attempts to explain how during the same period the Semites of Mesopotamia introduced their long barrel-vaulted churches among the timber-roofed basilicas of the Mediterranean area.

The fourth chapter describes the ' styles ' which succeeded that of Early Christian art in the West : Romanesque, Gothic, Renaissance. It reviews in chronological sequence elements which we have already seen existing side by side in the fourth century. This is a theme which I shall expand in *Beiträge zur vergleichenden Kunstforschung* (Introduction to Part I).

The fifth chapter conveys a warning against the prevalent over-estimate of representational art. The non-representational art of Islam must have had a prototype in that of Mazdaism, the whole principle of which, as a creation of the North, was antagonistic to the Southern spirit, as I explain in my *Altai-Iran und Völkerwanderung*.

The sixth endeavours to prove that at the beginning, and even as late as the fourth century, Christian art was non-representational in the decoration of its churches. It shows how precipitate it is, on the mere evidence of the Sarcophagi and the mural paintings in the Catacombs, to pronounce Early Christian a branch of the classical stem. Only the supposition of an original non-representational system can render the later iconoclastic disturbances intelligible.

In the seventh chapter I try to explain the reasons for the outbreak against pictures. Semitic art, outbidding that of Greece, had begun to personify all things and sundry ; it transferred to the sphere of Christianity the spell-binding methods of representation which a pagan despotism had first devised. It was opposed by the ancient Aryan concept of the universe, which we may still see shedding the light of Northern magic in the South through landscape-mosaics which do not attempt to render nature.

In the eighth chapter I separate out the purely artistic results reached in the preceding sections, classify them, and point out the gaps which I detect. I endeavour to convince the reader that archaeology must give up its false methods, the philological and historical, based on texts or the chance survival of individual monuments, and the philosophical and aesthetic, which evades the facts of evolution. The history of art must work itself free from the mere comparative study of monuments ; it must concentrate upon the work of art and its values, absolute and evolutional, and so find a path of its own. Only then can it take its proper place among the sister sciences older than itself. I hope to pursue this subject further in my *System und Methode der Kunstforschung*.

I have throughout avoided questions of the day, whether political or religious. Names are rarely mentioned. I occupy myself rather with opinions expressed on new facts and principles which, as experience shows, will yet be contested for decades to come. This book marks a pause, it is retrospective ; the writer trusts that it may elicit the criticism of individuals or groups of scholars in general agreement with his line of thought, though not pursuing it from the artistic standpoint alone. But there will remain a few representatives of art-history with whom he can hardly hope ever to reach agreement.

Illustration has only been employed where it seemed really to further the general understanding of the subject. The book has been kept within limits by substituting for references in notes a bibliography at the end, including both my own works and those of my colleagues ; here the reader will find references in abundance alike to monuments and to texts. Both in bibliography and illustration a knowledge of the Western material and its literature is assumed ; but it is much to be desired that any prospective collaborators in research should begin by completely mastering the works mentioned on pp. 4, 5 and 6, above all *Altai-Iran und Völkerwanderung*, and *Die Baukunst der Armenier und Europa*. What happens when this is not done is only too clearly seen in certain ' reviews ' of the last-mentioned book.

The eight lectures forming the basis of these chapters were written in the country during the summer of 1918, and delivered in the University of Upsala, March 24 to April 7, 1919, with the accompaniment of lantern slides. The method of oral delivery, with its opportunities of enforcing the emphasis at the right points, was naturally of service to the writer ; it helped him to sift and order his leading ideas. He was consequently desirous of revising his work in accordance with the experience thus gained. But there were obstacles to such a course. Firstly, the Swedish translation was completed ; secondly, throughout the winter of 1918–19 the writer had been occupied almost exclusively with the significance of the North for the artistic development of Europe ; the new subject thrust the old aside, and the material of these lectures was already less vividly present to his mind. All that was possible was to insert in the two last chapters of this, the original German edition, a summary and survey written after the lectures at Upsala had been delivered.

JOSEF STRZYGOWSKI.

VIENNA.
October 1919.

TRANSLATORS' PREFACE

THE translators have not found it easy to produce a satisfactory rendering of *Ursprung der Christlichen Kirchenkunst.* The style of the original does not lend itself readily to an English version, and it has been almost impossible to find concise equivalents for some of the terms employed. A few short passages of purely ephemeral reference have been omitted ; otherwise the book remains substantially as it was written. The proofs have passed through the author's hands.

LONDON, 1923.

TABLE OF CONTENTS

LIST OF ILLUSTRATIONS

Origin of Christian
CHURCH ART

I

The New Horizon

ART translates inward meaning into visible form ; it uses the creative skill of man to free it from the limitations of life. Under its religious aspect it involves a compromise between the artist and the visible world, due to the yearning of the human soul for positive belief. Christian art receives its name from a Founder whose life was so intent on an invisible world that neither construction nor presentation of form had part or lot in it ; it sprang from the spiritual need, the love and the joy of young communities which grew up on all sides, in the North no less than in the South, to the East of the Holy Land no less than to the West of it. The several arts of these communities were so blended as to form a new religious style. To all those who reject the old superstition of a Roman art one and indivisible, the first four centuries present a spectacle of the utmost variety and independence ; forms and types developed side by side in complete freedom. Uniformity was impossible until communities merged into Churches and individual States brought Churches under a single organization, as happened first in Osrhoëne, next in Armenia, and later in Rome and Byzantium. Until the conversion of Rome, the Christian community in Persia, the second empire in the then world, maintained an independent existence.

It is clear from the above how necessary it has become for research to put Rome for the time being in the background. We are not really qualified to resume the study of Christian art at the old starting-point until we have made the round of all the countries important to the problem of its origin. Not till we have done this are we in a position to follow the clues which by good fortune the centuries have left in Rome, while in the East and in the North all traces have been swept away by the storms of barbaric invasion or by the hostility of other creeds.

It is unscientific to pick out any single source, whether it be found in a community, a Church, a State, or an artistic tendency,

and announce that it alone determined the origin of Christian art.
The early expansion of Christianity was no less rapid than that
of Mithraism, Manichaeanism, or of Islam. While the two
former spread towards the West, and the decisive development
of the third took place in the East, Christianity moved in both
directions, a fact which historians of art are not the only persons
to disregard. Christianity in the first years of its growth embraced
a vast territory inhabited by peoples widely differing in culture,
among whom those of the Mediterranean coast-lands formed
a minority, representing, intellectually, perhaps a third of the
whole. The other two-thirds were Semites and Iranians, both
Eastern peoples ; and it will be one object of the present book to
show how much these two achieved for the growth of Christian
art during the thousand years after Constantine. It must be
remembered that at first there was neither East nor West in the
modern sense ; the distinction began with Islam, and with the
subsequent division of the Christian Churches which left the
countries of the Orthodox Greek Church, as it were, stranded
between the Catholic West and the Orient. The resulting triple
partition of the world must not be confused with the threefold
division which formed my point of departure.

It is still a very general belief that at the beginning of
Christian art the decisive voice lay, if not with Rome, at least with
the Roman Empire, or with Hellenism. Those who so think
overlook the fact that the Roman frontiers ran only just on the
far side of Lebanon and Taurus, and that even before the dawn
of a Christian art Hellenism had begun to give way outside
these frontiers even more than within them. Alexander the
Great, uniting the Mediterranean countries with Persia, created
a great South-Aryan system extending as far as India. This
system was completely dissolved in the period between the first
and fourth centuries of our era through the spread of a strong
rival force which had grown up in the ' Semitic wedge ' dividing
the Eastern and Western branches of the Aryans in the South.
Iran and the Mediterranean, above all, Parthia and Rome, stood
once more confronted, like two irreconcilable worlds ; all
intervening territory, the very lands which had given birth to
Christianity, the lands not sovereign but subject, were imprisoned
between the home of Mazdaism upon one side and that of an
official Hellenism on the other. But what they lost in political
influence and power they recovered by the profession of Chris-

tianity : Syrians, Cappadocians, Armenians, with the populations of the adjoining Iranian territory to the East, and the Greeks on the West, together created in these first four centuries a Christian art of cardinal importance for the development of the Middle Ages and the succeeding period, down to the building of St. Peter's by Bramante and of the church of the Gesù by Vignola. The great Mediterranean cities, Rome at their head, may soon have created to their own satisfaction a so-called Christian art. But the lead was quickly taken by the peoples of Hither Asia, wedged, as we have seen, between Iran and the Roman Empire, whose artistic forms were instinct with vital force. These nations were in contact with Christianity at so early a date that in their case it was possible for Christianity to become a state religion as early as the third century : thus both Edessa and Armenia took this step earlier than Rome. This is a decisive fact not only in political but also in artistic history ; we must not suffer our attention to be diverted from it because prevalent academic opinion does not take it into account.

The earliest research in the field of Christian art discovered its origins in Rome. It is thus easy to understand how even as late as 1880 the recognized horizon hardly extended beyond Rome and Italy. This was about the period when the seniors of the present generation began their work. It was a time in which our teachers kept us puzzling by the month together over the origin of the basilica, and we lived trustfully in the belief that the catacombs—above all, of course, those of Rome— were the birthplace of Christian art. The effect of all this is still perceptible in the manuals, for example in Sybel's *Christliche Antike*. It is true that Russian scholars did draw attention to Constantinople, and Dobbert, a native of the Baltic states, represented the same view in Berlin, but on lines then described as iconographical, which allowed small scope to central artistic problems. The result was the creation of a vague borderland between Rome and Byzantium, not unlike that still conceived to exist between Roman and Western mediaeval art. All the initiative was awarded to Rome ; the only matter in dispute was whether the transformation was effected by the decay of Roman culture from within or by the victory of Germanic barbarism from without. Every one breathed a sigh of relief as soon as he contrived to escape from the Dark Ages to the green island of the Renaissance. Only there, on the firm ground laid by the humanists, did the historian of art feel himself really at home ; from there only could he steer the true artistic course. Antique art, Italian personality—only from the interactions of these two forces, so the dogma ran, could the new perfection spring to life. Vasari was the prophet ; Jacob Burckhardt's works on the Renaissance were the scriptures thrust into every student's hand.

It is clear that the horizon of about 1885 is still commonly accepted to-day. Wherever the history of art was changed from a field of free competition into a preserve of official bodies, an oath of allegiance had to be exacted. All the forces of mediaeval-ism have been exerted to secure the application of a strait jacket. If I now treat the origin of Christian art from a fresh standpoint, I do so in avowed antagonism to this stagnation of a faculty which had unique opportunities for using the comparative method to lift scholars over the pale of the usual classical education and teach them without prejudice to patriotism and without economic hazard the true position of their country in the world.

But this is not the place in which to criticize the official administration of art, or to oppose the prominence of those entrusted with the charge of public and private collections ; my subject is the present condition of research. Since 1885 the horizon has been so far extended that many now avoid this whole field of investigation from the belief that its very extent debars them from honest collaboration. We have therefore first of all to consider this enlargement of the field.

First there is the geographical expansion. It began with a migration from Rome to Byzantium ; we contemplated the growth of Christian art from a new point of vantage. But the surviving monuments of the new Imperial city are comparatively late, hardly a single one dating from before the fifth century ; what we seek above all are remains of Constantine's own time or that preceding it. So we advanced to the great cities of the East Mediterranean littoral, and first of all to those pre-eminent in the Hellenistic period, to Alexandria, Antioch, and Ephesus. But what remains to us of these cities ? In 1901 my book *Orient oder Rom* set them in the foreground ; Ainaloff published his *Hellenistic Foundations of Byzantine Art* about the same time, making Alexandria his point of departure. It was the pre-supposition of Wickhoff's *Imperial Art*, that Alexandria and the East only came into the front rank from the fourth and fifth centuries onwards. Kraus, inverting the procedure, gave Alexandria the lead in the earliest period and Rome only in the fourth century. As late as 1901 I was still drawing attention to Asia Minor and Syria, and above all to Jerusalem. In *Koptische Kunst*, my catalogue of the Cairo Museum, and in my book *Hellenistische und Koptische Kunst in Alexandria*, it was already recognized that in all save representational art Christian and Mohammedan Alexandria was only repaying what it had borrowed from the East long before. I began to go deeper with *Kleinasien, ein Neuland der Kunstgeschichte*, and with *Mschatta*. I showed the existence of an Early Christian vaulted architecture and of an eastern stream of influence in decorative art which even in the centuries before Constantine was penetrating westward by way of the triangle of North Mesopotamian cities, Amida, Edessa, and Nisibis. A number of independent essays followed, till in 1910 the volume *Amida* resumed the story of vault-construction, proved the origin of the barrel-vaulted church in Mesopotamia, and extended our knowledge of the decorations first revealed at Mshatta. Whoever wishes to understand the results attained and the extension of the geographical horizon has only to glance at the literature which now appeared : Diehl's *Manuel de l'art byzantin*, Dalton's *Byzantine Art and Archaeology*, Kaufmann's *Handbuch der christlichen Archäologie*, Toesca's *Storia dell' arte italiana* and Wulff's *Altchristliche und Byzantinische Kunst*. But all of these books still remained more or less at the stage of *Orient oder Rom*, or *Kleinasien, ein Neuland*. My later works were hardly at all discussed ; in Wulff's case, from the firm conviction that Early Christian art, as Ainaloff assumed, had its origin in Alexandria. My book *Amida* remains unnoticed ; from more than one side the attempt has been made to cripple its effect by depreciatory criticism.

But the catchwords ' Alexandria ', ' Hellenism,' ' Rome ', relate only to the western half of the regions concerned with the origin of Christian art. They do not include Edessa and Armenia ; they ignore Mesopotamia and Iran, the countries where Mazdaism was the religion of court and state on just the same footing as the cult of the Greek gods in the West. People get round the difficulty by including these countries among the Hellenistic, and then conveniently forgetting their existence. Ever since 1902 I have repeatedly called attention to the fact that Hellas died early in the embrace of the East. To-day my outlook is wider.

Our idea of the regions important for the origin of Christian art must undergo a drastic change. By the side of ' Rome ' and ' Hellenism ', the West and East of the ancient Graeco-Roman world, we have to introduce new territories, first Iran, the region beyond the Tigris ; next, the Euphrates Valley, the Semitic centre between Iran and the Mediterranean. We can no longer make shift with the loose phrase ' The East ', confining it, as is usually done to-day, to the east Mediterranean littoral, which means the great cities of Alexandria, Antioch, and Ephesus with the inland countries in their sphere of influence. This central region of growing Christian culture had two other regions on its flanks, one on the west with Rome as capital, one on the east (Persia) with Ctesiphon. We usually see nothing but Rome, or perhaps a little of the Greek religious battlefields in the Mediterranean area, much as we do when considering conditions within the Christian Church to-day. We wholly overlook the fact that before Rome adopted Christianity as her official religion, and before Byzantium confirmed the Greeks in their old pre-eminence in the East, there had taken place a peaceful expansion of Christ's teaching which found its main support in quite another quarter.

This was the line followed by the three books published since 1910, first *Amida*, then, in 1916, *Altai-Iran und Völkerwanderung*, and, in 1918, *Die Baukunst der Armenier und Europa*. Behind the coast-lands of the Mediterranean rises as the real originator, the compact empire of the Parthian and the Sassanian, where at the beginning of Christian art, Christian communities were more freely tolerated than in Rome. The development of events in this part of the world was fixed by definite geographical conditions.

As soon as Syria and Armenia, Anatolia, Mesopotamia and Southern Persia, and, finally Northern Iran, were united by the possession of common ideas, physical conditions themselves compelled the emergence of a new cultural centre. This actually happened in the Early Christian period. What the Mediterranean was to the Graeco-Roman world, that the triangle of cities, Edessa–Nisibis–Amida, became for the nationalities of inner Hither Asia : Constantine might have been well advised to found his second capital here instead of on the Golden Horn. The real Syria and Asia Minor turn from the coast and look to this centre ; a Hellenistic highway to India and China once traversed it, and when barred toward the East, carried Oriental influences back in the opposite direction. In Christian times the Hellenism of Persia and India was already driven into the background by the reactions which will be treated in their turn in the course of the present volume, yet it was an influence which can no more be neglected in considering the origin of Christian art than, for example, Celtic Christianity in the West. In the radiant focus of Edessa–Nisibis–Amida I see the second, the Aramaean centre, round which the Semites gathered, just as the Western Aryans of the South concentrated about the Mediterranean, or the Eastern Aryans in Iran and in the Christian outpost of Armenia. If North Mesopotamia had no political capital such as the other regions possessed (Osrhoëne with its chief city Edessa was swept away as swiftly as Palmyra), this was only because this frontier-land between Rome and Persia was too fiercely disputed, perhaps also because neither rival understood its full importance. This Semitic nucleus has a value differing in character from that of Armenia, which was disputed in like manner by the same powers. Both belonged more properly to Persia than to Rome, yet both abandoned in favour of Christianity the Mazdaism of Iran which the Sassanian princes exploited for imperial ends. Thus North Mesopotamia lost the political importance which was naturally its due, to become the centre of an Aramaic–Armenian–North-Iranian world united by the bond of Christianity against the Persian. These circumstances alone rendered possible the full conversion of Edessa and Armenia as early as the third century. Everything justifies the assumption that fixed types in church building were here developed before the fourth century, a time when in the Roman Empire Christianity was barely tolerated or had only just begun to make itself felt. The supersession of the Greek style of the Mediterranean by the vaulted architecture of the Syrian and Armenian area is only intelligible on the theory that this had already reached maturity.

I. *Geographical Influences*

We can see why these regions prevailed over the Mediterranean area in art if we cast a glance at the building materials of the countries now being christianized, and at the construction to which they led. While Hellenism and Rome were content with the timbered church, in the East geology and vegetation forced men to rely upon other materials and methods. These conditions introduced two important values afterwards not less highly prized in the West, one economic, the other religious.

Iran and Mesopotamia, the region comprised in Early Christian times under the term ' Persia ', built mainly in un-burned brick. This necessitated vaulted construction. Archae-ologists who study the ancient East assume, indeed, that the roofs of Mesopotamian palaces were always timbered. Whether they are right or wrong, it is certain that Armenia, from which the necessary timber was brought down the Euphrates and the Tigris, was deforested at an early date, and at the period with which we are concerned was itself compelled to adopt vaulting in all construction upon a large scale. In Mesopotamia, Babylonian and Assyrian methods survived as long as builders remained true to the passage-like hall for which the barrel-vault was the one possible roof. Here originated the barrel-vaulted church with transverse axis which formed one point of departure for vaulted construction in the West.

It was otherwise in Iran. There the dome was indigenous. In my book on Armenia I have endeavoured to show how this came about. It would seem that in Iran a decisive influence was exerted by East-Aryan prototypes in wood-construction, such as we can still trace in the Ukraine, in Kashmir, and in India. In these countries the builder roofed a square plan by corbelling with short beams. As soon as this style of construction entered countries without timber, like Iran and the Armenia of Christian times, this corbelling was executed perforce in unburned brick or in rubble-concrete. So began first the polygonal dome, then the regular dome, with the transition from the square to the circular plan by means of squinches. For the further develop-ment of the dome on pendentives, the reader is referred to my book on the architecture of Armenia. The decisive cause of the improvement was the early erection of the dome in Armenia on supporting arches in place of on the four walls. In course of time the barrel-vault and dome produced a transformation in the Hellenistic timber-roofed church, first in the Byzantine area, subsequently in the West, and this provided the key to the whole course of architectural development down to and including the Renaissance. It has seldom happened that any style of building of oriental origin and wide distribution in the East has failed to penetrate the West. There are, of course, exceptions, among which I may cite the remarkable broad-naved church of Eastern Syria formed by a series of rib-arches one behind the other, and roofed with stone slabs, a type perhaps adapted from the architecture of Arabia.

It was a positive misfortune for studies then in their infancy that the distinguished Marquis de Vogüé, in his exploration of the Christian East, should have chanced precisely upon Syria, a region in which Hellenistic influence became predominant despite the underlying Arab tradition in the local house building. From such a starting-point the generalization was sure to follow that this Greek predominance was universal in the East. It is easy to imagine how painful was the surprise to find a belief which had grown into a comfortable habit denounced for distorting the whole perspective in the development of Christian art. Instead of personally putting the matter to the test, some of my colleagues were content to approve the meaningless objections raised by doctrinaires. The predominance of Hellenism had become their axiom : they still stand to-day where I stood about 1901 ; Alexandria, Antioch, Byzantium are for them the sole creative centres.

But since then we have advanced to a more accurate understanding of the compromise reached by Greek and Semite ; we have followed the destinies of Hellenism in the East, and are to-day in a position to distinguish contributions made in the infancy of Christian art by the national architectural forms of Mesopotamia from those of Southern Arabia, Armenia, India, and Iran. Let me take one example, the vault. Greek architecture never admitted this form as a constructive feature on an extensive scale. It appeared on the contrary wherever timber was scarce and brick building imposed its own forms. Early examples are seldom preserved except where unburned brick had been superseded by the more durable burned brick or stone. People therefore jump to the conclusion that the Greeks were the first to transform vaulted construction from popular into monumental art, and that this construction began in stone. As a matter of fact it was brick vaulted construction which, in the field of Christian architecture, superseded the old Hellenic forms. It can be shown that vaulting had no firm foothold in the Mediterranean area in the infancy of Christianity but was an oriental importation abandoned as soon as connexions with the East were interrupted. This change occurred in the fourth century alike in Rome and in the great Hellenistic cities. In East Syria the Arab tradition preserved the rib-arch and stone roofing. But barrel-vaulted churches were only erected in numbers east of the Euphrates, and domed churches only east of the Tigris. These are the regions which appear to have influenced architectural development in Armenia and Cappadocia. Prehistoric vaulting I omit, as lying beyond our present scope.

Even more instructive is the history of the column and architrave, the pier and the arch, and of their relations to each other.

In East Syria you can still see how arch and column were brought into connexion ; how after the foundation of Constantinople capitals of antique type were modified in the quarries of Proconnesos on the Sea of Marmara to fit them for carrying the arch, and how they developed on the lines habitual to Oriental brick construction with its interior enrichment by decorative lining ; how the round arch was succeeded by other types, the horse shoe, the pointed, the oviform, to which diverse conditions had given rise in the East, and how various other changes took place to which reference will be made below.

II. *Historical Influences*

The history of art has followed the example of other history and of philology. Like these, it has hopelessly entangled itself in Latin Europe when treating of the West, and the Greek Mediterranean area when concerned with the East ; it has adopted a classification of periods in Christian art which those who view things from the standpoint of the great world-religions can only regard as erroneous and an obstacle to a right understanding of the facts. Western Europe is treated as already the centre of the world in Early Christian and Islamic times, a notion fostered both by Humanism and by the Church, and now bearing its rich crop of bitter fruit. The educated Celt, German, or Slav is still blind to the real state of affairs ; otherwise he could not but regard history from his proper standpoint as a man of the North, and classify its periods accordingly ; he could not but abandon the traditional southern classification into Antiquity, Middle Ages, and Modern Times. If I am to classify as a student of art, then the only division I shall make will be between the time when the East triumphed over Hellas, and rose to predominant place, and the time when the West attempted to win its independence.

On these lines, the transitional period begins when Semitic influence transformed Hellenic into Hellenistic culture ; Iran and the North completed this movement by their orientation towards a mediaeval culture. Christianity was the climax of this penetration. The lead no longer lay with the Hellene, but with the Semite and Eastern Aryan ; in formative art it lay with vaulted construction and a decorative system opposed to that of the Greeks. Those who are obsessed by the classical tradition of the schools dismiss as a dilettante anyone who holds these views ; they apply to him trite old phrases of St. Nilus : his ideas are those of a babe and suckling. To-day Europe is in just such a state of transition as that which prevailed when the Semitic and West Aryan elements of the new Christian world first stood on their defence against Northern and East Aryan culture ; now as then we see an instinctive resistance to a contrary force which is not understood. It is the attitude of the Italians to northern or ' Gothic ' art, which the North in its innocence proceeded afterwards to ape. In their youth both Winckelmann and Goethe gave free course to their northern blood ; their later tincture of cosmopolitanism came to them only after they had learned to know the South.

From this point of view I can regard Christian art as only one of the attempts to create a new spiritual unity by the contact of the three Aryan worlds, Western, Eastern and Northern, with Semitism. This unity, so long as it remained independent of Church and State, or at any rate was not involved in their attempts after material conquest, gave a powerful stimulus to artistic imagination through the compromise which it effected between man and the world.

In so far, reflection on the origin of Christian art may gradually inspire new and impressive lines of research. It is in the power of formative art to bring into so clear a light this active influence of the Aryan North and East upon the overripe Southern world that a reaction upon other fields of knowledge may reasonably be expected. It is in its power above all to show how it required ages of war between North and South, East and West, to bring into being against ' antiquity ', Semitic and Greek, the culture which we half contemptuously call mediaeval. And that war is far from ended to-day.

We have to think not of any chronological division in the ordinary sense, but only of a transition by which, after its surrender to the Semites in the age following Alexander, Hellenism, the fine flower of antiquity, entered a mediaeval phase, through contact with Iranian (East Aryan) culture. It will be shown that this took place about the time of the birth of Christ. The mediaeval phase will last until the North succeeds in overcoming the Semitic-Roman conception of Church and State. It is for all of us to consider how much progress has been accomplished in this direction, and whether there is a prospect that the purely northern view will prevail.

After the great migrations and the forward movement of the East, there was a time when the North was actually in a fair way to impress its genius upon the life of Europe ; this was the time when the cities of the West reached the supreme point of northern expression in their ' Gothic ' art. But Rome made an end of Gothic. She used the interest of the Italians in their ancient history as a screen for her ambitions ; by unearthing old Semitic and Graeco-Roman traditions she succeeded once more in paralysing the North by driving it into the arms first of humanism, next of the Counter Reformation, and finally of absolute monarchy. Art ceased to touch the life of the peoples ; even to-day we hardly know what it may really mean to man.

It is characteristic that the two groups of persons who seek to elucidate the beginnings of Christian art, the classical archaeologists and the newer historians of art, should be unable to agree among themselves. It has been rightly said that the first group views things from the point of view of Antiquity, the second from that of the Middle Ages, so that the interest of the one centres rather in the decadence of antique forms, that of the other in the origin of modern ones. The result can only be a one-sided outlook for both, quite apart from the fact that neither can obtain any insight into the regions of real significance for our purpose, regions historically, geographically, and culturally distinct, but generally mislabelled by inclusion under that vague term ' the East '. Thus much we have already learned by our consideration of the historical and regional factors ; our inquiry into the decisive cultural factor will carry the matter yet further. A survey of this third element will shed additional light on the adjustments between North and South, East and West, in the province of early Christian church art.

III. *Social Conditions*

With the extension of the horizon in space went another extension, little noticed, and due to the conviction that the origin of Christian art can never be understood without a knowledge of East Aryan and Northern social conditions. The beginnings of Islam, which was really a great migration from the South, and the Germanic descent from the North have always suggested this line of research, which I sought to inaugurate in *Mschatta* and *Amida*. It soon appeared that the two movements were not disconnected. In other books—*Die bildende Kunst des Ostens* (1916) and *Altai-Iran und Völkerwanderung* (1917)—I tried to prove the possibility of the connexion. If it is still the general belief that all this has nothing to do with the origin of Christian art, it will be the business of the present book to bring about a change of opinion, but the full development of this question will be found in another work, *Die Baukunst der Armenier und Europa* (1918).

Let us begin by a glance at the attempt, first made some ten years since, to contract the horizon by introducing the idea of a Christian classical art. The aim here was to represent the Christian movement as solely dependent upon the Graeco-Roman element. A somewhat wider connotation than usual was given to the term classical by the pretence of including in its sphere those Semitic lands within the borders of which the Aryan culture of Hellas ripened. But as a matter of fact the inclusion was ignored. The idea of a Christian classicism as a decisive factor in Early Christian art had its birth among the classical philologists. The theory followed upon the generalization of results obtained from investigating the Hellenistic sources of Christian art ; it confined itself almost exclusively to what is called representation, the objective rendering of things seen, especially human beings, in their recognized natural forms. We are told that the Hellenism of Alexandria, Antioch, and Asia Minor advanced to Rome, where it is accessible to us in the surviving monuments of sepulchral art. Greek art in its last decline assumed a Christian dress. Everything beyond sepulchral art, first and foremost church architecture, the most decisive factor of all, is more or less ignored because it happens not to be Greek in origin ; there is only one exception to the ban, that purely practical building, the wooden-roofed Hellenistic basilica, though in its decoration even this is only

Hellenistic in so far as its columns were collected from older structures, which thus served the builders as quarries, as they later served the architects of the Mohammedan mosques. The vaulted church of the East, however little the West was able to follow it in construction, set a new fashion in decoration by the example of its rich linings ; this fashion prevailed even in the case of the basilica, despite the representational style of the art reserved for its walls. But the theory of classical Christian art is guilty of yet further oversights.

The Aramaic mind, from its centres in Edessa and Nisibis, set to work to provide a Bible-illustration which even the illiterate and those ignorant of the liturgical language could understand. Christian art itself has essentially as little to do with this picture-writing as with Christian classicism. Artistic quality does not consist in such representation, but in the nature of the spiritual content, and in the forms designed to transcend objectivity, supposing the artist himself to have been moved by any such aim. Thus in place of Christian classicism we get Christian Semitism. Such an idea as Christian classic art could never have entered the mind of the true student of ancient art ; it could only have suggested itself to the classical archaeologist. The true student would have discovered that Hellenic art ceased the moment artists began to abandon the symbolic manner, first by exaggerating truth to Nature, then by doing the exact opposite, 'representing' without Nature, and constructing by means of the vault. The art-student could therefore never have brought down the limit of classical art so late as the time of Justinian ; he would be more likely to fix it at the time of Alexander, and then assume a transitional period, in which observation of Nature was first accentuated in the Semitic fashion, then died out in a counter-movement, while all the time there were coming into the foreground structural forms alien to Greek tradition but eloquent of the growing influence of Iran. The change gradually deprived the Greek temple of its commanding position ; it lived on indeed, even to our own day, with its façade and its orders, but only as a survival. The real sequence of events is as follows. In the period after Alexander and about the time of the birth of Christ we mark the beginning of a new age even in Rome, an age which at first relapsed into the ways of the old Semitic East, then gradually found its true course in that artistic sense of the Northern peoples and the pastoral nomads which drew its inspiration from

Iran. Christianity was able, it is true, to muster in its defence a last rearguard of Hellenism. But Islam surrendered wholly to the new influence, for though it found its most perfect expression in the cities, its expansion was by way of the deserts ; pastoral nomads carried it across the world. We could never have failed to understand this truth had we not suffered an exclusive devotion to classical studies to narrow our minds, had we not pored ourselves half blind over books, losing sight of the events which disturbed the system of the Hellenistic and Roman World-Empires and replaced their policy by the new aspirations of Christianity and of Islam.

At the time of the Arab conquests Hellenism itself was classical no longer. Nevertheless the Iranian spirit rose against it in unconditional opposition. Borne by the migrant peoples of the North and East, this spirit began by overthrowing Rome, then allied itself in Constantinople, as previously in Edessa, Armenia, and Jerusalem, with the Semitic element in Christian art, and finally achieved its full development in Islam. The new art which, after its entry into the West, we describe as mediaeval, was first developed in the period between Alexander and Mohammed. Its only connexion with classical art was through a subsidiary branch preserved by chance in the Catacombs ; in reality it wrestled with Hellenism and gave it a fall, triumphantly establishing the Iranian element in architecture and decoration, and in representational art the new Semitic methods. Hellenism could only be kept alive by the efforts of learned reaction. It says little for European originality that in the sixteenth century classical art should have won a new lease of life with the Counter-Reformation and the art of the contemporary Courts, and that to-day it should still preponderate in the education of our youth. . . .

The above review of the condition of research, based on a consideration of regional, historical, and cultural influences, brings us to the following general conclusions. Hitherto the study of Christian art has been almost exclusively in the hands of archaeologists. Of these, one group, the specifically Christian, made the Catacombs its starting-point for centuries. Its members believed that they could solve the problem of origin by the help of the oldest Roman monuments, the underground mural paintings, the sarcophagi, and the timber-roofed basilicas. In recent years a second group, that of the classical archaeologists, has turned its attention to Christian monuments, just as classical philologists have directed theirs to patristic literature. This was the group which invented the phrase ' Christian classical art ', the watch-word of its studies, a phrase which reveals perhaps more clearly than anything else the one-sided character of such research, despite all efforts to assert the contrary. A third group, not far removed from the last, attaches significance to Byzantine Hellen-ism, and thinks to have discovered in this the creative spirit and guiding principle of development.

For the specialist who applies the comparative method in the artistic field Christianity rises against a background formed by the art of other faiths; it is the last religion established by a personal Founder before Islam, beginning, like that faith, in a frontier-region between the two Great Powers, Rome and Persia. He therefore considers the appearance of Christian art not only in connexion with Hellas and Rome, but equally in connexion with the older great religions of the world, Mazdaism and Buddhism, and with the younger religion of Mohammed. The archaeologists base their development of Christian art upon readings of texts coloured to suit their views and upon monuments surviving in the Mediterranean area. The specialist is convinced by his method of wide survey and comparison that this procedure leaves the origin of Christian art dependent on passages in books or the existence of single monuments, and further that it makes Graeco-Roman bulk so broadly as to hide beyond recognition all trace of other influence under the rank growths of an antiquated humanism.

IV. *Christianity in Persia*

This false interpretation of events involves an issue of decisive importance. Christian and classical archaeologists like to believe that the teaching of Christ spread only to Carthage, Alexandria, Antioch, and Asia Minor, and, both by sea and land, to Rome and Gaul; they overlook the fact that it spread just as rapidly towards the East. In the Acts of the Apostles, written in the second century, there is a list of peoples of surprising comprehensiveness which has much to tell us on this point. Among the crowd of Jews who streamed to Jerusalem to carry the new doctrine out into all the world we read of Parthians, Medes, Elamites, dwellers in Mesopotamia, Judaea, Cappadocia, Phrygia and Pamphylia, Egypt and Libya about Cyrene—and

Romans settled in these parts. The Romans close the list; the Persians head it: are they really as negligible a factor in the spread of the new teaching and in the origin of Christian art as the accepted theory takes for granted?

At the beginning of the Christian era Mazdaism dominated the religious belief of the East in just the same way as Hellenism dominated that of the West. The manner in which the cult of Mithras spread throughout the Roman Empire and that of Anahita over the whole of Hither Asia proved that it must be reckoned among the world-religions. Armenia was Mazdean; in Persia proper the doctrine of Zarathustra was exploited for political ends after the Semitic fashion by the Sassanian dynasty, which made it the State religion to prove their national monarchy established by the grace of God. Are we to suppose the immense religious force of the Zend Avesta, exerting through Persia and Armenia so widespread an influence towards the West, a negligible factor in comparison with Hellenism at the birth of Christian art? Opponents will meet this question with another: where is the evidence for a Mazdean art? I will refrain from citing the Persian rock-reliefs, where Ahuramazda is represented either mounted or on foot. Another question is really of more significance: is it so certain as is commonly supposed that Mazdaism had no widely distributed and popular art?

The idea that a whole religion can have renounced art is inadmissible, and the facts are against it. The aims of religion and art are too alike for the one to dispense with the other; both seek to establish and to reveal an invisible inward world of human hope beside the actual and visible world around them. I say nothing of prehistoric beliefs, or those of existing primitive peoples, though these too seem hardly ever able to dispense with symbols which may be regarded as the beginnings of formative art. In this book I am dealing only with the two main types of historical religion: that which emerged from dim beginnings in the forcing-houses of southern culture, and that revealed by personal founders, issuing more or less from the beliefs of northern peoples and pastoral nomads, and wholly or in part displacing the first. To say nothing of Moses, it is no mere chance that Buddha and Zarathustra, both Aryans, stand at the head of the list.

Works of formative art are among the most important sources of evidence for all religions. The Egyptian spirit is essentially opposed to the Hellenic, but both achieve their highest in their works of art ; every one knows what the monuments left by Asoka did for the expansion of Buddhism, and what those left by Constantine did for that of Christianity. Not long ago we learned for the first time from the funeral monuments of the Han period the nature of the state worship established by Confucius ; in the ' philosopher landscapes ' of the Sung period the critic detects the influence of Taoism, perhaps also the trace of Indian thought. The art of all these cults represents ; and we are so used to finding their religious ideas in their artistic creations that Islam, the only familiar world-religion which does not represent, is left out of the account, as something abnormal in the religious sphere and to be neglected with impunity.

In my book *Altai-Iran und Völkerwanderung* I attempted to show that in the perfected style of Islam there still survives that non-representational northern and nomadic art known to us through the work of prehistoric times and that of the later Teutonic and Turkish tribes. In the period of the great migrations, both these races advanced towards the ancient forcing-houses of culture, just as the Greeks, Celts, Persians, and Indians had done in pre-Christian times. Originally none of these peoples represented ; they first learned this mode of artistic expression in the South. The student of art is inclined to think that the contrast between North and South may be explained by the transition to a higher stage of culture. In the South, man passed immediately from the culture of the earlier Stone Age into a social system which sought to cast a spell upon the object by representation, as the primitive hunter attempted to do when he made pictures of his game. In the North, on the other hand, formative art developed out of the handicraft of the later Stone Age. It enclosed space in borders and filled it with ornament which for the most part followed from the nature of the material and the process adopted, ornament which was therefore geometrically designed for the purpose of pleasing the eye.

Judging from the ornament of Ostrogothic and Lombard metal work and sculpture in Italy, from Irish illumination and from northern antiquities generally, but above all from the oldest Scandinavian wooden churches, the student of art cannot but infer that the North hardly knew Christian ' representation ' at all. For the moment we may leave in the background its pre-Christian art, of which the roots are to be found in Celtic and Germanic religion.

To this northern group, or to that of the pastoral nomads, belongs Mazdaism, the only world-religion born in the sixth century before Christ on the confines of the North, but destroyed by the united advance of southern religions, Buddhism, Christianity, and Islam. Like these, it owed its origin to a personal founder ; its scriptures, burned by Alexander, but later collected in the Zend Avesta, were in use among the Iranian peoples for more than a thousand years. Neither the Indian sacred books nor the Bible could make head against them ; the Koran alone succeeded in displacing the Avesta after the Persian religious spirit, represented by the cult of Mithras and by Manichaeism, had proved itself a dangerous rival to Christianity even in the West. It is strange, but no one seems to have reflected that like all other religions, and especially those originating in the South, Mazdaism must have had an art. The circumstance that none of its monuments have been preserved or discovered, at any rate in wide distribution, no more proves that such an art did not exist than the similar lack of documentary evidence. A little while ago, whoever dreamed of the monuments of all kinds recently discovered in Chinese Turkestan ? Yet there they are, and in such overwhelming abundance as to make it incredible that we should have remained so long without the faintest idea that so brilliant an art existed. For this ignorance we have to thank the perverse method of our research, which only accepts as worth notice, or admissible for scientific work, what we can see embodied in surviving monuments. Since Winckelmann's day, everything possible has been done to rediscover the antique ; but in the meanwhile the other gaps in our knowledge have been ignored. Such a gap, and a wide one, hides from us the creative activity of Iranian Mazdaism in the first period of Christian art. I have therefore made it my special task to investigate it and to ask the following question : has Christian art really no constituent features allowing us to pre-suppose the existence of a Mazdean art ? The argument by presupposition will be found running like a red thread through the following chapters.

While still fresh from the impression of a new world opened to us, let us now consider a pronouncement like the following : ' Classical antiquity finishes its course in Christian art, and ' accomplishes its destiny. As far as painting and sculpture are ' concerned, the art of the imperial age, including the Christian,

' moves on a descending line ; there is no suggestion of new
' development ; we find no well-spring of youthful energy, nothing
' but the decay of hoary age. Beauty survives only in the earliest
' productions of the period. For the rest, the significance of all
' this work is not to be sought in its aesthetic quality, but only
' in its subject matter, in the origin of a Christian iconography
' and in its value as a key to early Christian thought. Yet in
' architecture, antiquity, and precisely Christian antiquity, was
' creative during the later imperial period ; it must be admitted
' that here it was still able to celebrate a final triumph.' Such
monstrous perversions of fact—I speak from the point of view of
the student of art—can only come from scholars buried in the
dust of antique learning. For what are the facts ? Long before
Alexander there were great national states in ' the East ', in
Egypt and in Mesopotamia. These gradually lost their national
character, and Egypt was eliminated as a creative force. Not so
Asia. The classical archaeologist fails to see that what made
Greece great, her Aryan quality, was first felt in its full vigour
at the birth of the two new world-religions, Christianity and
Islam, and not in the Semitic area, but beyond it in Iran (I leave
India for the moment out of the discussion). With these religions
it matured its powers, with these it flourished, and by their help
ended by achieving the artistic conquest of East and West alike.

The problem to-day no longer concerns the rival claims of
Rome and the East ; it concerns the Aryan spirit in East and West,
its assimilation of religions which had grown up on Semitic
ground, its flowering through their formative art. Just as
Christianity took final shape among the western Aryans, so did
Islam among the Aryans of the East. The subject of the present
book is limited to the period between Christ and Mohammed.
But in this period Christian art itself was penetrated by the
East-Aryan spirit ; its whole development towards its approaching
ascendancy in Europe is only intelligible if we grasp this hitherto
neglected fact. Early Christian art was only antique, that is, Greek
and Semitic, in those features which crippled its development, in
the timber-roofed basilica, and in the monotonous objectivity
of its representation. Architecture and its decoration, which gave
art life and growth for more than a thousand years, which formed
the germ of its development, was entirely in the hands of the
East ; those northern Aryans who had come into contact with
the South understood the Oriental forms, adopted them, and

perfected them in freedom from the oppressive influence of Semitic monarchism. These are the true facts about the development of Christian art : in the light which they throw, let any man decide whether the creative force rose from the well-springs of youth or from the places of senile decay. What Hellas was to the art of antiquity, that Iran was to the art of the new Christian world and to that of Islam. So at a later time the northern spirit informed the art which we call Gothic.

It must be remarked of the history of research in the field of Christian art, that those who pursue it, whether they reject or approve, have always kept within the limits which I have progressively defined ; in following the plan of my life's work, they have never advanced beyond me and so proved their comprehension of my task as a whole. They have been drawn on step by step, first by my work on Constantinople, then by that on Egypt, Asia Minor, and Syria. At the present moment we are crossing swords over Mesopotamia ; to-morrow it will be over Armenia, the day after to-morrow, over Iran. Each time they will begin by resistance and proceed by invading my claim and trying to drive me out. The day may come, I may yet live to see it, when they will envisage my course as a whole and at last begin to join their forces with mine instead of blocking my path. Speaking generally, we have at present advanced no farther than agreement as to the significance of the Hellenistic cities on the east shores of the Mediterranean ; first Alexandria, then Antioch and Constantinople with their closer relations to Asia Minor ; in short they accept my point of view down to the publication of *Kleinasien* in 1904. On the other hand they still reject the high antiquity of vaulted construction in inner Asia Minor and Mesopotamia, ascribe the initiative here also to Antioch, and even give Alexandria the credit for features of a pronounced Iranian character ; they therefore question the existence of any vaulted buildings before the seventh century, and explain them by hypothetical later reconstruction. I trust that the time has now arrived when instead of contenting themselves with manuals uncertain of their ground, people will rather listen to the specialist who has given thirty-five years of his life to the problems of development in this field of research. The bibliography at the end of this volume may incite my readers to adopt this course.

The church-building of Christian Persia had two distinct characteristics : it employed the vault from the very beginning ;

it decorated walls with linings. The vaulting may be either domical or of the barrel variety. Both kinds seem to have existed independently when Christian church-building began, but not to have been used together until the Church in the Mediterranean area demanded a building with a longitudinal axis. I am disposed to ascribe the origin of the barrel vault more especially to Persian Mesopotamia, that of the dome to Iran. The distribution of vaulted churches supports this view, a matter to which I will return later.

What vaulting is to structure, that the lining of the vaults and walls is to pictorial art. Properly speaking Iran knew nothing of the graphic arts in the narrower sense, since it did not represent, but confined itself to pure decoration. The Iranian style is thus at once and fundamentally distinguished from that of ancient Mesopotamia, which covered walls with representation. We all know the wonderful naturalistic reliefs in alabaster from Nineveh now in London, and the bodyguards in glazed earthenware from Susa in the Louvre. But in addition to such representations of natural forms, Mesopotamia had splendid ceilings with repeat-patterns enclosed in borders. Was this also purely Semitic? If in Mesopotamia we find representation and purely decorative ornament side by side, we must insist upon the fact that originally the ornament occurred alone in north-eastern Iran, and marks a stream of influence wholly Aryan. Even the Greeks when they migrated into Hellas, and before they came into closer touch with southern art, had, it would appear, only a geometrical and non-representational art of this nature.

It has been generally deduced from the study of Islamic art that its manifold designs and patterns were accumulated by voluntary contributions from all parts of the Hellenistic world and attest the penetration of monumental art by the various industrial crafts. Those who offer such an explanation reveal a profound ignorance of Iran. It may be said in their excuse that in their treatment of Persian art they set out from the monumental art of the Achaemenian and Sassanian South, where first the Semitic element, and afterwards the Hellenistic, drove back and overgrew the Aryan. But after all it is still quite possible to infer the nature of this Aryan element from buildings in which various kinds of wall-covering have been reproduced in stone, and the evidence of their existence thus preserved. Such monuments are Mshatta, part of the façade of the great mosque at

Diarbekr, and the Stûpa at Sarnath in India. It is true enough that Iran itself has so far yielded very slight traces of the pre-Mohammedan period ; but this is explained by the fact that the building material was unburned brick. When this fell into ruin, the lining of the walls fell with it. We have also to remember that systematic excavation with an eye to this kind of discovery has yet to be undertaken. When our Austrian expedition wished to excavate at Naishapur, the Franco-Persian agreement was put in force to stop our work. But the excavations at Samarra have confirmed the theory which I first conceived in Egypt and later developed in my books *Mschatta* and *Amida* ; that the moving force in the art of Islam came immediately from northern Mesopotamia but ultimately from the more distant centres of Iran.

V. *The Asiatic East*

In conclusion I will add a few words on the historical expansion of Christianity towards the East, first into the Persian Empire, then beyond it into India and China. In the West the new faith had only stopped with Ireland and the Atlantic. Its expansion in the East was just as wide : Chinese Turkestan is about as far as Ireland from the Holy Land. Here the exploration of the last two decades has yielded fifth-century fragments of a Psalter in Pehlevi, and of another Psalter in a Syro-Persian dialect, while Sogdian MSS. afford a glimpse of early liturgy. This variety of races thus represented among Christians in these remote regions may perhaps serve to explain why it was that Christianity was never politically as creative as Indian Buddhism, or the immigrant Manichaeism which entered Central Asia by the same Persian route. In the eighth century, indeed, the Nestorians did very nearly bring about a change in this state of affairs. In China a decree of A.D. 638 proclaims their arrival with sacred books and pictures, and the erection of a church in the capital Si-ngan-fu which in the eleventh century was known to the Chinese as a ' foreign Persian temple '. The priests came ' from the gold-bearing districts ', perhaps Tokharestan and Bactria, of which the capital, Balkh, was then a great centre of Nestorianism. The emperor Kao-Tsung (A.D. 651–84) caused Christian churches to be erected in all the ten provinces of China : some of these were restored in wood and stone by Hüan-Tsung (A.D. 713–56), who also caused services to be held in the Hing-King palace.

Su-tsung (A.D. 756–63) built churches in Ling-wu and four other places ; Tshi, a priest from Raja Griha in India, who had risen to high office at Court, once more restored the old churches, added to their number, and gave them so rich a decoration ' that they resembled the plumage of the pheasant in his flight '. In his time (A.D. 781) was erected the *stele* in the capital, in the inscriptions on which all these facts are recorded in Syriac and Chinese : ' Great palaces of light and unity (churches) covered the length ' and breadth of the Middle Kingdom.'

This East-Iranian Christianity entering China through the country beyond the Oxus and through Turkestan, and found flourishing there in the seventh century, started from the district of Edessa and Nisibis on the middle course of the Tigris between Diarbekr and Mosul. We learn much of this Parthian region from the *Acta* of St. Thomas. The above Chinese description, 'a foreign Persian temple,' has already given us a clue to the style of the churches. More precise is a remarkable passage in the Bar Saba legend of Merv.[1] Here the first church in that place is said to have been built on the plan of the Parthian palace at Ctesiphon, traces of which would thus appear to have been still visible in the Middle Ages. It may be assumed that the Parthian palace type is represented by the two surviving examples of Firūz Abād and Sarvistan in the province of Persis, where the central part of the building consists of one or more square halls covered by domes. We shall find the earliest churches in Armenia immediately connected with halls of this type ; for the moment, however, we are only concerned with the antiquity of church buildings in Iran.

Along the east bank of the Tigris extended a province of which the early Christianization and the art are so well attested by historical evidence that its neglect by workers in our field is a matter for some surprise : this district was known as Adiabene, with its capital at Arbela. The most important document for the early Christianity of this region is the *Chronicle of Arbela*.[2] The writer is Mesihazekha, a pupil at Nisibena in the middle of the sixth century when Abraham (A.D. 509–69) presided over this school of Eastern Christianity. His chief source was the teacher Abel, important to the historian of art as one of the witnesses to Christianity in the Parthian period, that is, before A.D. 226. Which

---

[1] Communicated by E. Sachau. [2] Edited by E. Sachau.

of us ever expected to learn of a church architecture flourishing beyond the Euphrates and the Tigris as early as the second century of our era ? My own researches in Armenia had indeed already forced me to this conclusion, but the *Chronicle of Arbela* brought direct proof. Abel the teacher, living about A.D. 200, may well have derived information from the episcopal archives of Arbela ; other facts he doubtless obtained from local tradition. There were churches in the place the builders of which must still have been remembered. The church of Isaac standing ' to this day ', that is to say the time of Mesihazekha, was built by Isaac, third bishop of the city (A.D. 123–36), and restored by Abbusta the eighteenth bishop (A.D. 450–99). We have no exact knowledge of its type ; the church was large and well proportioned ; when it was restored, it was enriched ' with all possible embellishment'. In memory of Noah, fifth bishop (*c.* A.D. 166–71), a second church, known as the small church, was erected ; ' its site was still known,' though by the middle of the sixth century it was itself no longer in existence. Its builder was perhaps the teacher Abel, if this personage is to be identified with Abel the sixth bishop (A.D. 171–*c.* A.D. 200) ; and within its walls the ninth bishop, Sahlupha (A.D. 235–41) was interred.

Facts like these give us some idea of the strength and wide distribution of Christianity in Persia, both Iran proper and Mesopotamia, enabling it to exert an influence far into Eastern Asia beyond the intervening region of the Altai. Nestorianism, which we found at work in China, was of relatively late appearance; it began with the opposition of the Aramaic populations between the Euphrates and the Tigris to the decisions of the Council of Ephesus in A.D. 431. Even before this, in A.D. 410, an episcopal constitution had been framed in Mesopotamia with the Catholics of Seleucia at its head, of which the sphere of operation extended beyond Media and Parthia into the regions whence the first priests entered China.

Christianity was transplanted into Southern Iran from Antioch by an exercise of arbitrary power. The eleventh-century Chronicle of Sööct, with which Graeco-Roman sources are in essential agreement, records that after his conquest of Nisibis and Antioch in A.D. 256 and 260, Shapur transported prisoners to Babylon, Susiana, and Persis, where he gave them lands and houses. In consequence, Christians became numerous in the Persian monarchy, and monasteries and churches were

erected. In later sections of this book we shall have to notice
the traces left by this Antiochene movement as it ebbed back
from the south of the Sassanian territory.

It was from the upper course of the Euphrates and Tigris
that the influence came which sought to dominate the National
Church of Armenia in the fifth century. In that country the
ruling Arsacid dynasty had established, about A.D. 300, a State
Church which was architecturally dependent on East Iran, and
derived its objection to representational art from the Mazdaism
hitherto prevalent in the land. When the Armenians invented
an alphabet of their own and set about the creation of an ecclesiastical literature by translating Syrian and Greek books, close
relations began between Armenian theologians and those of
Nisibis and Constantinople. The effects of this are marked in
the province of church architecture by the efforts of the Armenian
bishops to replace the national type of church, with central dome
and radiating limbs, by the barrel-vaulted church with long nave,
and to substitute North Mesopotamian or Greek wall-paintings
for the old non-representational style of decoration. Only the
abandonment of Chalcedonism [1] gave their opportunity to the
opponents of these innovations, who were not only strong in
popular support, but were also represented, if somewhat uncer-
tainly, in the Armenian Church itself. For though the Parthian
Arsacids died out, driven from the throne in A.D. 428, the
architects of the Nacharars were still able to impose the long nave
on the national form of church (see below, p. 68). In Armenia,
at least, we clearly mark the triumph of the national style of the
fourth century over the ecclesiastical influences of the fifth, after
a struggle lasting for at least a century. A similar observation
may be made in the case of East Syria ; there too the national
Arabian mode of building was pressed back in the fifth century,
only to be more strongly reasserted at a later time. But in Syria
Christian architecture came to an end as early as the beginning
of the seventh century with the crippling of the Byzantine
Empire, and was finally displaced by that of Islam. Asia Minor,
on the other hand, remained Christian for another five hundred
years ; while in Armenia, from the ninth to the eleventh century,
the arts reached a high development, this kingdom remaining
permanently Christian in despite of Mohammedan suzerainty.

[1] The Council of Chalcedon held in A.D. 451 condemned the monophysite
heresy.

These were the regions from which domed architecture passed to Constantinople, to the Greek Church, to the Balkans, and to Russia, while Mesopotamia transmitted the barrel-vaulted type of church with long nave to the Latin Church in the West. Brunelleschi once more recovered the old tradition of domical building, which in the hands of Leonardo, Bramante, and Vignola became the predominant style in the Europe of the late Renaissance.

II

Community, Church, and Court

THE revelation by the artist of the beliefs determining his personal outlook on the world should form an essential part of every religious movement in the field of art. Such revelation there was in the case of a Leonardo, a Michelangelo, a Giorgione, a Dürer, a Rembrandt; but even by them it was only made at times when they were creating independently and following their own nature. As a general rule the patron steps in between the artist and religion, sometimes in the shape of an individual, at others of a corporation, above all, naturally, in the shape of the Church; the patron intervenes either in a general way through an official right to prescribe and judge, or in his individual capacity, himself giving the commission for the work. The result of these relations is a material restriction of the artist's genius which must not be left out of account when we consider the origin and early growth of Christian art. Can a religious art allowing full personal freedom be said to have existed at all in the early Christian period, or was all artistic creation from the very first under such constraint?

A general tutelage of the earliest Christian art on the part of the Church or the Court is incredible. Before anything of the kind could have occurred, a Church would have had first to be organized; it would then have had to win so great a power over the masses that even the creative artist would have been forced to obey its authority. But the outstanding feature of the earliest Christian art was its purely religious development among communities distributed over different nations. This aspect of the question I find imperfectly considered in the literature of Christian archaeology. It must, however, become the subject of scientific investigation, since it is more than possible that art, at first isolated by differences of nationality and geographical position, developed under the impulse of spontaneous aspiration. The

Church in the meantime increased in power, but was seldom creative. Its course was to retain such artistic elements as accorded with its aims, and to reject everything which did not.

The first of these two kinds of growth presupposes a high level of moral and intellectual life ; it presupposes an eagerness to solve the riddle of existence, and artists with ideals beyond the aims of every day. But does not the very creation of religions by personal Founders itself involve the existence of this high level ? Religions, even that of the Greeks, which grow gradually from obscure beginnings, only attain the power of artistic expression by slow degrees ; on the other hand, religions established by Founders may at the very outset reach the supreme point of their artistic achievement. Christianity is a religion of this latter kind ; about A.D. 400 its foundations were already completed.

But here we must carefully distinguish between the East and the West. In the West it is probably quite true that the rigid organization of the Roman Empire suppressed all national movements. In the East, on the other hand, this central organization was not effective beyond the coast-lands of the Mediterranean. In the interior lay the different ethnical groups represented by Cappadocians, Armenians, Syrians, Jews, Egyptians, and beyond all these the second great power of the age, Parthian and Sassanian Persia, with an official religion, Mazdaism, more tolerant than the State Hellenism of the Romans, and admitting a freer expansion of Christianity than any sanctioned in the West. The case of Armenia shows us how these conditions reacted on the peoples wedged in, as it were, between East and West. Here an Eastern Christianity overthrew Mazdaism and was accepted as the religion of the State before any such change was contemplated by Rome.

Thus even in late Hellenistic times the Christian art of the East was rich in features which could only have grown up naturally in countries living their own national lives. In architecture, such a feature was the use of vaulted construction, resulting in the principal types discussed in the next chapter. In decoration there were the contrasting systems of representation and abstract ornament, and, within the limits of the first, the symbolic and the realistic styles, to be discussed in Chapters V to VII. All these groups enjoyed their independent existence during the first three centuries ; in the East the independence continued during the fourth. In the fifth century the ecclesiastical organization, now established in the Greek and Aramaic areas, attempted to subject the local and popular influences ; in the sixth century the secular power, in alliance with the Church, followed the same course, commanding the vastly greater resources of imperial Constantinople. In the East the beginning of deca-dence coincides with the appearance of Islam. On the outbreak of iconoclasm, the forces which had been developing an art averse from Hellenism shook the foundations laid by Church and Court. This led to a fresh division of the artistic world. Great individual developments ensued both in the West and in the Mohammedan East, while Constantinople, placed between the two, ate the stale bread of old traditions. This view of evolution in Christian art will be established in subsequent pages ; here I must lay stress on the fact that it is based solely on many years of experience in the study of the actual monuments.

None, therefore, should be surprised to find things wearing an aspect very different from that which they used to present in the exclusive light of literary evidence.

I. *Christian National Art down to* A. D. 400

Just as there was never a single and uniform Christianity, so from the very first there was never a single stem, far less a single root, from which Christian art sprang. On the contrary, the time when there was still no uniformity in the Church and still no Christian State was precisely that when the controlling factor was the national spirit, which varied from one people to another. According to the received idea, Christian art rose as a homo-geneous growth from Hellenistic and imperial Roman ground. We have seen that these limits must be extended. The moment the geographical horizon is widened, the vital and creative force is discovered in local genius. Race, nationality, and economic condition count beyond question for more than political and intellectual connexions. Historians of art seem to have lost the power of reckoning with these essentials ; with their narrow European standpoint, their purely classical and philological outlook, they hold it rather unscientific than otherwise to take any cognizance at all of these important matters. My own belief is that without a fundamental study of these things an answer to the problem of the origin of Christian art cannot and should not be attempted.

Christ appeared in Judaea, under religious conditions already determined when the Jews were still a wandering people. For the study of art, the important fact about the Jews is not that they were Semites, but that they never created an art of their own. The case of Judaism resembles that of Islam. Mohammed appeared among Bedouins, nomad Arab herdsmen, who had no more art than the Jews ; in any case neither people possessed that representational kind of art which we have come to regard as characteristic of Jewish life.

Semitic art, as a species, flourished in river valleys and among their settled agricultural populations. These peoples created Church organizations and States with their corresponding artistic tendencies so deeply rooted and so indigeneous as to ensure a regular and progressive development. Conditions were different for nomad herdsmen, as I showed in my book *Altai-Iran*; I shall return to the subject in the fifth chapter of the present volume.

When in 1901 I put the question : The East or Rome ? and later added the second question : The East or Byzantium ? I was thinking in the first instance of these Semitic or Hamitic peoples who determined the course of ancient history in Mesopotamia and in the valley of the Nile, peoples whose national sense increased in strength in Christian times and influenced the world through the great cities of the eastern Mediterranean. More than ten years' work on Mshatta, Amida, Altai-Iran, and Armenia fundamentally changed my point of view. I still hold that at the beginning of Christian art the Semites played a decisive part. Most important among them at this time were the Aramaeans of the northern parts of Syria and Mesopotamia, the Nabataeans forming a link which connected them with the Copts. Hitherto, when we have spoken of the Christian East, we have really meant these Semites of the interior behind the Hellenistic coast-lands. The time has come to modify the once suggestive formula ' the East or Rome ', in so far as the growth of our knowledge is now leading to the analysis of the term ' East '. In making any change I have in view not so much local as racial division. Behind the Semitic world was a world of Aryans. In Christian times Eastern Iran was inhabited by a great population not to be measured by the same standards as the Semitic peoples. Perhaps we shall best understand the true nature of the Aryans of Iran if we compare their art with that of the Hindus. These Aryan immigrants into India knew no representation ; they adopted it from the natives of the country, just as the Mediterranean Greeks had adopted it from the Semites. The Eastern Aryans knew nothing of representation. The Achaemenian, and later the Sassanian, court adopted the Semitic representational manner ; but the people, though their art had been much enriched by pictorial motives, yet remained true to their surface-filling ornament. Now this loyalty to Aryan and northern feeling had a part to play at the beginning of Christian art. If the Iranian point of view had already influenced the Semites and the Greeks, the origin and early growth of Christian art become unintelligible without it. As Islam issued from a southern people with no representational art, quickly finding its main support in Iran and among the nomad herdsmen of the Iranian North-East, so Christianity issued from the Jews, a nation in like case, and found before long its strongest support among Persians and Armenians, both East-Aryan peoples. In the case of Islam, the bond of union was always the Arabic tongue. In that of Christianity, it is true that in the Mediterranean area the Greek and Latin languages formed the bond of union. But in the East there were national groups wholly independent of the Mediterranean peoples, who translated the scriptures of the Greek Christians into their own tongues— Aramaïc, Armenian, and Pehlevi. In like manner artistic forms were exchanged. My work on the architecture of the Armenians and its influence on Europe initiated research with regard to one only of the above three national groups ; the present book will deal more comprehensively with the subject. For the moment I am concerned with the racial question in a general manner.

When Christian art came into being, the Jews were no more independent than other Semites ; they were completely subject to Aryan peoples—in Mesopotamia to the Persians, in Syria and Egypt to the Romans. The fact leads us to observe that even at this period we have to draw a sharp dividing line between Eastern and Western Aryans. From the separation of the two sections by the Semites, it resulted that they could only have a common frontier where the Semitic wedge came to an end, on the upper course of the Euphrates and Tigris, that is, in Armenia and, to a certain extent, in the North-Mesopotamian triangle of cities : Edessa, Nisibis, Amida. Was it mere chance that the first Christian states came into existence precisely at these points of contact, in Osrhoëne and Armenia? Be this as it may, the fact had momentous consequences for art.

In A.D. 323 Rome raised Christianity to the dignity of the state religion; but when soon afterwards Constantine founded his new capital on the Bosporus, he arrived too late for his action to affect art, just as before him Rome had come too late to meet Greece as a rival in the intellectual and artistic fields. Christian art was already in growth or full existence, and ' Christian classical art ', which means West-Aryan art, was helpless to prevent the triumph of the East. The two factors which made this a certainty were in the first place the presence of the great Semitic centre of Aramaean North Mesopotamia; in the second, the support of the Armenian people, the extreme outpost of East-Aryan culture.

Thus in the search for the origin of Christian art we have to divide the surviving monuments into three groups. First, that of the Mediterranean area, which itself falls into two subdivisions, a Greek and a Latin. Egypt belongs to this group only through Alexandria and its immediate sphere of influence; Syria only through her coast-lands, with Antioch as their intellectual centre; Anatolia, in like manner, only through the littoral and through its western half. There is in the second place the intermediate Aramaean region, with its unrivalled intellectual centre in Edessa–Nisibis; it includes Mesopotamia and the interior of Asia Minor, and comes into touch with the real Egypt through inland Syria. In the third place there is Iran, revealed to us through literary sources as extending its influence to East Asia, but so far as surviving church-buildings are concerned, as yet only known to us through its western offshoot, Armenia.

The threads first run together in the Hellenistic centres on the Mediterranean littoral, next in Jerusalem and Constantinople, when the two cities were re-founded in the time of Constantine.

Further, the compromise between the West-Aryans of Asia Minor with the East-Aryans of Armenia and the Semites of North Mesopotamia is a most notable factor in the origin of Christian art. There may still be talk of a ' Christian classical art ' of the Mediterranean, culminating in Alexandria, Rome, and the maritime cities of Asia Minor. But it will no longer be permissible to ignore the existence of a Christian Iran, and of

Semitic Christians who made their influence felt in art after a fashion which had been quite impossible to the Jews. Such, more or less, were the racial and national foundations of Christian art in the first three centuries, and even in the fourth, Rome for the first time brought Christianity into imperial politics.

The artist working in a country having an artistic sentiment of its own is able to provide a free religious community with forms corresponding to its needs, for instance, with an acceptable type of church ; he is in harmony with national feeling and ideas, and within the limits which they impose is free to obey his unconscious impulse. No autocratic patronage compels him ; the result is that his work develops a local character, stronger and more durable than any general bond, political, linguistic, or intellectual, imposed from above, as in the case of the Hellenistic or the Roman system. Even when new Christian Powers arose, like the Byzantine Empire, it was long before the assertion of their strength made any serious impression on the different nationalities of the East. In my own belief the whole fourth century still belongs to the epoch of individual national movements, at any rate in the province of art. As we shall see below, two occurrences give a clear indication of attempted ecclesiastical control : the penetration by the long church of regions originally unfamiliar with it, and the dissemination of figure art through lands unacquainted with representation. It was, apparently, not until the fifth century that the long church began to influence the national style of Armenia and Mesopotamia ; in Eastern Syria, at any rate in the three-aisled type, it was rather earlier : single-halled churches need not be considered, since they may be found anywhere, with any kind of roof. The intrusive art of representation which entered Armenia at the same time, whether from Edessa–Nisibis or from Constantinople, has no longer the bright symbolic character which it bore among the Greeks, but had already assumed the didactic and directive manner of Semitic art ; of this we shall have more to say in a later chapter. Here, too, the change was not felt before the fifth century, a point which admits of demonstration. Thus down to about A.D. 400 the several Christian communities, united in national groups, had developed Christian art on their own lines ; the fifth century marked the first attempt to bring these separate units under the control of a common Church. As in other cases, so in this, my first insight into the truth came from Armenia. A third movement in the direction of uniformity, the transformation of classical naturalistic art into diffused ornament in a single plane, resulted from purely artistic rather than from ecclesiastical causes.

Speaking generally, we may therefore accept it as a fact that the period of growth in Christian art came to an end about A.D. 400. It was then that the artless naturalism of this first period yielded to a new taste leading less to creative work than to an eclectic treatment of forms which in the first Christian centuries had grown up for the most part from national seed. We may note the same thing in the case of other creeds and civilizations. Indian Buddhism in substance perfected its art contemporaneously with Christianity, and began its expansion only a little earlier. In China the period of growth came to an end about A.D. 800, in Mohammedan countries about A.D. 1000; in both cases all subsequent art lived upon that of the earlier period.

II. *Church Art of the Fifth Century*

Thus, in my judgement, Christian art starts with the permeation of national groups by a spontaneous religious feeling free from ecclesiastical control; herein lies the fundamental difference between my attitude and that of other scholars toward the views which have hitherto prevailed. It is, indeed, true that the wall-paintings of the catacombs and the reliefs of the sarcophagi have actually been judged in the main by the standards of a time as yet uncontrolled by the Church; but this has not been the case either with Church buildings or their decoration. Yet every student has now begun to see that before the Peace of the Church in A.D. 313 there were already in existence both communities, and buildings adapted to their requirements. In spite of this no one drew the following unavoidable conclusion. The first three centuries had been so prolific in the creation of types that the Churches into which at the close of this period the communities had developed, found themselves confronted with fixed usages which they adopted without question. These usages, however, soon acquired a permanent authority through an original association with the Founders of the Churches, with individual apostles, with missionaries, or with princes such as Abgar, Trdat (Tiridates), or Constantine. The Church itself found it hard to make headway against them when the positive necessity for change was shown by subsequent experience gained by contact with the masses and by liturgical development. The study of Armenia satisfied me as to this conflict between the inherited traditions of the fourth century and the demands in the next century of a Church pressing towards universally valid forms. I conclude that the course of events in Mesopotamia was probably identical. We see the same struggle repeated at a much later time when the pioneer architects of the new S. Peter's at Rome envisaged a centralized structure with radiating arms, while the Church demanded a building with a long nave. On this occasion the original influences which the Church rejected won in her despite a momentous significance for architectural development.

It is characteristic of a Church claiming wide allegiance that it seeks to invest with a validity beyond the natural limits of place, time, and environment, the architecture and the representational art which have approved themselves and become customary in the chief seat of its activity ; it attempts to impose them everywhere. This course of action made on the one hand for consistency in development, on the other it was a source of conflict. Let me cite a typical example from Armenia. In that country, during the fourth century, the people had adopted as its church-type a centralized domed building in complete independence of outside influence. But when the representatives of the Armenian church sought union with the now powerful Greek and Syrian community, and were received with only too open arms, a type quite different from their own, the long church without any dome, was declared the one admissible form, and in the fifth century was actually forced upon them by this foreign influence. Naturally enough, friction ensued ; only so can we explain such enactments as Canon 182 in Armenian Church law (Canon 22 of the Successors of the Apostles), which runs : ' Only the bishop orthodox in faith may design the plan ' of a church, or the Chorepiscopos or the Peredut with the ' bishop's consent. If any presume to plan a church without ' the bishop or Chorepiscopos, we ordain the destruction of the ' plans. Should, however, an unauthorized plan be sanctioned, ' we recommend that it be again submitted for approval. Thus ' shall the designing of the church be blameless.'

The Armenian canons are incoherently arranged, and it is hard to assign to any particular one either a date or place of origin. Canon 182 must in any case be earlier than A.D. 719, the date of the fifth Council at Dwin. But since it is an apostolic canon, its substance should go back to the earlier centuries of Christianity, though it is perhaps unlikely to date from before the fifth. It is another question whether the canon was from the first actually followed in Armenian church-building. Agathangelos certainly describes S. Gregory laying the foundation walls of the *martyria* at Vagharshapat with rule and plummet in his hands. This passage may afford the simplest explanation of the nickname given to Nerses III—*Shinogh*, 'the builder', even apart from his active encouragement of construction. Be this as it may, such points are worth notice as proving the strong interest taken in the work by the patron, here the Church and its rulers. But the long congregational church introduced by the bishops in the fifth and sixth centuries was not constructed in Armenia in the usual Western manner with a timbered roof, nor was the barrel-vaulted roof employed after the Southern fashion. Barrel vaults were used, indeed, but with a central dome. The efforts of the Mediterranean Church after sole authority appear as early as the fifth century in the insistence upon a long nave ; but the consequent disputes led to compromises, which fell out differently in Armenia and in Mesopotamia, in Syria, and in Asia Minor.

With the official intervention of the Church in problems hitherto left to individual communities and their architects, a prescribed taste came into existence ; compulsion was exerted to give permanence to a solution already accepted : this throttled creative effort and brought ' styles ' into existence. The above-cited Armenian canon clearly illustrates this point. In Rome, research has not revealed facts equally important to the genesis of Christian art, because in Rome no discord could arise between an indigenous architectural type and that of an intrusive foreign Church. Discord was equally impossible in Constantinople and other ecclesiastical centres in Asia Minor, Antioch, Alexandria, and Carthage. Here the Churches maintained active intercourse among themselves, and decorated their severely practical and simple basilicas with forms which, in so far as they were widely distributed, developed on the common lines of Hellenistic art. Nevertheless it is far from being proved that the timber-roofed basilica, preserved in so many Roman examples of early Christian date, was their one recognized form.

The school which followed Ainaloff in ascribing to Alexandria a general leadership in creation had already deduced the existence, in the field of architecture, of individual forms more or less closely related to vaulted building. Moreover, it is by no means certain that the abrupt decline of vaulted architecture in imperial Rome at the beginning of the Christian building period occurred to an equal extent in the great cities of the East. The octagon of Constantine at Antioch, and the same emperor's buildings at Jerusalem and Constantinople, suggest, at the very least, notable exceptions, to be explained partly by the persistence of the Hellenistic tradition as to vaulting, partly by the coming of the domed and square-planned church of Armenian origin. At Ravenna, Bishop Ursus seems to have vaulted his basilica about A.D. 400; at Milan, Ambrose probably followed the same course.

An organized Church will always be in favour of placing restrictions on the progressive artist; its goal is not freedom but uniformity. But even in the fifth century and in the Mediterranean area there were several Churches, and their quarrels over religious hegemony sufficiently explain the general situation. Further, Alexandria and Antioch had not risen to greatness because the West and Rome supported them, but because they had attracted to themselves the trade of the East which brought with it oriental motives in art. These motives they handed on to the West, chiefly to Rome and Constantinople, which in this way received many new ideas at second hand.

The churches of Carthage with their three aisles and double columns have a tentative character which hardly attests a strong indigenous art. It is practically impossible to say how far the initiative may here be due to Alexandria, for ancient Alexandria is almost completely destroyed, and documentary sources are few. Judging from the remains of churches above ground and those laid bare by excavation, we might infer a marked contrast between monastic and city churches. The former expressed national aspirations and were in close touch with the art of North Mesopotamia, Armenia, and Iran. In the cities, on the other hand, churches were built in or near the ancient temples, like Thebes or Denderah, and here the timber-roofed basilica remained the model. The sanctuary at the grave of S. Menas in Lower Egypt belonged, indeed, so definitely to this Hellenistic group that Islam was able to provide itself from this source with columns for its mosques on a liberal scale. But, generally speaking, the national art of Egypt won the upper hand with the spread of Christianity ; it stood closer to the art of Syria-Mesopotamia and Armenia than to that of Greece, and triumphed in the monasteries against the cities. This is shown alike in the architectural types of Upper Egypt, and in a very common form of church decoration imitating in stone the effect of oriental wall-linings ; the builders were not content to use the ordinary Greek ornament.

Syria was divided into two parts. The littoral and Jerusalem attracted all the artistic talent capable of executing the imperial plans. A widely distributed national art is only found in East Syria, but with such a wealth of monuments dating from the fourth to the sixth century that we are well justified by the general tenour of development in assuming a flourishing art of the same character in regions where no buildings of the time are actually preserved, or attested by inscriptions. On the analogy of Armenia we shall regard precisely this period of three centuries as of capital importance ; there the indigenous development lasted out the fourth century, while the fifth and sixth centuries witnessed a general attempt to impose the Mediterranean type of basilica with timbered roof. We are here only concerned with the native style of architecture in Syria, which apparently leaned upon Arab tradition and found a permanent home in the stone country of the Hauran. Here the construction of a church shows a line of wide rib-arches, all supported on piers projecting from the wall. Apparently the side walls were carried up as high as the crowns of the arches and the roofing was then done with stone slabs. Similar methods prevailed in domestic building. I need not go into further detail, since from the seventh century onwards this architecture falls out of the development of Christian art. But probably the Syrian example strengthened the tendency to support arcades upon columns, observed quite early in isolated instances like Spalato and Pompeii, and destined ever afterwards to remain characteristic of Christian architecture.

Like Syria, Asia Minor also fell into two divisions : a national central region in the interior, the affinities of which were with Mesopotamia and Iran ; and a littoral, entirely in Greek hands, and one of the regions from which in Early Christian times Hellenism derived its principal support. In Asia Minor, more than anywhere, the Hellenistic spirit came into immediate contact with another national genius, strongest in those provinces of

Pontus, Cappadocia, and Cilicia which form connecting links with Armenia and Mesopotamia. In the coast-lands timber-roofing prevailed in architecture and representation in pictorial art; in the interior, vaulted construction and non-representational ornament. Constantinople reflected both aspects of this two-sided Anatolia. Down to the fifth century it went with the Hellenistic littoral; it then yielded wholly to the East, till iconoclasm threatened all that remained to Hellenism, now that the timbered roof was replaced by the barrel-vault and dome. Nothing but a regular 'Renaissance' availed to keep Byzantine art apart from that of Iranian Armenia, a revival which brought back Hellenistic-Semitic figure art in the decoration of the now predominant domed church. The spirit of Edessa and Nisibis triumphed; orthodoxy adopted painting as its most effective instrument for influencing the masses; in this 'Renaissance' instruction was everything, and art had little voice. Thus Asia Minor lost with its dualism its importance for the development of art. Armenians and Seljuks possessed themselves of the old Ionian soil; the old languages, spoken and written, partly died out; to-day in Anatolia there is a large Turkish-speaking population of Greek descent. In the same way the whole of Egypt succumbed to Arabic.

But in the fourth and preceding centuries Asia Minor was richer than any other land in national characteristics; achieving its best in all directions. In the Hellenistic area sculpture was at so high a level that Praxitelean types were adopted to embody Christian ideas. It was the same with painting. The Psalter was illustrated with miniatures conceived in the Pompeian manner, and marked by an attractive symbolism. Yet in immediate neighbourhood to this Greek world was the utterly different world of the Semite and the Eastern Aryan. The custom of wearing clothes figured with biblical subjects, attested by the rebukes of Asterius of Amasea, suggests a Semitic rather than a Greek taste. In the interior of Asia Minor the Mesopotamian barrel-vault and the dome of Armenia and Iran are the decisive forms rather than the Hellenistic timbered roof.

We must, therefore, draw a distinction between the inland regions in Egypt, Syria, or Asia Minor, representing the wide-spread indigenous element, and the coast-strips with their ecclesiastical capitals. These are either old metropolitan cities like Alexandria, Antioch, and Ephesus with its district, or else temporary residences of Roman emperors, like Ravenna and

Milan. They are all borrowers; none are creators, though indeed their populousness admitted of buildings on a scale unheard of in the lands actually providing the types, and effects sometimes attained were such that the original importation is almost undiscernible. There was a time when we believed these cities the creative centres of Christian art; for the period before A.D. 313 we thought principally of Alexandria, for the next period, of Antioch; while for later times we gave the first place to Constantinople and to an Asia Minor regarded as purely Greek. The advance of knowledge with regard to the East has wrought a fundamental change in these beliefs. The old Hellenistic capitals were in Christian times emporia for the interior in a double sense. They did not merely sell their merchandise to countries now reawakening to a sense of national life ; they also adopted and incorporated Mediterranean art, the architectural forms brought to their knowledge, a point of much greater importance to art-history. In architecture the way was thus prepared for the coming of the domical building, with the dazzling ornament of internal surfaces. Representational sculpture was deprived of its former dominant position by the influence of the inland countries. A new intellectual centre, Edessa-Nisibis, took from painting its symbolism and substituted a historical and didactic manner. Until Christianity became the State religion, the various ecclesiastical capitals retained their leading place.

Let us sum up the argument. Down to about A.D. 400 church art was represented in the East by independent national groups ; in the West, there was in architecture a general approximation to the Hellenistic hall of assembly, which by retention of the wooden roof, the longitudinal axis, and the gabled façade, still more or less preserved the tradition of the ancient temple. After A.D. 400, a movement began in the East which ceased to have any immediate connexion with religion. It sprang rather from the practical brain of Fathers of the Church, just as in later times the secular art of Constantinople sprang from the predilections of a Court. The people were at once to be instructed in the faith and dazzled by magnificent display ; this was the astute policy of the Aramaean and Greek scholars in Antioch, Edessa, and Nisibis, and, at a later time, of the Byzantine Court. Out of it arose the millennial reign of a spiritual and temporal autocracy in the old Semitic sense, authority in Church and State claiming to act together in the name of God.

III. *Autocratic Policy of the Court*

Architecturally, the effort on the part of the Church during the fifth century had issued in a uniform type, that of the wooden-roofed basilica. But as early as the fourth century Constantine had of his own initiative produced a Church architecture unique in the Mediterranean littoral, and intelligible rather as a continuation of the earlier Hellenistic-Roman vaulted style with important additions from Armenia and Mesopotamia than as a development of the modest and severely practical buildings erected by the communities of the time. Constantine and his successors rescued something of the great Hellenistic and Roman vaulted style for the benefit of the growing Christian movement. Compared with the building done by Churches and communities in the recognized fashion of the hour, the imperial creations give many proofs of individuality. Now, as in earlier times, they challenged the artistic talent of the world ; they displayed in isolated and conspicuous examples the new forms first carried westward by the Goths after the entrance of the northern peoples into the sphere of Christian art ; they developed the vaulted architecture which we commonly describe as Romanesque and Renaissance over an area embracing at least the whole of Western Europe. But in the East something different grew out of the style adopted by imperial Byzantine art and the allied art of the Byzantine Church ; this was the orthodox church type which everywhere remained unalterably attached to the dome. The two following chapters will be devoted to a discussion of this rich development ; our immediate business is to consider the significance of Court influence on art, especially that of the Byzantine Court.

Criticism makes the first period of great Christian art begin from A.D. 313, when Constantine abandoned the former Greek State religion for Christianity. In doing so it fails to see how important to the development of Christian art was the fact that in this political move Edessa had anticipated Rome at the beginning of the third century, and Armenia at the end of it. The older ' Founder's religions ', Buddhism at their head, had followed the same path : none of them attained a great creative art until a king associated the new faith with his political ambition, leaving thereby an inestimable heritage to posterity. But none of them invented new types of buildings any more than Christianity. Novelty is not beloved of State religions. Their way is rather

COMMUNITY, CHURCH, AND COURT 43

to enslave the artist in the service of their ambition, and to make the achievement of his own ideals difficult; to demand of him first and above all skilled and willing craftsmanship, and, like the Churches, to subordinate in him that expression of personality which is the foundation of all true creative art. The result is that the indigenous artist dies out, and no record of his activity remains unless he happens to have been directly under court patronage. It is the aim of State Churches as far as possible to keep art uniform in the interest of their arbitrary aims, to cripple the natural development which comes of competition, and all the variety created by difference of place, period, and social environment. The rise of three distinct styles in ancient Hellas was only possible in the city States before the time of Alexander; in like manner we shall only understand the great development of Western art in the so-called Middle Ages, when almost every district in France evolved its own architectural forms, if we realize the leading part played by individual monasteries and the advanced civilization of the towns.

The transition from individual believers to communities, small and large, is relatively easy. A Church first grows intolerant when she has the State at her back, when she is used as an instrument by the temporal power. Establishment at first strengthens a Church, but by degrees it leads to the subjection of religion by the secular power ; God is constrained to necessities of State. This sequence of events is easy to follow in the case of Constantinople. To begin with, the Church alone gained by the proclamation of Christianity as the State religion ; she alone took up the battle with local particularism. Justinian was the first emperor to force both Church and Art into his service. Though Alexander the Great laid the foundations of absolute monarchy in the modern sense of the word by his action in Persia and by his visit to the Temple of Jupiter Ammon, it was Christian emperors in Constantinople who first succeeded in enslaving the Church; it was they who began the policy, still surviving in certain countries, by which she is involved in state affairs, and thereby divorced from her true spiritual function.

The Church which has accepted the supremacy of a Court abandons the art which it cannot keep for itself or the art which it has trained to uniformity ; it must perforce place it at the service of the ruler who demands an effective parade of power and a display of dazzling magnificence. When this happens, we begin to find interiors gorgeous with costly materials and mural decoration which completely subjugate the devout spectator. Such interiors spread as an imperial fashion through all parts of Byzantine territory; their provision acquired great economic importance for the capital on the Sea of Marmara. The trade in marble columns fashioned at the quarries on the island of Proconnesos carried such sculpture from Constantinople all round the Mediterranean and Black Sea basins. It familiarized every region accessible by harbour, river, and connecting land-route with the modes of ornament created for imperial use; it brought back the riches of all these countries to the capital. If we remember the imperial monopoly in purple, in silk fabrics, and similar things, we readily understand why this splendour turned everywhere to the imperial advantage. The decoration and furnishing of churches became one of the most valuable commercial assets. Basilicas like that of Parenzo, or the churches which served as quarries for the building of mosques at Kairwan near Carthage, or in the Temple Area at Jerusalem, might, all but the bare walls, have been imported ready-made from Constantinople.

In this way there came into existence a kind of Imperial art, the Byzantine; an art economically more productive, though scarcely more creative, than that of the Roman empire. At a later period Baghdad in its turn traded the products of its art from the Indian frontier to the Atlantic; the beautiful wood-carving of the *mimbar* and the glazed tiles of the *mihrab* in the above-mentioned great mosque at Kairwan come from Baghdad. But it would be an error to suppose that Rome, Constantinople, and Baghdad were anything more than marts for the exchange of works of art. The pierced carving of the *mimbar* and the *mihrab* tiles of Kairwan are shown by their style and quality to be of Iranian origin; the rich decoration of the Proconnesian capitals in the Ravenna churches or that carved on Egyptian lime-stone along the Nile valley attests the same descent. Courts are like sponges; they absorb everything within reach and force it into the arteries which nourish their strength.

In that great emporium, Constantinople, two churches rose as unique examples of imperial craze for splendour; both of them go back to Justinian, as did the Church of the Virgin in the Temple Area at Jerusalem, where Solomon in an earlier day sought to eclipse the buildings of all neighbouring princes. Justinian in his turn was not content to excel Solomon alone;

he had to outdo his predecessor Constantine, who had shown how a Christian prince could also erect splendid monuments in glorification of royal power. The Churches of S. Sophia and of the Holy Apostles are in a sense only successors of the structures erected to proclaim the triumph of Christianity. I will now consider the sumptuous buildings of these two emperors from the point of view represented in this volume.

Constantine demanded that the basilica of the Holy Sepulchre should not only be more magnificent than anything elsewhere, but also so exceptional as to surpass the best that any other city could show. The chief architect was a certain Zenobios ; if it is true that he placed a dome over the crossing which served as a model for all western buildings, then there must have been two domed structures close together on this site, one over the sepulchre, the other over the long basilica. Further, a trefoil-ended building was begun over the cave of the Nativity at Bethlehem ; a dome was erected over the spot on the Mount of Olives from which Our Lord ascended, and so on. A whole series of buildings rose which must have produced an impression of great individuality, compared with those which we may conceive to have stood in contemporary Rome ; examples, conspicuous far and wide, of the resources which the imperial power of the day could draw indifferently from East and West. Jerusalem and Syria did not even supply all the materials, for the columns were assembled from the most various regions. The effect of the buildings erected by Constantine in his new capital must have been much the same. The octagon at Antioch, which was the model of S. Vitale at Ravenna, must have more nearly recalled the eight-foiled type of Armenia than the original plan of the Baths over which it was erected. Wherever in the Mediterranean area imperial policy touched architecture, we find some exceptional feature in the form of the building. It was ecclesiastical influence which first substituted the uniformity of the long plan in the two centuries succeeding Constantine.

Then came Justinian. His architects were from Asia Minor, but we should seek in vain in their native cities, Tralles and Miletus, the types which they adopted. The younger Isidore is heard of at a later period in the district between the Orontes and the Euphrates; it looks as if not only he, but also the older Isidore and Anthemius had in their time studied their profession on the borders of Armenia and Persia. For the Church of the

Holy Apostles was just such a many-domed type as is represented by the palace of Firūz Abād in Persia, and the church once occupying the site of the Halabiyeh mosque in Aleppo, where five domes were so arranged as to form a cross. In the wooden churches of the Ukraine we find the dome similarly used in groups of three or five even to this day, a point to which I will later recur.

IV. *The Church of S. Sophia*

This supreme monument of Eastern Christianity has never, like S. Peter's at Rome, inspired a host of imitations. It stood in a majestic loneliness until the Turks, in their characteristic way, once more took up the tradition which it embodied. In conception the church is purely Armenian; a central dome over a square plan is supported by semi-domes abutting on the sides of the square. It is true that the Armenian niche-buttresses are replaced on the north and south by vaults between massive piers which allowed the introduction of galleries; but the architects of the Ottoman conquerors were quick to recognize the original design, and, in the huge mosques built in imitation of the church, to restore the Armenian four-lobed plan.

S. Sophia, as we see it, results from the demand of the Church for a long nave even in a building with only a single dome; by the introduction of galleries into an Armenian plan, it meets the need felt alike by Church and Court for a hall of assembly on an imperial scale. The Armenian plan is impressive, and the combination of Iranian decoration and Greek organic structure notably contributes to the almost overpowering effect of the interior.

Justinian's other churches, both those which survive and those known by the descriptions of Procopius, all show a like exuberance of cosmopolitan features. We have already noticed the Church of the Holy Apostles. S. Sergius and S. Bacchus at Constantinople is an octagon inscribed in a square, itself transformed into a square by great niches in the Roman manner, and surmounted by a ' melon dome ' such as we find in Armenia. S. Vitale at Ravenna has an eight-lobed plan, probably copied from that of Constantine's octagon at Antioch, on which I shall have more to say. The common run of churches built before and after Justinian bear an aspect quite distinct from that of these buildings. To these churches I will next proceed after a few words on decoration.

Splendour in decoration was as little known to the old Greek religious architecture before Alexander as it was to the Armenians in their earliest churches, or, in much later times, to the architects of early Gothic churches in the north. The Hellenic spirit expressed itself by noble sculpture, the mediaeval through effects of mass and space. The Armenians knew only facings of dressed stone, with occasional painted ornament in the interior. It was the same in Syria and Asia Minor. In Mesopotamia and in Egypt, on the other hand, decoration was richer. These lands of the great eastern monarchies were the real homes of that desire to enhance artistic effect by decorative splendour which only the resources of despotism can satisfy ; the monarch sets the mode, and all the world tries to follow it. So the Phoenicians gave Solomon the idea for his temple, and the temple in its turn was eclipsed by Justinian's church. If we read the description of the building written by its panegyrist Paul the Silentiary after its dedication ; if we bear his account in mind when we contemplate the effect of the interior, still marvellous to-day despite the whitewash of the Turks, we shall have to confess that for sheer splendour the utmost which the Jesuits have achieved falls short of the Byzantine miracle. All is resplendent with the most precious material, from the floor of the church, through the walls and vaults, up to the crown of the dome. If imagination adds the woven fabrics, the hangings and the like, the objects in gold and silver, the other metal work, and the hanging lamps, which once completed the picture, we may form some conception of the magnificence attained by this Christian art. Justinian did not, of course, originate this trend towards splendour ; his part was systematically to assure its triumph, and to force Europe ever afterwards to walk in the way which he prepared.

This determination to enhance by decoration an achievement already good in itself also characterised the representational art of the time ; in this field, no less than in that of architecture, it worked in opposition to unadorned truth and to the grandeur of simplicity. The Court insisted that the subjects on which the eyes of the congregation were focussed should be imperially conceived. We remember the two scenes in S. Vitale at Ravenna, and how in that church the type of Christ had to be made imposing enough to deserve the homage of a Justinian and a Theodora ;

we recall the figure throned on the sphere of the world, with
angel body-guards, dispensing grace and receiving worship in
a pose of formal and rigid majesty, his hand resting on the
mystic scroll sealed with the seven seals. We remember the
overwhelming splendours of the remaining mosaics, which seem
to clothe a dogma itself in all the hues of a peacock's plumage.
We have to admit the success of the method. Justinian drew
upon the resources of the whole world that his church-interiors
might fascinate the believer; his artists wrought the material
with the ease of supreme accomplishment in the service of his
overweening will to power.

We like to imagine that the political centre of Christianity
after A.D. 313 was also the source of the creative spirit in formative
art. But art implies personality. Now a seat of Government
may produce personality in the sphere of politics, of which the
aim is material domination. To personality of this kind art
seems the best means of decking ambition in the garb of beauty,
just as religion is the best means of cloaking it with virtue and
nobility. But the personality which inspires art is not like this.
It flourishes less at courts than anywhere else in the world. For
at the seat of power everything is subordinated to politics; the
forces willing to accept this fact are always welcome; those
which are not willing must either emigrate or remain aloof.
The legends about the erection of famous buildings are instructive
in this connexion. They describe the patron as keeping most
jealous watch over his architect, and even compassing his death
to prevent any repetition of his design.

In centres of political ambition art passes from the hands
of creators into those of actors; it ceases to be an end to itself,
redeeming us from reality; it becomes play-acting, a making-up
to please inordinate wealth and power. The surest signs of a court
art are magnificence, and a change in the artists' motive from
expression of feeling to the production of dazzling effect. This
effect must needs rely on monotonously repeated forms and
subjects, in order to mould a public opinion docile to its purpose,
an opinion prepared to remove the control from the individual
creator and to hand it over to the bureaucrat. In this connexion
let us consider the dictum ' that Christianity came to be the
Indo-Germanic religion, in which the peoples embodied their
deeper feelings '. In Constantinople Christianity was not such
a religion; it was more nearly so in Rome, which had been

freed from the presence of a court. In Rome we shall find among the surviving mosaics traces which point away from Constantinople back to the centre of East Aryan feeling. In the North, Christianity remained a blessing to mankind only so long as the Church did not dominate the State and the State did not find a willing instrument in the Church.

The history of art has made its own path easy by concentrating upon finished ' styles ', and by leaving undiscussed all those early stages of germination which marked the successive forces at work in nation, Church, and State during the Early Christian period. It has disregarded the local, historical, and social movements which forced a material constraint upon the architect and his work, movements against which the individuality of peoples or persons had hardly a chance of success. The measure of development is given on the one hand by the free forms established by the several communities down to about A.D. 400, on the other by the trammels and exacting demands of Church and State. Research will in future have to become more and more familiar with these distinctions. For me, the effort to attain such knowledge is the real scientific work, whether it is possible or not for any single scholar ever to attain it. But without this aim things pass from a pettiness into a stagnation which threatens to destroy the importance of our studies. Our province becomes the hunting-ground of men who either fail to understand the crucial monuments, or else employ them to illustrate ideas good enough in themselves, but properly belonging to other fields of research. Such was Lamprecht the universal historian ; such are the archaeologists in their several spheres. It is high time for students of art to widen their horizon and get the reins once more into their own hands. They must not neglect their proper objective to lose themselves in critical analysis of monuments or texts, in which each will have to take his part. Problems of form are only a fraction of this.[1]

[1] In 1919, while these sheets were in the press, I received E. Göller's rectorial address at Freiburg on the division into periods of ecclesiastical history (Die Periodisierung der Kirchengeschichte und die epochale Stellung des Mittelalters zwischen dem christlichen Altertum und der Neuzeit). It shows at bottom so clear a realization of my conclusions from the Catholic standpoint, that I may perhaps hope to see the good results observable at Upsala repeated in circles nearer home. The difference of view is still wide, especially now that I have attempted to give Mazdaism the influential part in artistic development which is its due. But the ban is none the less removed, and I can only wish that all

I must now indicate the fundamental features in Church architecture already discovered by Christianity before about A.D. 400, and serving as prototypes for subsequent development. It will be a later task to point out the trammels and exacting demands of Church and State, in despite of which, after the lapse of about a thousand years, they finally attained their triumph in the West. To this task I can do no more than allude in the next chapter, though it may yet be granted me to devote a part of my life's work to this question.

who desire a closer familiarity with the problems discussed in these pages should read Göller's address by way of supplement to what I have said here. The question 'The East or Rome' is there placed in its true perspective in regard to my work on Armenia ; the procedure is in marked contrast to that of a hasty critic more closely connected than Göller with my line of research, whose recent pronouncements have only served to confuse the issue.

III

Local Variation in the Early Christian vaulted Architecture of the East

ARCHITECTURE begins from natural conditions of climate and soil ; later it is directed to definite aims, wanders far afield, following natural lines of communication between peoples, and satisfying the demands of power and wealth. In the crucial early period of Christian art there was no dictation of particular forms, such, for instance, as the old views on origins assumed in the case of the timber-roofed basilica, once regarded as the sole point of departure in church building. Only some world-wide power, such as a State or Church, could have dictated after this fashion ; Christ, an individual, without worldly power or influence, assuredly could not have done so ; and how, in any case, could uniformity have been enforced during the period of geographical subdivision which followed His coming ? Half a millennium had to go by before Christianity wielded any such strength either in Rome or in Constantinople, and even then neither city could ignore all that had come into existence in the meanwhile. It was precisely the modest first attempts in Christian art, in all their local divergence, which really governed the whole subsequent development. It was, indeed, within the power of Church and State to adopt or reject, to impose combinations or to fetter by their laws the ambitions of individual genius. But in the field of art the familiar forms of the earliest period remained quite as influential as the personalities of the Fathers or their pagan predecessors in the field of religion. Since, however, art is subject to less narrow limitations than language, the sphere in which it is born and works is far wider not only than that of language but of any other expression of life.

Christ came at a time of intellectual and spiritual satiety, no less conspicuous in Judaea than in the Hellenistic cities and in Rome ; it was a state which threatened to engulf all civilization alike in East and West, involving good and beautiful, ugly and bad, in one common ruin. Hitherto students of art have assumed that this ruin was actually accomplished; I myself once so believed, in so far as I held that at first initiative belonged solely to the great Mediterranean cities and to Rome, which together embodied all the creative power given to Christianity in its cradle. These views were expressed in my book *Orient oder Rom*, published in 1901. But the experience gained later in Egypt, Syria, and Asia Minor put me upon the track of other centres independent both of Hellenistic and of Roman influence; in these was developed an art which became the nursery of Christian architecture and of its original decoration. The first of these centres was Persia, the empire next in power to that of Rome, and, as we have already noted, more tolerant than Rome, so that in its territory Christianity was openly professed and not exposed to persecution.

The present is the appropriate place in which to trace the effect of another cause important in this connexion. The country then known as Persia included regions which had developed diverse architectural types, severally adapted to the various materials at their disposal and old traditional methods of building, types which flourished less through the patronage of the Diadochi and their courts than through their hold upon the affections of the common people. Unfortunately so little remains of pre-Sassanian times that proof of their existence can only be reached by retrospective inference.

It was with the utmost difficulty that students of art-history could be induced to widen their horizon even so far as to include the monuments of the Greek as well as of the Latin Church. We may, therefore, expect a long time to pass before they recognize the national movements which took place beyond the Greek coastlands of the Mediterranean. Against my harmless ' Amida ', they started a regular campaign which can but end in failure. There is only one course open to the student who sets out not from preconceptions but from the monuments themselves.

As early as the third century, Syrians had founded a State Church of their own, with Edessa as its centre. Though this Church was soon suppressed by Rome, yet neither the architectural facts recorded in the Chronicle of Edessa nor the significance of the theological school at Nisibis can be swept aside or explained away as results of dependence upon Antioch.

This school was an independent organization at a very early date, more open to eastern than to western influence, though it is true that it afterwards belonged directly to the Greek Church and was indirectly connected with the Latin through Cassiodorus, who in his monastery of Vivarium followed the model of Nisibis. It was, in fact, a Semitic centre flanked by two Aryan regions, inspiring the movement of art in the fifth century towards representation, while the Aryans on either side of it had even earlier assumed the leadership in building and decoration.

This is explained by the fact that the Semitic centre (not to be confused with the Jewish home of Christianity) already possessed a fully developed Church when it first made its influence felt. The Byzantine Court in the sixth century concentrated all powers in its own hands. In this it followed the example of the old Semitic monarchies, of which the tradition had survived, and now helped the Church to arrest the development of an indigenous and popular art. Yet in the end victory lay neither with Rome nor with Byzantium, but precisely with this creative lower stratum. The vaulted architecture of the East affords definitive evidence of this. It developed a vigorous growth through the greater freedom which Eastern Christianity at first enjoyed.

Organized religion is apt to cause persecutions, first at home, when one form of belief oppresses another, next abroad, with the rise of state churches at the beck of the temporal power. The student of art should closely observe both kinds. We have to remember that until raised to the position of state religion in the Roman Empire, Christianity was regarded as completely harmless in Persia, and allowed to expand at will. Persecution on the part of Persia only began when first Armenia, then the Roman Empire in West and East, transformed themselves into Christian States. This explains how the Christian Church in Persia flourished as early as the second century, and how it is that we hear, for example, of church buildings in Adiabene beyond the Tigris at a time when Roman Christians were still concealing themselves in catacombs, or holding their services in the palaces of aristocratic converts. This is surely the reason why church-building in the East should have begun earlier than in the Mediterranean area. Hitherto we have misunderstood the whole development because we have always applied to it the standards made in Rome.

The general notion to-day with regard to Christian architecture resembles that which I held myself in 1901 with regard to Christian art as a whole, that it originated in the great cities of the East-Mediterranean coast, especially in the ' cradle of Christian art ', Alexandria.   But this gate of Egypt represents more perfectly than any great Hellenistic city the sterile cosmopolitanism characteristic of the Late-Roman world as a whole. Of its own initiative Alexandria never got beyond the timber-roofed basilica.   As long as the regions really inventive in domed and vaulted construction lay beyond the range of our knowledge, it was possible to credit Alexandria with the invention of everything.   But to-day the case is altered.   In what follows I shall ignore the timber-roofed basilica as a type, in order not to make this book too cumbrous.   A whole library exists devoted to the subject ; every ' History of Art ' puts it conspicuously in the foreground.   What I wish to do in the present place is to show that it can be quietly left out of account, and still no fundamental proof be lacking of the continuity between the architectural development of the Early-Christian East and that of the Middle-Christian West (' Romanesque ' and Gothic), or that of Renaissance architecture in Italy.   The old profession of faith, that the basilica was the original building used for public worship in East and West alike, was rashly reaffirmed at the very moment when plain proofs to the contrary were beginning to emerge in Armenia.   It may be true of the West ; but even on the eastern coast of the Mediterranean exceptions appear, and no feature of the timber-roofed basilica penetrated the interior of Hither Asia except the tendency to lengthen the nave.

The duration of movements in religious art varies within wide limits, according as creation is free to individuality, or fettered by some general law.   In the first case, though differences of soil, climate, race, or people may give rise to local varieties, all can flourish and continue to exist indefinitely, side by side. But in the second case time will destroy the enforced uniformity and bring in changes from the world of variety which will end by undermining the law.   In Early Christian times we observe a notable contrast between the conditions affecting East and West. The East starts with a great number of local types, and after about A.D. 1000 passes to a few fixed ones.   The West, on the other hand, begins with a single fixed type, and after about A.D. 1000 adopts in succession the two main features which had long co-existed in Armenia, the vault and the dome. If we survey the distribution of types in the East during the fourth century, we find in Iran and Armenia the dome over the square plan, in Mesopotamia the barrel vault, in the Mediterranean area the timbered roof. Syria alone, in the Hauran where there was no wood, replaced the timber roof by one composed of stone slabs supported upon rib-arches.

Such were the types of wide distribution ; by the sixth century the Eastern forms penetrated Constantinople to the complete expulsion of the timber-roofed basilica. In the period down to A.D. 1000, the eastern dome and vault appear in isolated instances even in the West. But it was only after A.D. 1000 that vaulted construction spread upon a great scale in the West, the Eastern style, or Romanesque, developing into two branches, the Northern, or Gothic, and the Southern, or style of the Italian Renaissance. Romanesque and Gothic are based upon the long nave ; the style of the Renaissance has leanings towards domed building, enriching it, however, in an incongruous manner with features proper to the Greek temple. In succeeding pages I shall deal with these main groups, adding by way of supplement exceptional cases found in border-districts, or transplanted by migration far from their natural centres.

But something more is required than distinction between the large group and the isolated instance. In the case of the groups, we must further distinguish between the place of origin and the area of expansion. In the East it would appear that in general building-forms originated in the same regions where they are found widely distributed. But the rule has its exceptions ; thus it does not apply to the timber-roofed basilica in Syria, or to the barrel-vaulted church with three aisles in Armenia and in the interior of Asia Minor. In the two latter countries groups were formed by adapting the vault to the three long aisles favoured by the Church ; but vaulted construction had its home in Mesopotamia and Iran, the long church in the Mediterranean area. The regions in the south-eastern corner of the Mediterranean, the Syrian coast, and Egypt are of exceptional interest in this connexion. Here there is a wealth of church buildings, and in addition to individual structures a variety of groups represented side by side. But hardly one is indigenous ; almost all are immigrants originating in other places.

Jerusalem, however, is the chief instance of such immigration.

Constantine rebuilt the city as a place of pilgrimage. Did he avail himself of local building-forms, or did he derive them from other artistic provinces ? What strikes us most is his free employment of the dome. This used to be explained on the theory that he derived suggestions from types represented at Gaza (temple of Marnas, or *Marneion*), in Rome (S. Costanza), or at Nocera. But is it really true that the source of inspiration was the round building with dome pierced for light at the top and supported on an inner circle of columns ? Assuredly not. We find a number of architectural types, some destined to a wide influence abroad through the mere fact of their association with the Holy Places, which caused them to be imitated over and over again. We shall return to this point in connexion with the Church of the Holy Sepulchre and the Church of the Nativity at Bethlehem.

In Egypt the state of Early Christian art before the Mohammedan conquest of A.D. 640 can be more easily understood than anywhere else. The forms habitual before this date continued in use ; a further development, such as that which occurred in Armenia, was impossible. Research, lasting for years, among the monuments of the Nile valley forced the conviction upon me that after the extinction of ancient Egyptian art, there was an end of creativeness ; almost everything was imported from Hither Asia.

The old attitude with regard to Early Christian vaulted building, with a few isolated exceptions, was simply a denial of its existence. When my *Kleinasien* appeared, it was declared that the vaulted churches of Anatolia were an exception to the rule and to be explained by local conditions. But outside Germany the true explanation soon began to find acceptance. The Berlin school and its adherents refused, however, to give ground, even after the publication of *Amida*. Far from it ; despairing efforts are made to this hour to bolster up a worn-out doctrine. The orthodoxy of the average theologian and the average archaeologist is too hard hit by the change. Though the problematic has long been replaced by the certain, people still prefer the study of phantoms to that of realities. Intelligent readers of my books on Mesopotamia and Armenia know better now than to believe the completely vaulted church typical only of Asia Minor. Another fallacy which must be abandoned is that which pronounces the absence of the vault in Syrian churches a proof of earlier date, its presence in Anatolian churches a proof of lateness. As a matter of fact, the whole Christian movement culminates in the vaulted construction of Central Hither Asia, as it culminated in the timber-roofed basilica throughout the Mediterranean area. Christian architecture is linked not merely with classical forms, but above all with the vaulted construction originating in Mesopotamia and Iran. If we regard this vaulted architecture of Early Christianity and the mediaeval vaulted building of the West as two bridge-heads, the bridge between them must cross the whole region of the timber-roofed basilica, which is more or less valueless for architectural evolution. I have attempted to build this bridge in *Kleinasien*, in *Amida*, and in my book on Armenia. To persist in regarding the facts there adduced as still doubtful and still requiring exhaustive examination by specialists is to treat the work of my whole career as not worth the pains necessary to its comprehension. The student of art history may learn from this example the attitude of philology, archaeology, and historical research towards novel and disturbing views. They can proceed critically and methodically so long as their especial line of study is not in question and no one ventures to oppose the articles of recognized belief. We hear again and again of the ' boldness and freedom of Hellenistic architecture ' in connexion with S. Lorenzo at Milan, S. Vitale at Ravenna, or S. Sophia at Constantinople. But it would be far more to the point were it recognized that these churches really represent the expansion of Iranian art on European soil, an expansion only rendered possible by the complete surrender of the leading Hellenistic architects to East-Aryan and Armenian influences.

I have made this short statement of my case by way of preface, in order that those unfamiliar with the controversies of recent years may appreciate the valuable material now offered them, and may not be seduced from the right path if subsequently they read that the guide who here addresses them is not worthy of credence.

I. THE DOME

Only one kind of dome is of wide and crucial importance in the development of church architecture, the dome over a square bay. The dome over a round or over an octagonal bay appears in comparison as the single instance, or as the transient form produced by temporal, local, or social conditions. It is untrue to assert that local classification is not feasible in the case of the dome in the East. To begin with, the circular and octagonal types only appear in the Mediterranean area, while the dome over the square is of purely Iranian origin. In Iran it appears with no abutment but that provided by grouping secondary chambers round a single dome or several domes in association.[1]

It was Armenia which in the fourth century first introduced for use as a church the square building with single dome and abutment by axial and diagonal niche-buttresses. The long church lends itself no less than the centralized building to division into local groups. In Mesopotamia there are the two main types of long church, one with longitudinal, the other with transverse nave ; in the Hauran there is the pseudo-vault ; in the regions still remaining Hellenistic in Christian times there is the timbered roof ; and this classification does not touch such further points as the difference between one-aisled and three-aisled buildings, between those with clerestories and those without.

When we come to consider other groups built for definite practical objects such as Baths, which do not require a single great room for a uniform purpose, but a division of interior space for differentiated activities, round and octagonal buildings at once take a leading place. The Baptistery, related in purpose to the Baths, is associated with this group, though it stands for isolation, or at most co-ordination with chambers designed for other purposes, such, for instance, as those for

---

[1] While the original edition was in the press, Erik Peterson drew attention to a remarkable employment of the dome by the Sabaeans of Mesopotamia. According to En-Nedim the Sṣabians proceed to a chapel constructed of burned bricks and having a domed roof ; there they make offerings to their God Hermes (?) or Ares : the text at this point is corrupt (Chvolsohn, *Die Sṣabier*, ii. 37). Perhaps a statement by Akhibar ez-Zemon may be brought into connexion with this. He relates that the first Hermes, a figure in the Sṣabian cult, erected a lighthouse with a dome at Hermopolis in Egypt, and that this dome changed its colour every day of the week (Blochet, *Rivista degli Studi orientali*, iii. 185). It would seem to follow from this that among the Sṣabians the domed building was connected with an astrological symbolism not originating with themselves, but coming down to them from earlier times. This makes the adoption of the dome in Christian architecture all the more remarkable, and the question arises whether there may not have been points of contact in the intellectual history of the peoples. The same question is suggested with regard to India.

undressing, and those for the gradual introduction of the worshipper to the assembly or the rite, or those at the sides of a church. There is now evidence for a square baptistery dated A.D. 359 in the Church of S. James at Nisibis.

The dome over the square is a form which seems to have developed from wooden construction after the Aryan immigration into Iran. That country was poor in wood, and their method of roofing wooden houses with short beams laid across the corners had now to be reproduced in sun-dried brick, just as we see it imitated in stone in India and Kashmir.[1] Thus a corbelled dome rose from four squinches at the corners of the square, leaving a lozenge-shaped opening at the top. The East-Iranian house, as described by Curtius Rufus, is thus constructed, and even to-day such units form the greater part of every Persian village.

We cannot at present say whether this type was actually transmitted to the Christian Church on North Iranian soil; the sun-dried bricks weathered quickly, the buildings did not last long, and ultimately collapsed into heaps of dust. Nor have excavations yet been made in the crucial area. Yet we may infer from the ruined palaces of Southern Persia that the development must have followed two lines; at first, as at Firūz Abād, domed cell was merely added to domed cell; later, as at Sarvistan, there is a dominant single dome. How far the Fire Temple may have shared in the development, we cannot at present clearly see.[2]

The dome seems at first to have been set upon the four walls by the help of squinches. When, however, the quatrefoil plan was introduced, and the solid walls were pierced by arches, the spherical pendentive came in. Above, in either case, rose a drum with windows, for the most part octagonal externally but round within. The windows, one to each face of the octagon, were originally large, but later became mere slips splayed inwards.

[1] As a supplementary note to my book on Armenia, p. 631, I may here draw attention to a Korean grave, illustrated in the *Kokka*, no. 276, which shows the spread of such reproduction to the East; the grave is usually assigned to King Heigen (d. A.D. 589). In the interior we see corbelling executed with granite slabs on which are painted beasts and continuous scrolls, a circumstance which leaves no doubt that its point of departure was the triangular area beyond the Oxus, the apex of which is towards India. For the portable wooden house of the Aryans see Fergusson's *History of Indian and Eastern Architecture*, 2 A 1, p. 403.

[2] Cf. Diez, *Churasanische Baudenkmäler*, p. 16.

A. *The many-domed type.*

This type originated in the Iranian dwelling-house. The palace of Fīrūz Abād has three domes along the transverse axis of the whole complex, between the entrance-rooms in the front and a court at the back. The disposition of the interior rooms along the transverse axis will demand our attention when we come to deal with Christian barrel-vaulted structures. This disposition persisted even after new liturgical requirements favoured the type with longitudinal axis, though the later Nestorian churches commonly have the row of domes on a long and not a transverse nave. The old church incorporated in the Halawīyeh Mosque at Aleppo may be of this type, should it prove to have had three domes down the longitudinal axis. It was a plan which became prevalent in Aquitaine, a point to which I will return in the next chapter; in the present place I am concerned solely with the main area of distribution, and only introduce the West in so far as isolated cases prove how far afield Asiatic vaulted types travelled even though they failed to establish themselves on any extensive scale.

The Church of the Apostles at Constantinople represented a combination of the longitudinal and the transverse plans by disposing the domes along both axes so as to form a cross. This church was destroyed by the Turks, but the type is copied in S. Mark's at Venice. S. Front at Périgueux is of the same type, the central dome at the crossing belonging to both axes, the longitudinal and the transverse. This arrangement has nothing to do with a second five-domed type, much favoured by the Orthodox Church, to which we shall return later.

It is an interesting fact that the long church with three domes in a line, and the cruciform type in which the two lines of domes cross each other at right angles are the predominant forms of the wooden churches in the Ukraine. It may be that Aryan timber-architecture here passed directly into Christian church-building; the persistence of the corbelled dome favours the supposition. It would be interesting to know why the wooden churches of Scandinavia show no analogy to these constructional forms of the South-East Aryans. In Iran the national custom of building with sun-dried bricks seems to have been transitional between the old Aryan method of wooden building and the Christian adoption of burnt brick for churches with several domes.

1   Mástara, domed square with apse-buttresses, *c.* A.D. 650 ; exterior from South-West.   See p. 61.

B. *The one-domed type.*

It seems to have been the tomb which even in pre-Christian times led to the free-standing square building with single dome. We may suppose the royal Arsand tombs in High Armenia to have been of this type, as also those of the two founders of the Christian State in that country, Irdat and Gregory, and those of their successors. The only surviving example is the Baptistery at Nisibis, near the Armenian frontier, erected in A.D. 359, probably on the site of the grave of S. James (*d.* A.D. 338); this is the most ancient ecclesiastical building in Mesopotamia. But the tomb of Theodoric at Ravenna compensates for what has been lost. The type did not develop spatially until it had to be increased in size in order to contain a Christian congregation. The enlargement was carried out in two ways : by setting several single-domed units in a row, and by the expansion of the single unit. The necessary abutment for such *martyria* was secured in Armenia by placing great niche-buttresses at the ends of the axes [1] to receive the thrust of the dome. There are two principal forms of the square plan with niche-abutment. One, which I shall call the ' niche-buttressed square ', shows the four niche-buttresses projecting from the four walls, which stand free as a visible square ; the other, to be called the quatrefoil, shows the square plan only in the interior, since the niche-buttresses meet each other at the corners without any intervening wall-space. Each type can be subdivided into further distinct varieties :

a. Subdivisions of the niche-buttressed square. These are of three kinds : that with niche-buttresses on the axes only ; that with niche-buttresses on both axes and diagonals ; and that without any niche-buttresses, the dome resting on interior supports.

1. *Niche-buttressed squares with the buttresses on the axes only.* This, the most important variety, was unknown to us until quite recent times. The first photographs of the simplest surviving example were taken during the expedition of the Institute which I founded in connexion with my professorial chair at Vienna ; this example is the Church of Mastara, dating from about A.D. 650 (Fig. 1, opposite). Except for the band of arcading beneath the restored roofs and the arched mouldings above the windows, it is without elaborate ornament ; it finds

---

[1] i.e. in the middle of each of the four sides.

a parallel in the Church of S. Gregory in the Haridsha monastery, which perhaps dates from the sixth century. A second variety is preserved in the Cathedral of Artik (Figs. 2–3, opposite) ; in this both exterior and interior are richly ornamented with blind arcading on engaged shafts ; a later example is the Church of the Apostles at Kars, erected in the second quarter of the tenth century. This last has blind arcading only round the dome ; but at Artik the decoration is such as to arouse the liveliest interest of the Western traveller. It covers two of the niche-buttresses ; the shafts are surmounted by cushion capitals, while triple interlaced bands are repeated on the cornices. The exteriors of these indigenous Armenian buildings produce an effect of strength and mass, mainly through their pyramidal form, the roofs of the four niche-buttresses leading the eye upwards to the dome crowning the structure.

This variety had a wide distribution beyond the limits of Armenia. We need feel no surprise to find it represented in North Mesopotamia (Deir es-Zaferan), as well as in Georgia. The richly ornamented niche-buttressed square at Amman in Moab is to be connected rather with the architecture of Iran proper. Here the niche-buttresses are square at the base and are carried over into a round plan by squinches, as in many other not purely Armenian examples. The point most important for us to notice in regard to relations with the West is that the niche-buttressed square can be traced across the Dobruja (*Tropaeum*) into the Czech country, where some of the most ancient national monuments are small-domed churches of this kind.

By the side of these national examples we may notice an adaptation of the apse-buttressed square due to imperial influences at Constantinople, perhaps immediately to the Court architect, Trdat, an Armenian, engaged upon the restoration of S. Sophia in A.D. 989. It is to be seen in splendid monastery churches, where we mark a tendency to replace the niche-buttresses by barrel-vaulted members. The best-preserved example is the Church of S. Luke of Stiris in Phocis between Helicon and Parnassus ; next to it that of the monastery of Daphni near Athens ; in the third place, that of Nea Moni on Chios, in many ways the nearest of all to the original type. The intrinsic splendour of decoration and allusions in texts lead us to conclude that these buildings were erected under imperial patronage.

2   Artik, cathedral, domed square with apse-buttresses ; South-West view.
See pp. 62, 95, 117, 146.

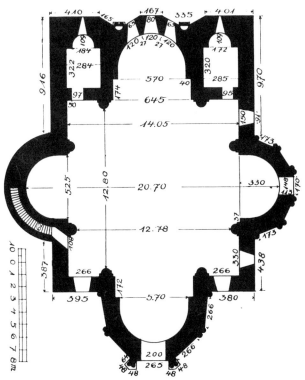

3   Artik, cathedral ; plan.   See p. 62.

2. *Domed churches on square plan with both axial and diagonal niche-buttresses* (i. e. with niche-buttresses both in the middle of each wall and at each corner). The niches at the corners are three-quarter cylinders, perhaps originally intended to strengthen the abutment of the dome, but soon pierced so as to give access to subsidiary chambers near the eastern niche required for liturgical purposes. These conditions are still apparent in Vaspurakan, where the Church of Achthamar (A.D. 915–21) seems to represent a later example of the original type. In Georgia there are at least two good surviving examples, the cruciform Church of Mzchet (about A.D. 600), and the Sion church at Aleni (about A.D. 1000), the creation of an Armenian architect, where the niche-buttresses with the rectangular corner-chambers are distinguishable even on the exterior. The model of the type is the Hripsimeh Church, and such complete examples are only to be found in Armenia : Awan, built about A.D. 570, has round corner-chambers, the Hripsimeh Church itself quadrangular, though here these and all the niche-buttresses are invisible from outside, since the whole structure is concealed within quadrangular external walls above which the dome towers on its windowed drum. In this one-domed group there developed a special Armenian form of external church decoration, affecting the niche-buttressed square ; this consisted of triangular slits designed to give salience to the niche-buttresses by vertical furrows of deep shadow, and comprised within a gable which gives the mass of the roof an essentially new aspect. In the interiors of this type the barrel vault is employed in connexion with the corner-chambers and the external walls ; it is interpolated between the square central bay and the niche-buttress, and serves also to accentuate the east-west direction of the main axis. This type is the most singular which occurs on Armenian soil. It has found no favour beyond the Armenian border, unless S. Peter's at Rome can be regarded as an example.

3. *Dome over square bays with axial niche-buttresses and central supports.* This variety has to-day only one representative in Armenia, the Cathedral of Bagaran, erected A.D. 624–31. In the inscription, the date is reckoned by the regnal year of Chosrau Parviz, and further, the oviform arch found with both the pointed and the round varieties betrays a Persian influence. Four piers originally supported a dome now fallen in, but once rising from squinches. High barrel vaults are interposed between these

piers and the niche-buttresses. The interior decoration is confined to narrow geometrical fillets, that of the exterior to arched mouldings over the windows, and a toothed motive on a slanting surface, such as at a later time we so often see used as a border at Venice.

The Bagaran type is known to have existed in Iran and on the route from Iran to Armenia. One example is seen in a corner hall, it must be admitted, of rather late date, in the palace of Sarvistan in Persis ; another is the now-destroyed praetorium of the second century at Mismiyeh in Syria, where it is modified in a Hellenistic sense ; a third is a church of the second half of the sixth century before the walls of Rusafa near the southern border of Armenia. The Armenian example at Bagaran is the only one in a region where the evolution of the type can be logically demonstrated. We conclude that a suggestion originating in Persia found its development in Armenia.

Now in A.D. 806 this type appeared on Frankish soil in the Church of S. Germigny-des-Prés ; it was probably, in the first instance, transmitted to France by Persian or Armenian archi-tects connected with the immigrant Goths from the Black Sea region. All the arches in this church are of the horse-shoe form, and the stucco decoration has Iranian features. The mosaic in the apse, with the Ark of the Covenant between angels, seems to find a parallel at Tekor in Armenia. A second example of the niche-buttressed square with interior supports is S. Satiro at Milan, erected A.D. 879, though here columns take the place of piers, and there has been frequent reconstruction. The type also exerted no unimportant influence on the drawings of Leonardo da Vinci, who may have become acquainted with it in Armenia itself. In general the West can only show a few scattered instances. In the east of Europe, on the contrary, this Greek-Cross plan with square central bay is of extraordinary importance, though it must be admitted that the niche-buttresses, as seen at Bagaran, are here generally omitted. It became the almost universal type of the Orthodox Church, and as such will receive fuller attention below.

   b. *Buildings composed of niche-buttresses only*. The large niches originally introduced in Armenia to buttress the four walls of the square-domed unit here touch each other without intervening walls, and enclose an (ideal) square, hexagon, or octagon ; thus arise radiating types with four, six, or eight niches in juxtaposition.

The dome rests on the wedge-like projections of the walls between every two niches ; it has a drum with windows, and a hemispherical cupola, covered by a pyramidal roof. We found numbers of such structures dating from the Bagratid period at Ani and Chtskonk, others, dating from the seventh century, at Agrak, Irind, and Eghiward. The type is probably one used for Baths, and must go back to pre-Christian times. I have adopted the name quatrefoil for a building of this kind with four niches. A quatrefoil may be either simple or have an ambulatory. In the West the first variety is to be seen at Biella and Galliano in North Italy, and at Montmajeur (Church of S. Croix) in France ; an example upon the road between East and West is to be seen on the Vistula at Cracow. The second variety has more importance. The most remarkable example in Armenia is the sepulchral chapel of S. Gregory at Zwarthnotz, erected, together with the adjoining palace, by the Catholikos Nerses III about A.D. 650 (Fig. 5, facing p. 66) ; here my assumption is that the tomb was enclosed in a containing structure. Excavation proved the existence of a great quatrefoil with ambulatory, clearly imitated in the ninth century at Bana and Ishchan, and in A.D. 1000 by King Gagik at Ani. In this group the quatrefoil is enclosed in a circle or a polygon. Armenia may, however, have possessed buildings in which one quatrefoil enclosed another. A connecting link exists on the road towards the west, in the so-called ' Red Ruin ' at Philippopolis ; a quatrefoil enclosing a quatrefoil is still preserved in the much-reconstructed Church of S. Lorenzo at Milan.

This example well illustrates the importance of Armenian discoveries as throwing light on the early growth of Christian art in Europe. S. Lorenzo has always been regarded as an enigma ; it has been too seldom observed that Italy can show a parallel case in the ' Minerva Medica ' at Rome, probably erected in conjunction with a villa of Licinius Gallienus (A.D. 260–8), and in the time of Constantine buttressed by two great niches. S. Lorenzo is a niche-buttressed square ; but the Minerva Medica is composed of ten niche-buttresses once supporting a dome upon a drum with windows. My impression is that this building, so abnormal for Roman imperial times, may be the work of Armenians, who were strongly represented in Rome. If so, this would be another of the proofs compelling us to admit the existence of Armenian domed buildings in variety in the fourth century, and simple niche-buttressed buildings even earlier. The hypothesis will give rise to much investigation ; at the same time it should provide an unhoped-for solution of the difficulty, insoluble as long as all attention was fixed on the Mediterranean area without a thought for the comparative material in the East, above all in Iran. Armenia now provides the connecting bridge by bringing the niche-buttress into the problem.

S. Sophia at Constantinople is itself related to the quatrefoil group with ambulatory. In their imitations of the building, the architects of the Turkish conquerors left out the galleries ; they placed their great niches on the diagonal axis, and so produced a regular quatrefoil. The amazing splendour of the interior decoration of S. Sophia, in which antique and Iranian elements blend, makes it difficult to distinguish the underlying plan ; but the logical affinities of the building now become clear. The nave, with its dome and two semi-domes, i.e. niche-buttresses, is so conspicuously Armenian that there can be no doubt as to the source from which the Anatolian architects derived their plan. Their problem was to build a Court church which should at the same time serve as an imperial hall of assembly ; the galleries were for the accommodation of women.

The second variety with contiguous niche-buttresses, the six-foil (Fig. 4, opposite), was widely distributed in Georgia, where it underwent the strangest transformations, one of which, represented at Kumurdo, has been repeated in a striking manner in the Attic monastery of Dau, though here too a gallery has been introduced. The chapel in the citadel of Marienberg at Würzburg, 'the oldest church in Germany', is a six-foil of the Armenian kind ; exact investigation of this chapel will show whether it may not prove to be a veritable landmark in architectural history.

The third variety, the eight-foil, is familiar through the example of S. Vitale at Ravenna. It is true that here, too, we must bear in mind the universal absence of galleries in Armenia, the country where the type is most widely represented and connected by the most numerous links with other church forms logically leading up to it or issuing from it. The variety with galleries makes its appearance as soon as the Greek area is entered ; we see this as early as the fourth century in the case of Constantine's octagon at Antioch, erected on the site of earlier Baths. This building, described by Eusebius, and often mentioned

4 Ani, Church of S. Gregory, mid-tenth century, sexfoil plan with triangular slits ; South-East view.   See p. 66.

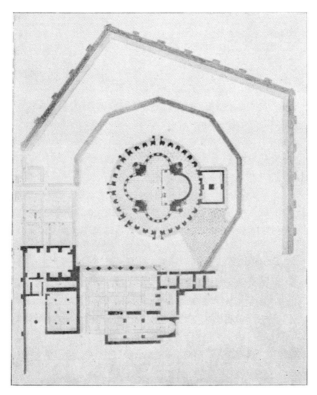

5 Zwarthnotz, Church of S. Gregory, c. A.D. 650, quatrefoil plan with ambulatory, and palace, p. 65.

by other writers, forms a link between Armenia and S. Vitale which has hitherto been regarded as, more or less, a copy of the Antioch octagon ; it would appear to have been an eight-foil with ambulatory. The simple eight-foil occurs at a late date in S. Michel-Entraigues near Angoulême. The idea of the type was taken up once more by Brunelleschi in the ' Tempio degli angeli ' begun by him at Florence, and by Leonardo in his drawings.

II. THE BARREL VAULT

We have already had to deal with this vault in discussing domical construction ; as far as Christian Church architecture is concerned, it seems to have originated in Mesopotamia rather than in Iran or Armenia. In Mesopotamia there is a whole series of churches vaulted exclusively in this style. Since examples of this method of roofing upon the most impressive scale are preserved in Sassanian palaces, for example in the celebrated Taḳ-i Kisra, it may well be indigenous, and have attained a wide development with the period of Parthian influence. At first sun-dried bricks were doubtless used, and the earliest examples will only be found by excavation ; the examples which now stand are of burnt brick, like the above-mentioned Sassanian palaces, or, as in the old Assyrian North, of stone and brick in combination.

A Parthian building, the palace at Hatra, in the desert between Tigris and Euphrates, about their middle course, shows a ground floor with barrel vaults only, constructed of rubble faced with stone ; the Arab method of roofing, as known to us from the Hauran churches, is only employed in the upper storeys. If we look back to yet earlier times, the uniform employment of the barrel vault in Assyrian and Babylonian palaces may be disputed, but the vault itself can be shown to have existed. Recent excavations have laid bare temple sites which may perhaps be considered prototypes of later church buildings.

A. *The church with transverse nave.* There were two regions which did not follow the Mediterranean area in beginning with the long church, but opposed to its advance a building remarkable for its breadth. One is East Syria, where a type originating in Arabia prevailed. Here we find a line of rib arches supported on piers ; the surrounding walls are carried to the height of the crown of the arch, and the roof is formed of stone slabs ; a series of such arched units forms a long hall. The Mesopotamian method was different. There the church consisted of a single transverse nave at right angles to the line connecting entrance-door and apse. To the occidental, the appearance of the exterior is unfamiliar, since on entering you have before you not the gable, as in the case of a Greek temple, but one whole slope of the roof, as in Chinese buildings. The best surviving examples are the Church of S. Jacob at Salah (Figs. 6–7, opposite), several monasteries in the Tur 'Abdin, and at Kesum near Edessa. The type may be connected with the church-plan of the early third century, when Christianity was for a while the official religion in Edessa, and is perhaps directly based on ancient oriental methods. It had no influence on the further development of Christian art, unless it be on the formation of the transept, especially in that Armenian variety called by me the domed transept, where a central dome is flanked by niche-buttresses or semi-domes ; this variety is admirably represented in the Church of the Virgin at Khakh in the Tur 'Abdin. S. Sophia at Constantinople shows in so far a distant affinity to this Meso-potamian type with its Armenian dome and flanking niche-buttresses, as it also has a domed nave ; though this follows and does not cross the longitudinal axis of the church. But as suggested above, the more direct affinities of S. Sophia are probably with Armenia. In the West the introduction of the transept may have been suggested by the Mesopotamian church with transverse nave.

B. *The long church.* The dome and the barrel-vaulted transverse nave dominate the oldest Christian church-building of the East. It is possible that a single-aisled long church existed at the same time. But in the fifth century the favourite Mediterranean form, the three-aisled long church, began its expansion, as we see both in East Syria and Armenia. In Syria, builders at first attempted to retain the old style of round arches and roof of stone slabs ; but here the timber-roof gradually gained in popularity. Barrel vaulting now first occurs in Armenia, probably through the influence of North Mesopotamia and Cappadocia. In these countries the three-aisled long church is almost always vaulted ; the timbered roof forms the exception, though it is found in parts of the Euphrates valley bordering on Syria, and examples occur in towns as far as Meiafarqin. But in the monasteries of the Tûr 'Abdin in Armenia, and at Birbir

6   Salah, Mar Yakub, church with transverse nave.   See p. 68.

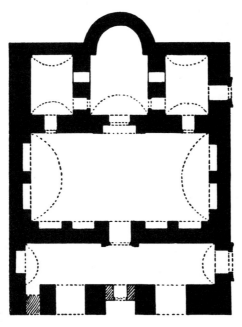

7   Salah, Mar Yakub, plan.   See p. 68.

8 Ereruk, basilica with ruined barrel-vaults, and façade towers.

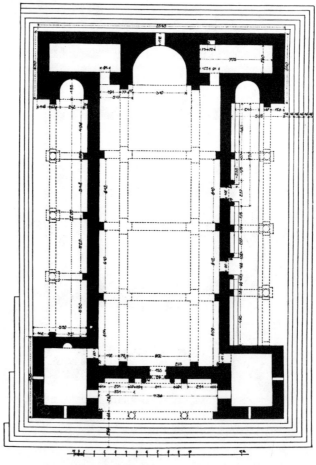

9 Ereruk, basilica ; plan. See p. 69.

Kilisse, only the vaulted hall-church is known, with, here and there, the regular vaulted basilica with clerestory. All the three varieties of long church are represented in the East by more or less numerous surviving examples. I am here considering only vaulted long churches, and omitting all three-aisled buildings with timber roofs. The one-aisled and three-aisled long church without clerestory, the hall-church, is widely diffused. Examples of the regular basilica with clerestory are rare. There is a single brilliant example at Ereruk (Figs. 8, 9, 19, facing pp. 69 and 91), as if to prove that the Armenian architect, whose proper interest was in the domed church, was capable of excelling in the foreign form also; the church is a regular basilica, homogeneous throughout, with a developed western façade between two towers. The portico or narthex at the west end, the aisles, and the high nave wall above the windows all have barrel vaults; and the lateral chambers on either side of the apse, which have more than one storey, have ascending barrel vaults of a type occurring in Asia Minor and at Como and Aix-la-Chapelle. But in all likelihood Ereruk is as early as the fifth century, when the Greek and Aramaean Churches sought to impose their types upon Armenia. Thus here, too, the theory is confirmed that the most important achievements in Early Christian art belong to the period between the fourth and sixth centuries. Ereruk ranks among the most consummate examples of the vaulted basilica in existence. The distribution of the vaulted long church will be discussed in the next chapter, which will be entirely devoted to this subject.

III. ABUTMENT OF THE DOMED BUILDING

Despite the intrusion of the long vaulted church, Armenia remained true to the dome. Everywhere within its own area, and beyond it in Constantinople, Salonika, and Egypt, it imposed its unit, the dome over the square bay on forms transitional to the long church, using niche-buttresses on trefoil-ended churches, whether single- or treble-aisled, omitting niche-buttresses but adding galleries in the so-called domed basilica.

A. *The Trefoil (Trikonchos).* Trefoils with single nave result when the western buttress of a niche-buttressed square or quatrefoil is replaced by a longitudinal or transverse barrel vault. The last variety, examples of which are preserved at Khakh on the upper course of the Tigris, and in monastery

churches in Egypt, may descend, as already observed, from the
Mesopotamian transverse-naved church, the barrel vault being
replaced by a central dome with flanking semi-domes. The nave
with trefoil end may therefore have a source other than the
cemetery chapel, the derivation suggested in *Orient oder Rom* ;
it may have originated independently in Armenia from the
niche-buttressed square when the needs of the Church called for
a long hall. This variety is represented in that country by
examples belonging to different centuries, and it migrated
westwards both by land and sea. The *cellae trichorae* of Southern
Russia, those in the Balkans, and in Italy, above all in Lombardy
and France, are like milestones marking its path ; on the Rhine
we find the tendency to develop three aisles, already pronounced
in Armenia. That country still possesses two large cathedrals of
this rich variety dating from the seventh century, Thalin (Fig. 10,
opposite) and Dwin ; in both the dome is placed in the
middle, in contrast to the usage obtaining where there is only
a single nave. At Kutais in Georgia, the first country into which
Armenian types spread, and in the Mesopotamian region of the
Euphrates and Tigris, we find such buildings observing this
essential law of the single-domed structure ; for example, the
long church with four niches and ambulatory at Resafa, and the
Church of the Virgin at Amida ; it is not certain, however,
whether in these cases the domes were of a permanent character.

B. *The domed basilica.* This type is exclusively confined
to Asia and the Balkans. It first appeared on the confines of
Armenia, moving South, and West as far as Salonika. It owes
its peculiar character to the fact that the Armenian single-domed
church, on entering the Greek area, had to meet the demand
for a women's gallery. The consequence was that the lateral
barrel-vaulted members were modified, as was the case with
the lateral niche-buttresses of S. Sophia, and two continuous
aisles resulted, at any rate, on the ground level.

At Meiafarqin, once, under the name of Tigranocerta,
capital of Armenia, the seventh-century Church of the Virgin
still recalls the Mesopotamian church with transverse nave ; it
is the type of S. Sophia at Salonika, which is an isolated instance
decorated in the Byzantine manner ; it proves the westerly
migration of Armenians and Mesopotamians in the period
before Justinian. Qasr Ibn-Wardan, in the Euphrates region,
and Khoja Kalessi in Cilicia, show the pronounced long type

10 Thalin, cathedral, sixth–seventh century, from South-West ; three-aisled trefoil-ended type ; the dome fallen in. See pp. 70, 214.

11   Ani, cathedral, before A.D. 989–1001 ; long cruciform domed type ; North-East view.   See pp. 72, 94.

co-existing with the transverse as early as the period between the fourth and sixth centuries. The type soon spread through Western Asia Minor, and has perhaps two representatives in the Balkans (Philippi and Pirdop), as early as the Salonikan example. In their present ruinous state these long churches suggest two-domed buildings, as does the Church of S. Irene at Constantinople. They, too, were probably also long domed basilicas, with galleries. S. Sophia at Constantinople, which I have already noted as an exceptional building, itself belongs to the series of domed basilicas; it is a quatrefoil transformed on basilican lines. Its galleries are a characteristic feature; had these been omitted, as they are in the Turkish mosques, the domed basilica with continuous aisles on the ground level would have been impossible. The name ' cruciform domed basilica' might be introduced for domed buildings which have a definitely basilican appearance, and have adopted, wherever possible, certain characteristics of the basilica such as a striking length of nave, and corresponding lateral aisles (cf. Odzun in Armenia and Mokvi in Georgia). The domed basilica at Meriamlik approaches most nearly to a Hellenistic style.

C. *The cruciform domed Church*. All transitional forms were finally superseded by this purely Armenian type. It developed either directly from the niche-buttressed square with interior supports (e. g. Bagaran), through the dropping of the niche-buttresses and a slight increase of nave length (e. g. Mren), or by the addition of a dome to the hall-church with piers (e. g. Tekor), the old long barrel vault and the new short transverse ones by themselves providing adequate abutment. The essential feature is that in the domed cruciform church, the dome rests upon four piers at the corners of a square bay and its thrust is taken by four barrel-vaulted limbs at right angles to each other and following the two axes of the cross. The result is a cruciform room with a dome rising from the crossing; in Armenia the dome is always in the middle, in other regions into which the type spread, either in the middle or nearer to the apse, according as the idea of a long church or that of a domed structure prevailed.

The type passed in the first instance to Asia Minor, and then, with the Armenian Dynasty, into Constantinople. The first emperor of the line, Basil I (A. D. 867–86), built his palace-church, the so-called *Nea*, on this plan. The type subsequently became dominant in Byzantine architecture, going wherever Byzantine influence extended, and it has to this day remained the consecrated form in the countries of the Orthodox Greek Church. I will not here follow up its distribution, because my immediate subject is the origin of Christian church-building in the West. In general it may be said that the triumph of the cruciform domed church meant the triumph of domical construction. The architects of the Renaissance were the first to bring about this change in western building. Deferring this point to the next chapter, I now proceed with the eastern types.

D. *The domed hall-church.* When the long-naved church was imposed upon Armenia in the fifth century (p. 7), the dome was added, and a type produced which bore in itself the seeds of Christian northern art in Europe (Gothic). Long ago old controversies as to the origin of the *opus francigenum* led to the notion that abutment by niches formed a first step in this direction, though no one had the slightest idea of the facts now known with regard to Armenia. When the Armenians wished to transform the long church, giving it at the same time a dome and spatial unity, they abandoned three aisles for one, and applied the piers supporting the dome directly to the outer walls ; the aisles now survived only as recesses without independent function and spatially belonging to a single domed hall, as was the case with the much later Barocco church. The piers applied to the interior walls have really the same significance as the Gothic external buttresses ; both are equally supporting piers.

A fully developed example of the domed hall-church is preserved in the cathedral of A.D. 668 at Thalish (Arudsh, Figs. 12–13, facing pp. 72 and 73). A building of this period is unlikely to be the archetype ; since the type affords the one satisfactory solution, we should expect the Armenian architects to have discovered it at the end of the fifth, or during the sixth century, when the conflict between national and ecclesiastical influences was at its height. The domed hall-church always retained the dome over the middle of the building. One of the most remarkable achievements in this style, the Cathedral of Ani (Figs. 11 and 21–23, facing pp. 71, 94, and 95), interposes very narrow arches between the piers bearing the dome and the wall, so that these dome-supports stand free. It is a delight, in a church earlier than A.D. 1000, to see the builder, the Court architect Trdat, carrying Armenian art so logically and so

12   Thalish, A.D. 668, domed hall-church, South-East side ; the dome fallen in.   See pp. 72, 214.

13   Thalish, the same ; interior from West.   See p. 72.

successfully past ' Romanesque ' to ' Gothic ' that many have
been at a loss to explain this cathedral in any other way than
as a reconstruction by a western master in the thirteenth century. The careful study of Armenian art has now proved
that the buildings of Trdat in the last quarter of the tenth
century uniformly show clustered columns and pointed arches ;
they still keep, indeed, the cushion capitals, but give the bases
of the colonnettes such deep mouldings that we again receive
a ' Gothic ' impression. If the above-mentioned Canon 182
of the Armenian Church had not interfered with free competition
among architects ; if the Armenian builder had not been too
closely confined to his walls by his technique of rubble faced
with dressed stone, his northern style might have yet more
definitely pursued the methods which the western masters
adopted or rediscovered down to the time of Vignola.

The Gesù, the domed hall-church of Vignola, the first
church of the Jesuit Order in Rome, finds its proper place at the
close of this section. We may at once compare it to Thalish,
a building nine hundred years older ; the only differences are
that Vignola's dome is nearer to the apse than to the west end,
while the lighting of the upper part of his church is not confined
to the windows under the dome. Vignola set his dome on the
axis of the church near its end, and lighted the nave throughout
its length from above ; while the Armenian always jealously
preserved that unity of space and lighting which belongs to the
very nature of the dome. We shall return to this church in the
next chapter, when we discuss S. Peter's at Rome.

Let us now resume the contents of the present chapter.
It conveys a false idea of development in church-construction
to assume that Christian ideas were first embodied in classical
forms, and then diffused these forms throughout the world.
The precedence habitually given to the Greek and Latin languages
is no less misleading than that accorded to classical architecture.
Aramaean, Iranian, and Armenian deserve, to say the least, an
equal, if not a privileged position, since it was they which provided
the real stimulus to development. If this is granted, we can better
understand how it was that when Diocletian reconstituted the
Roman state, he had no choice but to substitute a Persian for
a Roman organization. The changes introduced by this emperor
did not affect the social structure alone, but equally the whole
fabric of art. If this truth was overlooked, and people refused

to admit the force of my contentions, this only showed that in the study of Early Christian architecture group-distribution and sporadic occurrence had not been properly distinguished. It showed, above all, that to this very hour students have allowed themselves to be prejudiced against my pioneer work by the academic views so obstinately retained in certain European capitals. In scholarship there are still unscientific influences at work convinced of their power to arrest the advance of learning.

It must not, however, be supposed that the question of 1901 ' The East or Rome ' still has the old importance to-day, or that a full agreement might be reached by changing the formula to ' The East *and* Rome '. There has never been any question of splitting hairs in this fashion. As far as architecture is concerned it should now be superfluous to add a single word. After the fourth chapter, dedicated to the West, we shall be in a position to judge whether the hypothetical element in our attitude towards decorative and purely representational art has not gained support by the certainty gradually attained in the field of architecture. For in this field we are no longer dealing with mere suppositions set up just to test the point whether things might not have been ordered in a certain way, but with facts which cannot but produce their effect upon a scholar's mind. These facts no longer allow men to persuade themselves on the authority of mere texts that things ought to have happened in this or that way. The specialist who investigates essential facts and their development by the comparative study of monuments has firmer ground beneath his feet than the philologist who presumes to compose history from written sources, and thinks by this means once more to confine the whole development to Roman ground. As soon as it becomes a question of artistic creation, Rome has nothing to say in the matter ; we shall see an example of this in the mosaics of Roman apses, on which I have something to say in Chapters VI and VII.

IV

The Succession of Periods in Western Architecture

IN accordance with the chronology above suggested, I do not regard Christian architecture, the origin of which forms my subject, in the narrow ' Early Christian ' sense, but from a wider point of view, passing beyond the Middle Ages to the High Renaissance, even to the beginning of those influences diffused over the whole of Europe by the Counter Reformation. The usual division is as follows : Early Christian period, down to about A. D. 467 or A. D. 568 ; period of the great migrations, down to Charlemagne ; Ottonian period, down to about A. D. 1000 ; lastly, the Romanesque, Gothic, and Renaissance periods. But this classification is only justified if confined to the narrow sphere of western civilization, and even so, it can only be admitted as part of the machinery of historical research. It becomes untenable as soon as the horizon is enlarged in the manner proposed in these pages. What really dominates all these centuries, considered from the point of view of art, is the struggle between East and West, or that between North and South ; in any proper classification this fact must be recognized, and in naming its several divisions we must take it into account.

In the previous chapter I purposely disregarded the basilica. I here in like manner disregard the survival of antique tradition in such familiar architectural embellishments as the column and the capital. It is a matter of observation that the introduction of antique ornamental features goes with a decline in constructive power ; at the time of the Renaissance we have the remarkable spectacle of a triumphant classical decoration, in great part imposing its laws upon a system of construction which followed quite different paths.

Before Christian church-building was openly permitted, that is, before A. D. 313, western art, whether generally influenced from Hellenistic sources, or particularly influenced by Rome, was in a fair way to accept the complete supremacy of the vaulted construction originating in Mesopotamia and Iran. Had the Western Church yielded like the Eastern, Europe would not have been arrested in its architectural development during a period of more than five hundred years. The collapse of western architecture resulted from the readoption of the wooden roof in place of the vault. If in this matter the Church had not followed the Temple, northern art would have been spared a wrong turning. The S. Peter's of the fourth century ought by rights to have inherited the style of the basilica of Constantine in the Roman forum; it should not have been necessary for Europe to wait until the sixteenth century to pick up the dropped thread under quite different conditions. What struggles and efforts fill the interval between the erection of the old S. Peter's and that of the new, before the Roman vaulted basilica, transformed in the Armenian sense, could continue its progress in the West !

The basilican architecture of the West may thus be divided into the following periods: the period of the wooden roof; that in which the eastern vaulted building was transmitted to the South; finally, that of independent development in the North, lasting until the domed building attained a compromise with the long-naved plan, and made its reappearance from the South, anticipating any northern attempt in the same direction. It may be that the future will solve the problem by discovering that the external buttressing which we associate with Gothic and the central-domed system of Armenia were created one for the other.

During the Early Christian period proper, the West was the passive recipient of types transmitted from the Mediterranean and the East. There can be no question of national styles in the western church-building of the fourth century. The common Hellenistic type of long building with wooden roof was predominant, and became the chosen form of the Roman Church. It may be called the fatality of western architecture that neither Constantine nor his successors built either of the two great *martyria* of S. Peter or S. Paul with vaulted roofs, or in the form of the domed basilica. We may suppose that the stream of oriental influence ceased in Rome when the building of Constantinople was undertaken, and the national architecture of the Armenians and the Mesopotamian Syrians began; while the groined vault, which had become a characteristically Roman feature, was no longer in demand in the construction of columned basilicas. Barrel vault and dome, the two essentials of church-building in the East, could not permanently establish themselves in Christian Rome. Yet the former had been transplanted to the western capital by architects like Apollodorus of Damascus, who had given them expression on the grandest scale in the Temple of Venus at Rome, and in the great Baths and Fora, all examples of vaulted construction in brick.

One reason why the timbered roof was so hurriedly adopted in Christian church-building may perhaps be sought in familiarity of the people with the type of the pagan temple. In the Iranian region such models only occur in isolated examples like the Temple of Garni in Armenia ; there was thus no general incentive to reproduce the model. A cause which might have been expected to dissuade Rome and the Hellenistic countries from adopting it was its inflammable nature ; the Christians wanted not a shrine or temple, but a building to contain a congregation, and the assemblage of large numbers under a roof of this kind was dangerous. It seems the fact that the timber-roofed basilica only established itself in permanence where the antique temple was widely represented. The regions which first followed Persia in employing the vault were not those in immediate relations with the Mediterranean area and its essentially Graeco-Roman culture, but, on the contrary, those connected through an active commerce with the main sources of vaulted architecture in the East. The decisive influence in dissemination seems, however, to have been that exercised by the mass migration of the Goths westwards from the Black Sea. This people and the craftsmen who went with them built vaulted structures in groups where hitherto there had been only single, if conspicuous, examples, as at Milan, designed to meet special needs of the Court.

In the Mediterranean area the retention of the timber roof involved that of another classical feature—the column. This must be regarded as a legacy even more momentous for Christian architecture than the wooden roof. For while the combustible roof was ultimately displaced through fears for the safety of the congregation, and through the pious wish to build for eternity, the column was never superseded.

The safer vaulted construction of the East had gradually to force its way against old prejudice favouring the type of the Greek temple. Progress was necessarily slow ; a process reaching its end in Persia as early as the fourth century, required more than a thousand years to struggle to victory in the West against the combined influence of Hellenism and Rome. And the victory was never complete; even to-day the North has to fight for its independence against the Hellenistic Southern style which triumphed so long ago in Europe. It was an event of deep significance when Christian architecture in the Mediterranean area transferred to the church, now required for congregational use, features from the pagan shrine intended to house the god's statue, a type of building derived from wooden construction; it was an event of no less moment when in contemporary Armenia a monumental type arose which in its turn failed to meet the need of the later Church for length in its places of worship. Between these two extremes, development verged from one side to the other until the West began to cover its churches with barrel vaults and multiplied domes, and then entered upon its proper northern path, while the Orthodox Church of Eastern Europe adopted the domed Greek-Cross plan as its consecrated form. In the East the centralized domed type triumphed over the long church. In the West the opposite was the case; the long axis was retained, and in this the timbered roof and column were more potent as determining factors than the eastern position of the altar adopted from Oriental sources. For the altar existed before orientation: even in the Syrian coast region the apse was originally at the west end. In later times orientation, which began in Armenia and Asia Minor, completely triumphed in the West together with the long nave. Even to-day very little is known of all these struggles for survival, the discovery of which was first made possible by study of the ruined churches on the eastern shores of the Mediterranean and in Armenia. In tracing the destinies of Christian art in the West, I begin with that region which, like Armenia in the East, was originally least affected by Southern influence.

1. *The wooden churches of the North.* The first question which we have to ask is whether the North was capable of itself arriving at vaulted buildings for congregational use. We may be permitted to begin by comparison with China and India. None of the three national religions of China required a hall to contain a congregation. There was, therefore, no incentive to build closed halls on a great scale; and since local beliefs did not demand buildings designed to last for ever, architecture naturally

failed to advance beyond the stage of construction in wood. It was otherwise in India, where wooden architecture predominated among the Aryans down to the time of Asoka, but gave place to a more durable form of construction when the idea of eternity prevailed, at any rate in the religious field. A permanent character was uniformly given to the constructed and free-standing stûpa with the stone rails enclosing the processional path. More than this, the interiors of temples became permanent, if only after the old indigenous fashion, so prejudicial to all organic development, by which space was enclosed not by the construction of walls and roofs but by excavation from the living rock. But in India wooden building still survived in the monasteries, in palaces, and dwelling-houses.

In the North the wooden house and hall of pagan times do not seem to have provided, as might have appeared obvious, the model for the Christian place of worship. Nature herself had from of old provided it under the open sky. Places for religious assemblage, roofed in like house and hall, only came in a short time before the admission of Christianity, and chiefly as a result of its introduction. I therefore doubt whether it is correct to assume from remains of temples in this part of the world, that the temple really served as the point of departure for church construction. It is hardly possible as yet to be categorical; but the North probably approached religious architecture along the path already trodden by Greece, though with the difference that the determining factor was not the imitation of a shrine to enclose a statue, but the production of an interior large enough to contain a congregation. This had a remarkable consequence for the whole North, Celtic and German and Slav alike; what was wanted to meet the needs of people living in small settlements far removed from each other was not a few great buildings but a multitude of small ones. The nature of the material employed counted for much; but a social or economic condition, the absence of cities, also had its own significance.

The character of indigenous church-building in the North is clearly reflected in the surviving wooden churches of Scandinavia. The student of Christian art is ill advised if he fails to begin his examination of Northern architectural remains by investigating these structures. In the North their position is analogous to that of local types in Iran, those ancient developments of Aryan wood-construction which formed the point of departure in my discussion of Armenian churches. Many facts of high evolutional significance have been overlooked or contested through an incapacity to distinguish between the constraint laid upon art by the religious movement from the South and the creative freedom of architecture in the North, at any rate until the immigrant southern influence became too strong to be ignored.

It is time that we began to take the large group of northern wooden churches into account. There were conflicts and compromises with the South which might well explain many obscure points both in the period of Oriental influence (Romanesque) and during the growth of the crowning (Gothic) style in northern church-building.

The wooden churches have more than one type. There is the simplest house-form with four walls and gabled roof, exemplified by the single-naved church at Hemse ; there is a type of square plan, the so-called Valdres type (Fig. 14, opposite), in which originally four masts seem to have been used in the interior. I proceed on the contrary theory to that of Dietrichson [1]; instead of regarding the wooden churches as copies of models in stone, and beginning with those which have numerous columns, I am inclined to construct their pedigree by placing the four-columned Valdres type at the beginning, and tracing the descent down to the twelve-columned type of Borgund, where the church was built about A.D. 1150 and received its present form in A.D. 1360 (Fig. 15, opposite). Here the four single masts are replaced by groups of three, the result giving that total of twelve columns characteristic of Aryan and Islamic wooden architecture from India to Spain. At Borgund we already find the long nave which, in satisfaction of liturgical requirements, was afterwards the condition of all further development. In any case, the introduction of masts in the northern wooden churches may have met half way the forward movement of the basilica from the South (Fig. 16, opposite). There must, moreover, have been in the northern system of wood-building some cause tending to the supersession of the barrel vault by the groined variety ; this cause is perhaps to be found in the method of supporting the clerestory and roof on spaced interior supports instead of upon the outer walls.

The wooden architecture of the North may ultimately

[1] *Die Holzbaukunst Norwegens*, p. 17.

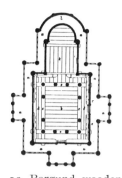

15 Borgund, wooden church; plan; after Dietrichsen. See pp. 80, 117.

14 Valdres, typical wooden church; plan; after Dietrichsen. See p. 80.

17 Triforium of wooden churches; after Dietrichsen. See p. 96.

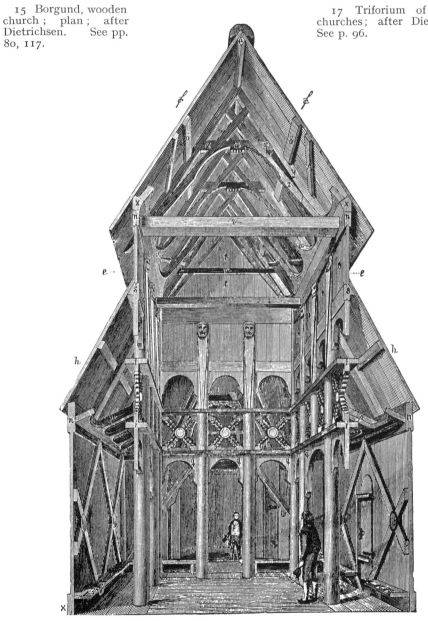

16 Borgund, wooden church; interior; after Dietrichsen. See pp. 80, 93, 96, 117.

derive from the same influences as the wooden churches of the Ukraine, the stone reproductions of wooden dwellings in the temples of Kashmir and a whole group of Indian buildings with domes built by continuous corbelling. I will take only a single piece of evidence, the so-called cushion capital of Romanesque art. It is a mistake to suppose that the Lombards invented the type and introduced it into Germany. The truth probably is that it was invented in Armenia and carried westwards into northern Italy. In the Ararat region of Armenia it is so densely represented that we can have little hesitation in describing it as an indigenous form. Yet it might be precipitate to explain its appearance in Germany directly by importation from Lombardy or Armenia. Most likely it appeared in Armenian and in German art from a common source, the wooden architecture of the Aryans. It must always be remembered that the North is every whit as cardinal in the movement of art as the Mediterranean area in the South. We cannot therefore conclude, just because certain forms appear in Armenia, Lombardy, and Germany, that one of these countries inspired the others, much less that all were inspired by the South ; quite apart from their mutual relations, all alike may have produced an identical form through mere technical necessity, for all had to deal alike with timber, the usual raw material of the North. We shall only begin the proper study of this wooden architecture when we at last bring ourselves to recognize its fundamental value both for the northern area itself and for the border regions towards the south, such as Armenia and Lombardy. It is to be hoped that the discoveries at Oseberg may point the way in this direction.

II. *The Oriental Art of Western Europe—Romanesque*

Just as the dome on a square plan spread from Iran into Armenia, so by ways at present not fully known the barrel-vaulted church came into Gaul from Mesopotamia and the interior of Asia Minor, there to undergo a development no less logical than that of the dome in Armenia. Exploration and research both in East and West tends to bring the Goths into the foreground as the disseminators of this vaulted style, that Teutonic tribe which taught the North its runes and once migrated, probably from Sweden, across East Germany to the shores of the Black Sea. Let us recall a single character in Gothic history, Ulfilas, the translator of the Bible, who came from Cappadocia, and accompanied the Goths across the Danube. But the tribe pressed forward even farther ; its paths led it into Greece, Italy, Gaul, and Spain. Wherever the Goths settled we find traces of their art on an extensive scale, though both Ravenna and Rome form exceptions. For though individual *martyria*, such as the tomb of Theodoric, are domed, yet in Ravenna the church for general assembly remained the timber-roofed basilica with long nave. It is true that Ursus appears to have erected a vaulted basilica, but, if so, it had no successor. The case was very different in Milan. There Ambrose himself must have resorted to vaulted construction, though S. Lorenzo alone survives to attest the influence which he introduced. We shall return to this subject below.

It was the Visigoths who laid in the West those foundations on which vaulted construction grew up with the help of ever fresh inspiration from the East. It may be true that the timber-roofed basilica predominated in Gaul through Greek influence, and among the Franks through Roman ; nevertheless the *manus Gothica* did not cease from its activities. In Spain continually, in France exceptionally, there arose buildings of ashlar which the texts repeatedly ascribe to Visigothic hands. The relations between the Goths and the East become convincing when we contemplate the Tomb of Theodoric at Ravenna, unique with its massive ashlar. The tombs of the Armenian kings in the citadel of Ani on the upper course of the Euphrates must have looked like this ; and it is related of the tomb of Sana-truk (between A.D. 75–110) that the Persians, when they tried to rob it in A.D. 350, were prevented from gaining entrance by its skilful construction and the careful joining of its massive masonry. The Armenians and the Goths were in contact with each other in Asia Minor and on the Black Sea. Ulfilas came from the Armenian borderland in Asia Minor; the language of his translation of the Bible shows many traces of Armenian influence.

While whole Teutonic peoples migrated into Western Europe from the East, there was a movement in the contrary direction not to be overlooked when we are considering the possibility that artistic forms travelled westward from the Black Sea and the Mediterranean. Just as in our own time the whole Mohammedan world would make pilgrimage to Mecca, so in the first millennium of our era every Christian girded up his loins to visit the holy places of Jerusalem. The Crusades are only intelligible as the end of a great movement which had a stronger mastery over the minds of men than we are apt to suppose. These continual pilgrimages, the itineraries of which were carefully mapped out, led at the beginning of the period into what was still the Promised Land of art. The sights which met the pilgrims' eyes were not lost to memory without leaving a trace ; on their way they saw the buildings of Armenian Cilicia, at the end of the journey the venerable monuments of Jerusalem and Bethlehem. We are just beginning to realize the possibility that the Church of the Holy Sepulchre was not simply a timber-roofed basilica with galleries, but a church with a dome over the crossing.

If this was so, the surprisingly early appearance of this type in Europe finds a ready explanation ; it cannot be questioned that Armenians were quite capable of constructing it in the time of Constantine.

The monasteries were also important agents in promoting a lively intercourse between East and West ; other contributory causes were the traditional political relations between Rome and Byzantium, and the continued interchange of views between the Churches in countries round the Mediterranean. Monastic institutions spread from Egypt, Syria, and Asia Minor, and every new foundation meant an intellectual and artistic influence. Thus no less a man than Cassiodorus adopted for his newly-established monastery, Vivarium in Southern Italy, the system of theological study[1] devised by the schools of Nisibis, and by this action ensured its transmission to the West : remains of his foundation point to the adoption at the same time of vaulted construction. Marseilles and its neighbourhood formed the terminus of a sea-route which very early rivalled in importance the land-route followed by the Goths as a means for the penetration of the West by Oriental influence ; from the seaports this route was continued in the interior up the Rhone and into the valley of the Rhine. It was not used by the Church alone ; it was above all a trade-route. It brought a swarm of Syrian traders, in whose train doubtless came many Armenians. In the preceding chapter we made acquaintance with a number of individual buildings which confirm the presence of Orientals in Western Europe, notably S. Germigny-des-Prés, which, so far

[1] The *Trivium* and *Quadrivium*.

as its type goes, might almost as well stand on Armenian soil, and in its decoration, both of stucco and mosaic, betrays no less clearly its connexion with the Iranian area. Another piece of evidence which points to Eastern influence is the statement that at this period Charlemagne sought the collaboration of Greeks and Syrians for the emendation of the Gospel text, a statement confirmed by the character of various miniatures in Carolingian manuscripts. There was thus no lack of intermediaries between the distant East and those West Frankish and Rhenish territories which played the leading part in the earlier Middle Ages. Nor were the above routes the only means of communication. Much reached the West not directly by land or sea, but indirectly through Upper Italy. From the fourth and fifth centuries, when they were capitals of West-Roman Courts, Milan and Ravenna had been centres of an intellectual and artistic life not unconnected with the prevalent Oriental influences. In the first three Christian centuries Rome had derived its artistic vigour from Alexandria; with the fourth century she continued to lose ground. But in proportion as Rome declined, Milan rose and pursued paths of its own. The landmark of these times, S. Lorenzo, points to the region in which the new art had its roots. As in liturgy and church music, so in architecture, the initiative lay not with Rome but with Hither Asia. We have already seen that the plan of S. Lorenzo, the domed square with niche-buttresses, is the primary unit in Armenian church-building. And reproduction of this kind could not have stopped here; S. Lorenzo may be exceptional; but vaulting in national church architecture must have been widely adopted at an early date. The relations of S. Ambrose with the spiritual leaders of the Greek Church in inner Asia Minor may well have embraced such matters as church-building and decoration, for the letters of the Fathers show beyond all doubt that these were subjects of correspondence at this time. Like Bishop Ursus of Ravenna, who before A. D. 400 built his vaulted Basilica Ursiana, S. Ambrose may have himself erected basilicas with barrel vaults. The decoration of the old cathedral of Ravenna, unfortunately replaced by a more modern church, is happily known to us through the description of Agnellus, which proves that the Iranian method of covering walls in the north of Italy, to which we shall recur, was usual. The nature of the decoration is described by the letters of Nilus of Sinai and Paulinus of Nola: the nave walls were ornamented with hunting and fishing scenes and figures of beasts; the apse had a landscape. For Agnellus, the ninth-century writer, these things had become an enigma; but there are still many traces in Ravenna of this more ancient phase.

It may be that in these early days the ground was prepared for the commanding and original position assumed at a later time by North Italy in the development of Western architecture, in so far as this part of the country became a centre of distribution for the Eastern vaulted style. To this various causes would naturally contribute; there were the direct relations between Milan and Asia Minor, and those between Ravenna and Antioch; above all, there was the presence of Armenians among the immigrant Goths. These Orientals were more intelligible than were the Romans to the Lombards, who on their arrival were still in the stage of building in wood; they became indispensable when the invaders adopted a new method of construction. I will say nothing here of the hypothesis that the artificers known as *magistri commacini* may have been closely connected with these developments; it is much more important that actual features in Lombardic building point to Armenia.

Among such features we may especially note the Iranian squinch, frequently used to effect the transition from the square ground-plan to the circular plan of the dome, and the employment of square tower-like drums with windows. But Armenian influence appears also in long-naved churches; it may, for instance, be detected in the so-called cushion-capital. In Italy this form seems first to occur on a stone sarcophagus at Lambrate; in this connexion we may recall the tradition, unauthenticated though it is, that Daniel, the favourite stone-mason of Theodoric, was an Armenian. When we also remember that at a later period no less than three Armenian cavalry regiments were quartered in Ravenna, we shall see that the presumption of a national influence is by no means impossible. It is, however, of more importance that the cushion-capital became a characteristic mark of the Lombard masters. It need not have come by a roundabout way through Armenia; but may have entered Italy directly from the North through the influence of wooden construction. It was not so with vaulting, which I shall now discuss in connexion with individual types and varieties of church buildings in the West itself.

A. *Barrel-vaulted churches.*

The dominant kind of vaulting in the West was at first not the domical but the ' barrel ' type. It is easy to see why : the long church was already well established before there was any idea of vaulting. But when vaulting was resumed in the West, solutions of the problem how to roof long churches with barrel vaults were ready to hand in Mesopotamia, in Asia Minor, and, after the fifth century, in Armenia. In Iran itself another method had been introduced, one based on the dome, in which a long hall is covered by a series of cupolas in a line ; this we shall find employed later in the south of France. After all this there need be little cause for surprise when we find the West treading in the footsteps of the East. I shall now discuss the several provinces in which there was originally a distinctive national character, concluding with a few words on the loss of individuality by the general adoption of the northern Gothic style.

The barrel-vaulted churches of the West have a nave only, or a nave and two aisles, with or without rib-arches. These features existed in the East in earlier times. But the vaulted basilica, that is, a three-aisled vaulted building with a clerestory, existed in the East only in isolated examples ; the same was the case in the South ; the vaulted basilica was widely distributed in the North alone. Should not this simple and fundamental fact in itself lead to the conclusion that South and East go together, but that the North follows its own path, starting from wooden architecture and the timber-roofed basilica, and finding its own northern solution in what we call Gothic ? I know that a hundred details prompt to the rejection of this hypothesis, but is it not advisable in our search for guiding principles at least to keep it before us ? The vaulted church without clerestory arrived in the West, so to speak, at a bound ; the vaulted basilica, on the other hand, reached its final development only by degrees. Does not this itself suggest the adoption of ready-made forms on the one part, and a process of free experiment on the other ? And is it mere chance that the adoption of the ready-made is found in the South and the systematic experiment in the North ? Did not the wooden churches of the North prepare the advent of Gothic by means of their tall, mast-like pillars in their interiors, which made clerestory lighting possible ?

a. Barrel-vaulted Churches with single nave. The starting-point here is the hall. The form is widely distributed in all the Oriental regions in touch with Mesopotamia. Nothing was known of this fact when the academic theory as to the barrel-vault in the south of France was first formulated. We were told that since antique remains show it to have been the prevalent Roman method of covering long rooms, the Roman method was the obvious inspiration for the French architect, and thus we arrived at 'Romanesque' art. This theory is contradicted by recent investigations in Armenia and Asia Minor and among the Visigothic churches in Spain, proving that the Eastern barrel-vault is not merely sporadic in the West, like the dome, but widely distributed, with numerous monuments in groups. In Spain a mass of important material has been discovered which my opponents would fain treat as they have treated the material in the East, refusing it significance for the early history of development on the plea that it is of post-Mohammedan date. The horse-shoe arch plays a special part in this discussion. This also is a characteristically Armenian form, and may probably be traced back to Aryan wood-construction. Its appearance in Spain at the same time as the vault is significant. No amount of critical gymnastics can permanently obscure the truth as to facts like these.

In Mesopotamia barrel-vaulted single-naved buildings, with or without rib-arches, are contemporary with the earliest Christian churches, and appeared in the second to third century ; they may well have been indigenous in Armenia as well, and the fifth century found them so numerously represented that examples still survive. It need not therefore surprise us to find them representing the most ancient element in the early church buildings of France, especially in the south, in Aquitaine and Provence, the heart of the Visigothic and Burgundian states. They are long churches with barrel-vaults and rib-arches, the nave leading up to a hemispherical apse. They often show Armenian characteristics ; they have polygonal apses and very massive walls ; above all, they reject the wooden roof, the tiles being laid directly on the extrados of the vaults ; we may add to the list their tendency to end the chancel with a trefoil. It is true that surviving examples are not earlier than the year A.D. 1000 ; but if once we grasp the possibility of a connexion with the Visigoths and their Armenian architects, fresh research may well bring earlier remains to light. Sometimes the pier-projection is replaced by that conspicuously Irano-Armenian motive the double pilaster.

Spain has also a whole series of one-naved buildings with barrel-vaults on rib-arches, and actually dating from the Visi-gothic period. The chief examples are the church of the Virgin at Naranco, a structure recalling the hall of the Tak-Ivan in the south of Persia; the church of Santa Cristina at Lena, and other buildings. Here we seem to have contemporary evidence which may be brought into direct connexion with the Oriental influence introduced by the Goths.

It is a fact not without importance that we find in the south of France a tentative movement towards the Armenian ' domed hall '. The vault is carried not by the walls, but on projecting piers in front of them, the walls becoming thinner, and the piers dividing the interior into shallow bays. As in Armenia, we here find buildings in which the treatment of space is handled in a masterly manner for which it would be hard to find a parallel. The chief example is the cathedral of Orange.

b. Hall-churches. In the case of the so-called Hall-churches, with three aisles but no clerestory, it is again commonly assumed that Roman buildings, such as the Bains de Diane at Nîmes, served as models. But we must observe that the hall-church is the common form of the three-aisled long church in Armenia and Asia Minor. Here again the old dogma must be retested in the light of new facts. The Roman barrel-vault is always supported by the walls, never, except perhaps in cisterns, on piers or columns. The most individual attempt to support the arch carrying the vaulted roof on a pier projecting from the wall was first made on a large scale in the east of Syria ; the earliest three-aisled churches with such piers may have originated in the interior of Asia Minor ; in Armenia they began in the fifth century.

With the hall-churches we reach a type which had a wider area of distribution. They spread from Lombardy and the Rhone valley, in the south into Spain, in the north along the Rhine into Westphalia. They also flourished in Auvergne, which introduced a hall-church with galleries, just as it adopted the galleried domed-basilica in opposition to the Armenian type of one-domed church. In its southern region the West begins with the hall-church, a logical development similar to that begun by the North with the basilica. I shall not here treat this subject in detail, but select only such points as properly concern the present volume.

B. *Churches with several domes.*

Allusion was made in the last chapter to a group of long churches in France apparently connected with similar buildings in Iran. We should no more regard these as of French creation than we should attribute, for example, the early church remains on Bulgarian soil to Bulgarian genius. Like the type of the barrel-vaulted churches with single nave, this type also is an importation, more ancient than the Frankish Empire, and probably of Eastern origin. These churches occur in the same regions as those with barrel-vaulted halls, and chiefly in Aquitaine; in Périgord they completely superseded the barrel-vaulted type. Armenia, as we have seen, was not their place of origin; they came from Iran, their route, so far as it can be traced, leading from the region of the Nestorian churches and of Aleppo to Constantinople. The employment of the pointed arch is additional evidence of this. It is remarkable that in the French churches the domes do not rise from squinches, but from spherical pendentives, though these are not constructed with wedge-shaped stones but, as in Armenia, with overlapping horizontal layers. The blind arcading in the interiors also points to Armenia. The chief group shows several such domes following the long axis of the church, but in the case of S. Front at Périgueux their cruciform arrangement resembles that of the lost church of the Holy Apostles at Constantinople and of the wooden churches in the Ukraine. There has been much controversy whether these French churches are or are not Byzantine. The answer is certainly in the negative. But they afford perhaps the best examples of a movement from Iran to Europe which did, indeed, pass by way of Constantinople, but died out in a region much farther to the west, where it found its chief representation. Like the Armenian domed churches, the churches of Périgord are distinguished by one common characteristic. Their primary purpose is to enclose space; the architects dispensed with decoration in the achievement of the desired effect; it is from their simplicity that these buildings derive their greatness. S. Mark's at Venice is a milestone upon their way from East to West, though here the splendour of decoration shows an intermediate influence, coming not from any area allied in feeling to Armenia, but from the Byzantine court. It was therefore an error to connect S. Front primarily with S. Mark's, even a greater error than to hold the old belief that the cathedral of Aix-la-Chapelle was no more than a copy of S. Vitale at Ravenna. For the effect of its interior S. Front should be compared with the cathedral of Ani, or with Thalish ; so also should Notre-Dame at Le Puy. When this comparison is made it will be seen how far East-Aryan conception in its impressive unity excels the West-Aryan agglomeration of spatial units.

In their attempts to discover the origin of these single-naved domed churches in France, writers have often brought the Crusades into the picture, and have drawn special attention to similar buildings in Cyprus, altogether overlooking Armenia, and Cilicia with its Armenian art. More than once these discussions have also brought into notice the almost contemporary movement connected with the Manichaeans, Paulicians, and Bogumils, which was ended by the crusade against the Albigenses. One imagines oneself transported to Armenia when one reads of the rejection of the Eucharist and remembers what struggles with the Greek Church centred in this point in the countries where this type originated. Much of the plainness in the decoration of these buildings, such as simple profiles and blind arcading, might be explained on the hypothesis of such a connexion. Evidence of certain Persian features is also not without significance.

C. *The groined vault.*

The groups hitherto discussed possess only the barrel-vault and dome. But developed Romanesque employed the groined vault. Must this be ascribed to the revival on Frankish soil of the Roman moulded variety, despite the fact that the South transmitted the timber-roofed basilica, and only the East the vaulted building ? This is the popular hypothesis. In my judgement the capacity for revivals, by which I mean deliberate restorations of Southern forms in the North, was lost for centuries, and in fact presupposes a very different intellectual plane to that attained in the early years of Romanesque architecture. Most people will perceive an underlying contradiction here.

18 Salah, Church of S. James, type with
transverse nave ; vaulting of nave ; photo.,
G. L. Bell. See p. 91.

19 Ereruk ; South view. See figs. 8, 9 ;
and p. 69.

20 Sofia, Church of S. Sophia, cruciform domed church with
three aisles ; plan ; after Filow. See p. 91.

The earlier suggestion of a Byzantine influence was nearer the mark ; it was at least so far correct that it derived vaulted construction from an Eastern source. This construction may have contained the germ of the groined vault subsequently developed by Aryan logic. The Greeks began with a wooden house, the Armenians with a walled square surmounted by a dome. What did the West- and East-Aryans of the South make of these elements ? What did the North make of the groined vault ?

The Goths brought to the Northern Aryans, among other things, a kind of vault well known to us in Mesopotamia (Fig. 18, opposite), and traced on its western migration as far as the church of S. Sophia in the capital of modern Bulgaria ; this was a barrel-vault in which the bricks are so laid as to suggest groining. For this reason the old cathedral at Sofia has been erroneously described as a Romanesque church with groined vaulting, and only on the strength of this supposition was it possible to dispute its age. Actually, it is a fine three-aisled domed church with trefoil end, and the cathedral of Thalin is hardly an older example. The dome-like roof is concealed within a square tower such as that of the tomb of Galla Placidia at Ravenna, that at Tekor in Armenia, and that at Khakh in Mesopotamia ; such a tower as that above the crossing in the church of the Holy Sepulchre at Jerusalem, in the church of the Saviour at Spoleto, and in many post-Carolingian churches in the West, especially in the region of the North Sea and the Baltic from the British Isles to Sweden.

The barrel-vaults at Sofia, which suggest groining, and are connected with the square groin-vaulted tower, may have travelled in the same way, though at present there is no tangible evidence. One thing only is certain, that alike in the Mesopotamian group and in the isolated example at Sofia (Fig. 20, opposite) the barrel-vault is first narrowed by building up the sides ; thus small squares are formed between the rib-arches, and these are covered from all four sides by courses of bricks parallel to the sides of the square. In this way four triangles are formed, the sides of which meet on the diagonals of each single square and unite in a small terminal square at the top. Now the simple groined vault of the West shows the same kind of construction at the springing of the vault, carried out by means of horizontal courses, each projecting beyond that beneath it ; it shows also the diagonal arches, that is to say, the triangles simply meeting in a joint. These arches do not project in the single and unbroken longitudinal vault, but come into being when this is met by transverse barrel-vaults of the same kind. A distinctive mark of this work is seen in the fact that the direction of the joints is no longer vertical, but parallel to the axes of the several triangles.

In the north of France and in Germany the groined vault is the starting-point of a logical development at the same moment (about A.D. 1100) when we may note tendencies towards a Proto-renaissance in the South. Surviving remains of antique architecture were here the sources of inspiration (Cluny, Autun). The old theory is now disputed that this movement had as a direct consequence the introduction of the sculptured human figure into Western architecture ; to this point I shall return below. However, an end was made of this incipient influence by a bold action on the part of the North which rid Western Europe for centuries of this retrograde Southern movement. Would that it had stemmed it for all time !

The striking and essential difference between the Oriental influence in France and Germany deserves careful attention. In contrast to the gay variety in France with its wonderful wealth of local difference, we find in Germany a purposeful effort after the uniform development of all available artistic values, only comparable to the similar activity in Armenia. A fixed type resulted in both countries, a long church, which in Germany had groined vaults, in Armenia dome and barrel-vault. Very striking are the resemblances in the mode of decoration, the well-defined unity of the interior, and the accentuation in the exterior of a clearly conceived design. Probably the genius of the North succeeded in asserting itself more fully in Armenia and Germany because these countries were less led astray by influences from the South, especially that of classical art. But what may be fairly described in each case as the national employment of the cushion-capital suggests other possibilities. In Carolingian times there must still have been a northern route between Armenia and the Rhine. Architectural features at Würzburg, in Bohemia, and Cracow attest the migration of Armenian forms such as the sexfoil, the conched square, and the quatrefoil. In this connexion we may note the popularity of the trefoil in Rhenish cathedrals. A comparison of the eleventh-century S. Maria in the Capitol at Cologne with the seventh-century Cathedral of Thalin awakens a lively desire for further investigation in this field.   Further, the conformation of the old cathedral of Cologne and the persistent tendency to such rich combinations in Rhenish cathedrals both find their explanation in Armenia, especially in individual features, such as the dome over the crossing and in the superimposed turrets for bells.   In France a single and logical development first came in from the North when the old forms adopted from the East had ceased to be effective.

III.   *The Northern Art of Europe : Gothic*

What we choose to call Romanesque in Europe is based upon a Southern form of church, the timber-roofed basilica, translated into terms of oriental vaulted construction.   Gothic represents the Northern version of this art.   The unfamiliar phrases, Eastern art of Christianity in the West and Northern art of Christianity in the West, will at first seem hard to accept ; but they fit the facts, and we shall soon grow used to them. The Gothic treatment of the long vaulted church resembled that of the Iranian dome in Armenia.   The dome rested first on the walls, then on free-standing piers within the walls ; finally wall and pier were linked by narrow arches, and a system of central supports created.   This kind of abutment was brilliantly employed in S. Sophia at Constantinople.   Like the Armenian domed hall, it is ' Gothic ', though with interior abutment and plain external walls.

The connexion with the foregoing orientally inspired development is obvious.   But I must insist with emphasis on the common mistake of ignoring the Scandinavian wooden churches.   These churches, in complete independence of the South, created their own church type in wood, a ' basilican ' type, and therefore without vaulting (Fig. 16, facing p. 80).   By their vertical development and their treatment of space they show various features which appear to be of some importance for the growth of vaulted architecture in the North.   If it is remembered that at the time when the groin-vaulted basilica originated, the central part of Europe must surely still have had a flourishing wooden architecture such as survives even to-day in Scandinavia, here and there in other regions, and of course in Russia, then we ought to consider the Seine valley in the light of a nursery for these

Northern developments no less than for those from other quarters. We shall come back to this subject later. Here I draw attention to a few features as conspicuous in this logically progressing art of the North as in Armenia under similar conditions ; the impression is thus conveyed that the development in both countries was only rendered possible by the promptings which both received from the Northern spirit. But there is also the possibility of an Oriental influence on the growth of Northern art, the introduction of which is usually ascribed to the Crusades. French scholars, Viollet-le-Duc, de Vogüé, Courajod, Dieulafoy, and others followed these tracks more than half a century ago, but much has only become intelligible through our new knowledge of Armenia. The fact deserves special mention that in Armenia there are buildings which Schnaase, Texier, Lynch, and others found inexplicable except on the supposition that they had at least been reconstructed or restored by a few ' Gothic ' architects from the west of Europe. The chief example of this has always been the cathedral of Ani (Figs. 11 and 21–23, facing pp. 71, 94, and 95). This church was begun before A.D. 989 by the great architect Trdat, and completed in A.D. 1001. The use of the pointed arch to support the dome and the absolutely western style of the four piers with their clustered columns (Fig. 23, facing p. 95) were the features which chiefly suggested the interposition of a western hand. In reality the appearance of these very features can be traced through their logical development during the period between the seventh and tenth centuries, just as certainly as the recessed Romanesque portal.

And, as a matter of fact, with the transformation of the old pilgrimages into the Crusades there began a change in relations which had hitherto been confined to the introduction of oriental artistic forms into the West. There now began a counter-migration. The distinction amounted to this, that the Oriental forms set on foot a movement in the West very fruitful in development, while the western forms in the East remained, at any rate in the domain of architecture, alien importations, sterile and without effect. This is well shown by the relations between Mohammedan art and that of the West. Whereas we may with probability discern the influence of this essentially Iranian art in certain forms of abutment, in the use of the pointed arch and of the pierced stucco window-slabs filled with coloured glass, we find on the contrary no evidence that Armenia or Islam adopted any

21   Ani, cathedral ; interior from North-West.

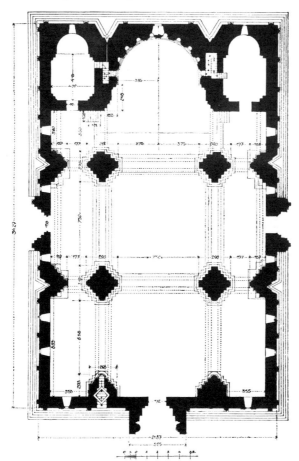

22   Ani, cathedral ; plan. See pp. 72, 94.

23   Ani, cathedral ; bases of piers with clustered
columns.   See pp. 72, 94, 95, 145.

24   Thalin, cathedral ; detail of South-West pier.
See pp. 95, 145, 146.

western forms. The Mohammedans carried off as a trophy a Gothic doorway from Akka and placed it in the Mosque of Kalaun at Cairo ; at Jerusalem they adopted much that was of western origin ; but they went no farther. It was the same in Armenia, where the comradeship of the Crusaders and the Rubenids of Cilicia afforded ample opportunity for exchange. There can be no question of a penetration of Armenia by Gothic forms ; an influence of Islamic and Armenian forms on the North through the Crusades is more probable.

What the cushion-capital was for the openly Oriental influence in Europe, a *Leitmotiv*, invaluable for comparative architectural study in Armenia, Lombardy, and Germany, such, in the case of the purely Northern influence, were the engaged shaft and the pier with clustered shafts. The engaged shaft is a vertical cylindrical member running up wall or pier, and having no connexion with the free-standing column. This, indeed, can only be clearly demonstrated in Armenia, where the column was never admitted as a constructional feature, whereas the engaged shaft had come in from the first with the Iranian domed building. In Armenia the shaft appears both in the interiors and on the exteriors of churches (Fig. 23, opposite), in the latter case generally double, and associated with the niche (Fig. 2, facing p. 62) and cushion-terminations at top and bottom, but also at a very early date in the demarcation of wall space within the church. But it was only in conjunction with the pier that the shaft acquired its great importance for comparison with the West. It was applied to the projecting part of the pier as a half-cylinder, or, as three-quarter-cylinder, placed in the corners between the projecting parts. The use made of it is thus exactly the same as in the West at a later period. In all this the shaft is not bound, like the column, by any fixed relation between height and diameter ; it is an unrestricted form, which in certain cases is indefinitely extended.

Another fact to be noted is that a kind of ribbed-vault was developed in Armenia, the origin of which is to be found in the porches placed in front of small churches when they were enlarged. Fig. 25, facing p. 96, shows such vaulting from the monastery of Aisasi, though it must be admitted that the example is a late one. We see two massive ribs in the form of pointed arches which embrace a small dome, and are buttressed by two quarter-arches. There are other similar combinations, and it is possible that such stone structures had prototypes in wooden buildings. So much for the features of importance for the comparison between western and Armenian types. As regards the wooden buildings indigenous to the North, I proceed to the following remarks.

It was suggested above (p. 80) that the wooden churches, by inserting tall mast-like supports, may have helped to prepare the way for the basilica advancing from the South. We may conjecture that the development was from the simple type with four columns to that with a group of twelve, and from this to the unrestricted use in rows. This involved a calculated system of meeting thrusts, which may have prepared the way for the crowning achievement of northern stone-construction, the so-called Gothic style. Observe how in the interior of the church of Borgund (Fig. 16, facing p. 80), the masts are buttressed by the frame-walls and the roofs of the aisles, and in Fig. 17, facing p. 80, the detail of a triforium, where the method of buttressing by the frame-walls is repeated in a somewhat clearer manner. It seems to me that here the approximation to thrust-receiving arches is no less clear than in Armenian or Romanesque buildings. Other valuable observations can be made on the articulation of the roof supports at Garde on Gothland. Such points as these should be indefinitely multiplied as soon as our eye for these matters grows sharper. My own country of Austria will certainly yield valuable results.

Fig. 26, facing p. 97, a house in the Upper Austrian town of Steyr, shows a characteristic example. It is just one among many which represent the local type of citizen's house, and illustrates the old indigenous wooden forms translated into stone. The inner court of the house is surrounded by open galleries, which, however, are not visible on the ground floor to the left. In their place we note piers before the walls, carrying long projecting brackets which support the gallery with its pillars carved in angular relief. This otherwise characteristic example unfortunately lacks the usual pierced screens, sometimes wrought in stone after the model of the old wooden prototypes. The influence of church-building need not be denied. But the essential point is that in spite of it the old domestic wooden style is everywhere to be found, the style which may have had far more influence than we think on the beginnings of church-building itself. Unluckily it too succumbed to the artistic ignorance of the humanistic movement behind Church and Court,

25   Aisasi, porch of monastery church ; Armenian ribbed vaulting.
See p. 95.

26   Steyr, court of a house ;   photo., Reiffenstein.   See p. 96.

and Europe reverted to the habit of aping classical models. Very few people at all grasp the fact that as a result of this reversion, real understanding of the nature of art and its value to life was in great part lost. In all fields of knowledge except those of science and technology, the belief that the imported is able to replace the indigenous has held its ground for centuries. The consequence is that not formative art only, but the whole of European life is under various aspects pretentious and insincere. To resume the foregoing : the Christian art of the North means at bottom the rebirth of a true European art, of a North-Aryan influence in a Europe which after the close of the Hellenic period had ceased to be independent and creative.

We have seen that northern art itself renounced its proper character in so far as it conceded to the human figure in architecture a place only equalled for importance in India. A distinction must, however, be made. In India the suggestion came not from the art of the immigrant peoples in the north of the country, but from that of the older population in the south, just as farther West it came from Egypt to the Greek art of Southern Europe. In North European, or Gothic, art, however, the essential lies not, as in India and Greece, in the human figure itself, but in the draped figure—not in the body, but in the covering given to the body by art. The figure itself is subordinated to form, as in East Asia ; natural shapes become merely the vehicles of rhythmical line. Moreover, these northern figures are in organic unity with the body of the structure. The consciousness that the various parts of the organism are thus naturally enlivened leads, independently of the human figure, to a luxuriant overgrowth of vegetable and animal forms unequalled in any other art, even in the South.

The North thus took the step from decoration to representation without fully subordinating the natural instinct of formative art to exact reproduction of Nature. Representation gradually triumphed, but was never carried to its logical extreme. That was only done when styles of Italian inspiration established art upon an intellectual basis.

IV. *The Italian Mixed Style (Renaissance)*

It was reserved for Italy to make Europe a second time acquainted with the East-Aryan dome, Italy which continuously maintained the closest relations with the Eastern coasts of the

Mediterranean.   Aquitaine had introduced the multiple domes of Iran ; it was for the Renaissance to recognize the essential merit of the single-domed Armenian plan, and to give it a permanent place in European architecture.   The course of development repeated that witnessed by the East in earlier times. A Leonardo and a Bramante established the principle that the dome is the centre of the whole.   Then the Church, as patron, won the upper hand and demanded a long building, and for the second time in the history of Christian art Vignola discovered in the ' domed hall ' the solution of the problem.   But since in the West the basilica was no less firmly established than the church with central dome in Armenia, the dome was not able to preserve the law of its being by maintaining its right position ; it was advanced to the East end, where the old dome over the crossing had stood.   While, therefore, in Armenia the long nave was imposed upon domical architecture, in Italy the dome was placed upon the long nave.   I will attempt a brief explanation of this development.

By buttressing the dome as he did, Brunelleschi may be said to have completed the Gothic cathedral of Florence in the Armenian style.   Looking at the East end from without, one might take it for the work of an Armenian architect.   The pointed dome alone has a Western air, though the shell of the cupola again suggests the East, and especially Islamic architecture.   In S. Lorenzo and S. Spirito, indeed, the affinities are rather with Romanesque, the Oriental style of Western Europe ; and here Brunelleschi adopted the dome over the crossing.   But in the Pazzi chapel he took a step which showed him in a fair way to full understanding of the square as the right form for the bay beneath the dome ; his plan for S. Maria degli Angeli in like manner shows that he had in mind the Armenian eight-lobed type. Alberti and Michelozzo, who had himself visited Cyprus, went beyond Brunelleschi ; their ideas carry yet farther the possibilities of the dome over a square plan.   Yet Leonardo, as his drawings show, was really the first who flung himself into the exploitation of domical building, though at first he had no thought of adapting it to churches ; a visit which he may have made to the Taurus country would be enough to explain these Oriental designs.   But the architectural tasks entrusted to him at Milan and Pavia in connexion with the cathedral, together with his activity in the service of Francis I, directly confronted him at last with these

27   Vagharshapat, Hripsimeh, A.D. 618, domed square with apse-buttresses
and angle-chambers ; South view.

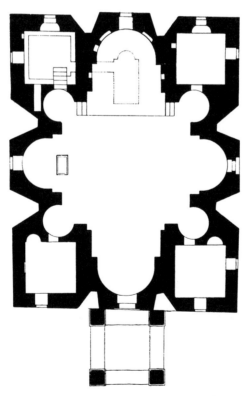

28   Vagharshapat, Hripsimeh ; plan.
See p. 99.

29 Ammān, square building with apse-buttresses; blind
arcade with formal ornament. See pp. 123, 124.

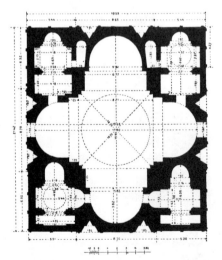

30 Ani, church of the Apostles; plan.
See p. 99

31 Korea, stone tomb;
structure of the roof; from
the *Kokka*. See pp. 122,
123, 124.

problems as related to church construction. His influence in any case seems to have brought Bramante to a point at which he permanently abandoned the Gothic style and entered the paths leading him to S. Peter's. In all probability Leonardo's later sojourn in Rome only matured the plans first formed at Milan.

For Leonardo the central architectural idea was the octagon ; but side by side with this appears time and again a plan corresponding to that of the Armenian ' apse-buttressed square ' with interior supports (p. 63). This type is, indeed, exemplified by S. Germigny-des-Près, and by S. Satiro at Milan, but both are derivatives from Armenian models ; Leonardo may just as easily have come into contact with the original type in Cilicia. Could it be shown that he was also acquainted with the plain apse-buttressed square without central supports, we should have abundant proof that this was the case. Unfortunately, Leonardo took the lamentable step of adorning the Armenian structure, not in its proper style, but with classical features after the ordinary fashion of the Early Renaissance. Significant evidence of the constructional ideas which he possibly derived directly from the East is afforded by the château of Chambord. Here, after the manner of Armenian and Mohammedan palace construction, he makes his dominant central point a domed hall of cruciform plan with barrel-vaulted limbs, the very plan which inspired Bramante's work at S. Peter's.

The history of this great church repeats as a solitary example the destiny of Early Christian art in Armenia. As was the case a thousand years earlier, a pioneer architect produced a monumental design, placing the central dome, as in the Church of the Apostles at Ani, above a quatrefoil (Fig. 30, opposite), but of necessity interposing barrel-vaults between the dome and its niche-abutments, because he disposed four chambers on the diagonals, as in the case of Awan or the Hripsimeh (Fig. 28, facing p. 98). Naturally, there is no comparison between the dimensions, but the plan in itself is certainly similar. Bramante's design was not originally intended for execution, and had to be modified in essential features before it could actually be carried out. Yet throughout it remained fundamentally Armenian, even when handed over to Peruzzi and Michelangelo. In the end, the demands of the Church for a long building were successfully asserted ; the architects gave way as they had done long before in Armenia ; and the result is seen in the S. Peter's of to-day.

In Armenia greater foresight seems to have been shown; the main point was never lost sight of that the dome had to dominate the whole interior, and be visible from the entrance in all its parts right up to the crown.

Leonardo and Bramante more or less represent the architectural point of view of the Armenians in the fourth century, though the dimensions of their buildings were very different. The work of Vignola corresponds to the phase upon which Armenian domical building entered after the fifth century under the influence of the Church, its final achievement being the domed hall. On these lines Vignola built his Gesù, the Jesuit church, the type of which spread with the order over the whole of Europe, and became the characteristic model for the Barocco style. The difference between his solution of the problem and that of the Armenians lies, as we have seen, in the fact that in Armenia the long nave supervened on the centralized domical plan, while in Italy the dome supervened upon the long nave. The results are essentially alike, though in Armenia the dome had the last word, in Italy the conception of the long church, the dome being transferred from its proper position to the bay before the apse.

Bramante seems also to have manifested that feeling for pure construction which we had occasion to praise in Armenian buildings, in those erected in Aquitaine after the Armenian manner, in the work of the severe German tradition, and in that of early Northern (Gothic) art, the feeling which wholly subordinates ornament to construction and spatial effect. The fashion of making façades, external or internal, by the employment of antique elements had not yet triumphed; it must have found little favour with Bramante during his earlier career, if only for the reason that he also aimed at combining unity of interior space with an impressive treatment of the exterior as an organic whole, producing its effect upon the spectator by the equal influences of all its parts.

The victory of the Renaissance throughout Europe was determined by the supremacy of Court and Church which was everywhere followed by the Counter Reformation. The Roman forms were tacitly accepted as alone suited to a policy based on power.

It is a favourite assertion that with the progress of development after Roman times the contrasts between Asia and Europe grew more and more profound. In the early Middle Ages in Europe the opposite was true; even in the sphere of formative art political rivalry demanded compromise, because the West never wearied of learning the tricks of impressive display practised by the Oriental courts.[1]   Let the question be asked, on the other hand, which method had the final word in architectural decoration, that in which spatial and constructional form were brought into ever closer harmony, or that which adhered to the columnar style of classical antiquity only abandoned by the West during one brief interval.   Here, too, the East had already completed in Early Christian times that breach with Greece and Rome which a proper regard for our own independence bids us open anew.

Now that we have evidence of an Early Christian vaulted architecture in the East, we have the chance of studying the historical development of art along these lines.   The old method was to proceed by basing everything on literary sources, and relying for the rest on general history; that is, by fitting the monuments anyhow into a ready-made frame without the least regard for possible gaps, which might disarrange the whole picture; let us hope that this procedure is done with once and for all.   Hitherto we have been engaged in writing mere history; now at last we can begin as specialists to apply the comparative method, observing each work of art on its own merits and for the essential values which make it what it is.   So long as the most important comparative elements were unknown, this method was excluded, and it was therefore quite impossible to grapple with questions of origin.   When such questions were in fact approached in the light of some theory like that of an imperial Roman or of a Christian classic art, the attempt was bound to come to grief through two causes, an inevitably one-sided point of view, and a palpable ignorance of the monuments in question.

In the first half of this book, ending at this point, the familiar old Christian buildings have been evolutionally considered, and the types set in their proper places in the order of development. In the second half, which begins with the next chapter, it will be our business for the first time to demonstrate the existence of the oldest branch of Christian art, till now to all intents and purposes totally ignored.   In the process the complete contrast between the usually accepted doctrine and my own will become absolutely clear.   In the succeeding chapters I shall again confine myself to the Early Christian period.

[1] Architecture in the West reacted to Eastern influences introduced by the immigrant Goths.

V

Religions without Representational Art

WE are apt to conclude from our own example, and from that of Ancient Egypt, Mesopotamia, Greece, and India, that all religious art is naturally representational ; thus we never reflect that the earliest Christian art cannot possibly have had this character, a point to be discussed in the next chapter. I need here only observe that while Hamites and Semites in the Nile Valley and in Mesopotamia had representational art, the immigrant Aryans were at first without the idea of copying nature, and only began to render deity in human form under the influence of the southern peoples. The same is true of India. Here Aryans were first induced to represent by the Dravidian and other indigenous populations, just as the Greeks had adopted the older Mediterranean art, the affinities of which were with ancient Egypt and Mesopotamia.

In my work *Altai-Iran* I sought to explain that this difference in practice results from a fundamental opposition of North and South in their attitude towards art, an opposition which may also be awakened by radically different economic and social conditions. Thus the nomadic herdsmen of the desert and the steppe base their art upon principles quite distinct from those adopted by the agricultural peoples in the valleys of the great southern rivers —those veritable forcing houses of culture. In the present volume I shall broadly define the manner in which this suggestion may influence our idea of religious art. In the province of architecture, we found that progress along these lines was blocked if we persisted in beginning with the Mediterranean area, with Rome and the earliest sepulchral monuments, which have hitherto cumbered the foreground of Christian art ; advance was only possible if we started from the opposite side, from Asia and from the North. We shall find things the same in the province of formative art.

The characteristic ornament of early Teutonic antiquities,

still surviving in the decoration of the Scandinavian wooden churches, has peculiar features shared by the art of Islam. Neither the ancient Teuton nor the Mohammedan made use of representation on any extensive scale. The investigator approaching the problem from the Asiatic side perceives affinities between their respective arts the moment he considers them from the angle of Altai and Iran. He observes that the nomadic herdsmen roaming between North-east and South-west, especially the Turks, had no representational art, and that the Aryan nomads roaming between North-west and South-east were in exactly the same case. The artistic motives which we find Teutonic peoples bringing with them across Europe at the time of the Great Migrations represent only the last phase of a very old development gradually becoming clear to us, a free development flatly opposed to that representational system of the southern peoples which has alone attracted notice in historical times. There is no question here of degrees of merit, as, for instance, between a mature and an immature art ; the distinction is one of kind, and concerns two different entities. Of these only one, the representational, has counted in the eyes of European scholars trained in the classical school of Greece and Rome, while these same scholars, even those of the North, have never really approached the other, though in the very nature of things it should have been their first concern.

When one hears the dictum that decoration in a single plane proves arrested development, while the plastic treatment of Greek art proves maturity, one can but say that such a statement betrays a fundamental ignorance of the distinction between representational and non-representational art. It is of the essence of non-representational art to decorate and fill a flat surface. The idea of filling implies another idea, that of framing. Representational art does not at first enclose its subjects ; it covers the surface without order, or obliquely, or in superposed zones, and at first itself begins by keeping to one plane. Non-representational art on the other hand, with an enclosed space to fill, never abandons the flat surface ; it is the human figure which forsakes the single plane as soon as it is framed. This distinction is fundamental as regards the two methods. Non-representational art was born out of handicraft ; it was from handicraft that art sprang into being in the North and among the nomadic shepherd peoples ; Gottfried Semper should have taken up his parable at this point. The origin of Southern art, with its representational ideal, is on the contrary to be sought in the subject ; from the beginning it pursued the imitation of nature. Non-representational art ignores alike reproduction of nature and disposition of forms in cubic space.

The conception which has hitherto prevailed could only have originated, one might think, in that partition of art-history which is concerned above all with the Mediterranean. The student using the comparative method cannot be content with it. His eye is directed rather to the gaps in our knowledge than to the disconnected remains known or preserved by chance. It further seems to him that by adopting this point of view, a man of the North abjures what is in his own blood for something foreign and acquired. Non-representational art is not more backward or more primitive than representational ; it is simply different. Instead of being proud of what we have done, we of the North ought rather to deplore our excessive surrender to the histrionic feeling of the South. To personify or anthropomorphize all and everything is to attempt the opening of every door with the one master-key ' Man ', and to recede far indeed from great Nature and her secrets. It is clear enough that the present generation has deliberately turned against representation. The Greeks introduced the human form into their art at a very early period ; it was their good fortune that they did it without ulterior motive ; the military states which had gone before them knew only too well why they gave a common form to God and King. Christians were once as far removed from representation as the Greeks were originally. The assumptions which underlie a fact consistently ignored have now to be considered.

Among historical forms of religion, Monotheism appears to favour a non-representational system. Judaism and Islam are examples ; we shall see that in its origins Christianity inclined in the same direction. If a non-representational method really meant no more than an elementary and undeveloped phase, it could never hold its own by the side of representational religions. Had it been only this, Hellenism would no more have accepted a non-representational Christianity than it accepted Islam, and the old representational art of Mesopotamia and Iran would never have tolerated a non-representational and popular Mazdaism. We shall come back to this point. The truth is that the sentiment of nomads and northern peoples resents the entrapping of religious impulse by means of representation, which they consequently exclude from their religion. I conceive the whole North of Europe and Asia as a vast funnel-shaped area, narrowing to a point in the region between the Black Sea and the Altai. The Aryan peoples who made their way southward through this tract carried with them the northern artistic feeling, which also traversed the whole South from East to West, from Central Asia to the west coast of Africa. In my book *Altai-Iran* I thought it possible to approach the art of these regions from the side of Islam. From the Syro-Egyptian angle, once the starting-point of Christianity, I felt my way towards the North-east, the quarter from which the whole artistic movement of Islam flowed back like a tide. If I had to begin again, I should prefer to start directly from the Northern side ; but as yet such a course might be premature, and in the present section I shall keep to the path already trodden. In a later section we shall learn something of a representational cross-current between Asia Minor and India.

1. *Islam*

Islam has no religious representation. Starting among the nomads of Arabia, it broke through the Hellenistic-Indian barrier in a north-easterly direction, and soon ceased to build with stone, after the fashion of Christianity, which preceded it in Syria, Asia Minor, and Armenia, adopting instead the Mesopotamian and Persian material, brick. It covered its brick walls in an un-Hellenic and un-Indian manner with geometrical repeating patterns, which originated in the use of diverse materials and crafts and produced their effect by openwork, by slant-cut surfaces, by sheen or colour, never by the plastic representation of natural forms in light and shade. All these patterns, all these kinds of work came into Western Hither Asia through Persian influence just as representation had entered the East through that of earlier Greece ; they in no way resulted from any gradual transformation of classical feeling, or any change of late-classical taste in the East. Greek architecture let its forms develop gradually like the human figure, so that formative art and construction harmoniously advanced together ; but Islam adorned the walls of places of worship with surface-filling design, not admitting the human figure even as a means of giving the scale for the parts of the building. Despite all religious schisms, the mosque at no time and in no place admitted representational pictures whether disposed in friezes after the Semitic fashion, or, as in Pompeii, as centre-pieces in the middle of a wall; the only Pompeiian style which we can at all compare with the later Islamic manner is the architectural, in which the whole wall was treated as a unit, or the style which counterfeits marble linings. The Hellenistic painter imitates lining in his frescoes; Islam never follows such a course. Rejecting objective form, it creates patterns that fill borders with rhythmic undulating lines, and larger surfaces with straight lines forming lattice, net, or interlacing diaper. The only Islamic ornamental form with objective meaning is the band of decorative Cufic lettering. This originated in the old Semitic country, but, like the builder's art itself, only received farther East the decorative transformation which gives it its artistic value.

I now treat as briefly as possible the art of the Mohammedan religious building, or mosque. Down to about A.D. 1000, the period which alone concerns us, the mosque was an open court surrounded by walls with roofs on the inner sides, the roof towards Mecca covering more ground than the others. At Medina, palm-trunks formed the original supports; in Syria and Egypt columns from Christian churches were employed, connected after the Arab manner by arcading, the roof being formed of any suitable material that came to hand. Under such conditions as these, there was small scope for an art with individuality, going beyond the simplest practical needs, either in the home of Islam, or in Syria and Egypt, the first countries into which the faith of Mohammed spread. If embellishment was desired, craftsmen were pressed into the service wherever they could be found, either in the district where the building was being erected, or from richer places such as Coptic Egypt or even Constantinople. Corporations of workmen for ordinary purposes were everywhere at the disposal of the conquerors.

It is characteristic of these times that Islamic art first attained individual expression in Persia; in the present place the bare fact can only be stated, the reasons for it will occupy us later. As long as the Ummayads in Syria were endeavouring to outbid the rulers of all countries, monuments were erected which betray their foreign inspiration in every line. In the Dome of the Rock, built to supplant the structure round the Kaaba at Mecca, the rock was enclosed within a circle of columns taken from a church, and covered with a wooden dome ; this was in its turn enclosed by a second circle of columns and an octagonal outer wall. The original decoration of the interior is represented by the spandrel-mosaics which reproduce purely Persian designs. In the great mosque at Damascus a central dome was flanked by aisles ; here too only the long members were modified in a Christian sense by the use of columns ; the structural type itself is represented on Iranian soil by an earlier building, Eiwan-i Kerka, or Taḳ Ivan. The dome mosaics show ' landscapes ', combinations of trees and other features with only a remote resemblance to nature, and intended rather to symbolize than to represent. Thus even in this early Syrian period these exceptional mosques, which differ so markedly from the usual Mediterranean type, were already penetrated by Persian influence.

The earliest group of systematically planned mosques appeared in Mesopotamia ; we may recall the fact that this was the country which originated the barrel-vaulted building of Christian times. Islam retained the open court of its earliest mosques, but the supports for the surrounding roofs could be no longer provided by columns collected at haphazard from Christian churches ; they had to be built up brick by brick. This brought order into Mohammedan art. Mesopotamia was the first place where surviving monuments show what we should call uniformity in decoration ; we see bands of ornament in stucco, carved or stamped, like the familiar designs in the mosque of Ahmed Ibn Tulun at Cairo, built in A.D. 872. It has been persistently maintained that, like the wooden panels carved in the same style, they are of Egyptian derivation. I fancy the excavations at Samarra have sufficiently shown, despite the desperate efforts made even here to prove the contrary, that in all this incredible wealth of borders and broad surfaces filled with geometrically planned designs of formal scrolls in lines or repeated in diapers, the East was the sole source of inspiration.

It has already been suggested that certain materials, like stone and wood, suffice in themselves to produce a decorative effect, while others, notably unburned brick, require facing to make them pleasing to the eye and to secure durability. Such facing may be carried out in stucco, tiles, mosaic, or other similar means. People are ready enough to admit that even mosaic has an ' oriental ' character, though in their view the essential point to notice is that the oriental could make little of his own invention : Greek wits were needed for its development. But before venturing upon such judgements we ought first to ask ourselves whether this mode of decoration was not intended rather to produce a general effect from a distance than to represent particular things through compositions designed for a nearer view. If so, should not quite different standards be employed in criticizing two distinct methods ?

The decorative facing of walls was known in the ancient East, and naturally in the first place in Mesopotamia. But there representational compositions were employed, running along the walls in horizontal zones. This is a style which cannot have originated in wall-lining, but must have been superimposed. It is essential to wall-lining that the wall must be regarded as a unit, that is, a framed surface to be filled with an ornament befitting this conception of its nature. In their ideas of wall-decoration North and South stand over against each other like distinct worlds ; the South bases everything upon representational art, the North begins with craftsmanship. For the moment no more need be said of the representational system; we shall revert to it in Chapter VII. In the present place I confine myself to ornament, the evolution of which was due partly to physical conditions, to the treelessness of Iran ; but in a greater degree it must be ascribed to a religious belief, the creed of Mazdaism.

II. *Iran*

In the late period with which we are concerned, we must recognize fundamental contrasts in art, similar to those which existed in a remoter antiquity. As we distinguish between Egyptian and Mesopotamian art, the one characterized by an organic treatment of architecture, the other by the habit of covering the walls of buildings with decorated linings, so we should now discriminate between the organic architecture of the West-Aryan Greeks, and East-Aryan (Iranian) architecture, with its lined and decorated surfaces. In the intervening Semitic tract of Mesopotamia, an uncertainty of procedure may be perhaps detected ; Greek types may appear, transformed in an Iranian sense. But except in the Sassanian region in the South, national feeling in Iran prevented the intrusion of Greek forms on any extensive scale ; it excluded the columnar style, acanthus ornament, and, above all, the representational system. After

Alexander, there was a perceptible infiltration of popular ornamental methods from Iran into the Mediterranean area.

The introduction of wall-lining is the most conspicuous
instance. This was probably adopted by ancient Egypt from
Asiatic sources. About 280 B.C. the so-called style of incrusta-
tion appeared in Alexandria, essentially the same as of the First
Style in Pompeii ; this style uses the slab of coloured marble
as the slab of tufa is used in Armenia. It was soon succeeded
by the architectural wall-paintings of the Second to the Fourth
Pompeiian styles, which came westward via Antioch and Rome.
These are fantastic architectural motives giving quantity without
quality after the fashion of much Indian work, and distributed
over the surface almost like repeating patterns. Semitic and East
Aryan art were never associated with these extravagances. Their
wall-lining and ornament remained independent of structural
forms, creating their own laws on the basis of material and craftsmanship. Their place of origin, as I showed in *Altai-Iran*, was
the north-east of Iran.

The Persia of the Early Christian period must be distinguished from the Persian State of to-day. It included Mesopotamia, which in Sassanian times (A.D. 226–640) had even the
honour of including within its bounds the capital, Seleucia-
Ctesiphon, situated in the territory of the ancient Babylon. We
have therefore to inquire whether this inclusion favoured the
spirit of the ancient East, or whether after all the advantage lay
with the intruding spirit of Iran.

It would appear that at this period Mesopotamia was just
as uncreative as Egypt ; in architecture it had the barrel vault,
in sculpture and painting its representational system. In the
province of ornament, we may infer from the Parthian palace of
Hatra, and from certain Christian churches to be mentioned
below, that Hellenistic forms were modified to suit an art of
surface decoration ; deprived of their organic meaning they were
confined to bands or ' friezes ', running in broken courses in
all directions. There was no creation of new forms.

The plateau of Iran is divided by a salt desert into two
absolutely distinct parts, a northern, the seat of Parthian power
between 247 B.C. and A.D. 226, and a southern, the country of
the Sassanian dynasty (A.D. 226–A.D. 640). The two parts
were connected on the east and west sides by the Indian border-
lands and by Mesopotamia respectively.

We are familiar with the art of Southern Iran through important surviving reliefs representing Achaemenian and Sassanian monarchs. In the gigantic barrel-vaulted hall of the Tak-i Kisra, that Mesopotamian wonder of the world, with its façade of blind arcades, we recognize the remains of a Sassanian palace, though nothing survives of the interior decoration. In neighbouring Persian districts are other ruins of similar style, though upon a much smaller scale.

The key to the problems involved is provided by early Mohammedan buildings in Mesopotamia, revealed to us by modern excavation. Remains of immense structures have been laid bare at Samarra telling us at last something definite as to the style and the appearance of the buildings which we may expect to find in the south of Persia : palaces and mosques with vast walls and piers of burned brick allow us to infer a despotic atmosphere in which the passion for magnificence could hardly be excelled by the Roman or the Byzantine courts in the utmost display of their arbitrary power. The excavations at Samarra brought to light a whole city of palaces and mosques extending by the Tigris over an area 33 km. in length by 2 km. in breadth, all built in a uniform style during the ninth century, and soon afterwards totally abandoned.

Here we find a wealth of wall-decoration. For the most part this consists of repeat-patterns on the stucco lining, either impressed in slant-cut surfaces by means of wooden stamps, or deeply undercut by hand to produce sharp contrast of high light and black shadow. Hardly any of the designs are indigenous to Mesopotamia ; those with slant cutting come from the Altai, those with vine-derivatives from Persia. Iran, its northern and not its southern area, was the real source of this decoration. Islam replaced the Mazdean religion of the Sassanian state. It is a point of crucial importance that the fundamental and permanent qualities of Mohammedan art were derived neither from Damascus nor from Baghdad, but from the area of Altai-Iran. My book upon the art of that region was written to establish this point. Here I need repeat but little from its pages, turning rather to the religious aspect of the problem, an aspect to which I was already at that time able to allude.

We have recognized in Edessa and Nisibis one religious and intellectual centre of Christian Oriental art, from which a Semitic influence was diffused throughout the world. But there was another and remoter centre on the frontier dividing Eastern from Western Asia, the influence of which, passing Pamir and Altai, extended by a northern route into Buddhist China. During the first millennium its position as an area where Indo-Aryan and Turco-Mongolian influences crossed lent it a significance the beginnings of which I sought to trace back to prehistoric times. Indo-Aryan elements are still to be detected in Islamic technique and Islamic designs, derived from wooden construction, Turco-Mongolian in motives of decoration borrowed from tent-coverings and from personal ornaments of metal.

Altai-Iran was confined to a study of ornament. My work *Die Baukunst der Armenier und Europa* rounded off the problem from the architectural side. We can only explain the Armenian building with dome on squinches over a square plan on the hypothesis of its introduction by the Arsacid royal house and the partly Oriental Nacharars, who used Trans-Oxanian constructional forms for their baths, palaces, and tombs. The region across the Oxus and Iran are the home of the dome on squinches over a square plan, and there it persists in the domestic architecture of to-day. In some Iranian villages scores of such domes are to be seen. Their distribution extends to the Buddhist temples of Chinese Turkestan ; it includes the palaces of Seistan and Persis, where the two well-known examples of Firuzabad and Sarvistan illustrate North Iranian domed construction as developed on South Persian soil ; a whole complex is held in equilibrium by the juxtaposition of individual domed chambers and barrel-vaulted halls. Only in North Iran, at Bus-i-Hor, can we show to-day the single dome in rubble-concrete with tiled roof, a type fulfilling all the conditions required for a further development in Armenia. In the province of decoration the sequence is no less plain than in that of architecture.

My starting-point is here once more the angle between Altai and Iran, the meeting-ground of Indo-Aryan and Turco-Mongolian influences. Let us recall the cardinal fact that both were non-representational. The Indo-Aryans soon surrendered to the contrary practice of the South ; in Mohammedan Persia, Chinese and Indian representation is frequently found. The Turco-Mongolians, on the other hand, remained, with few exceptions, true to their old non-representational methods down to the penetration of their territory by European influences in recent times. During the first millennium devotion to non-representational art was a trait of the genuine Northern nature among the Persian and Turkish populations ; it was this which rendered possible the union of the two artistic streams, that of the Northerners of Iran and that of the nomad herdsmen. From this source sprang the power of a movement which came into the light of history from the East, a movement which succeeded in maintaining itself against that art of Southerners, Indo-Chinese and Semitic-Hellenistic, both, as products of a hot-house culture, making representation their principal aim. Once more Armenia gives us a glimpse of the period before Islam, although this mountainous volcanic country did not adopt the Iranian methods of covering blank walls. The Armenians preferred to use the tufa and lava of their own country in place of stucco, glazed tiles, metal, or carved wood; a lining of plain stone was their sufficient decoration. Yet in certain places on their buildings we find employed forms of ornament characteristic of East Iran, vine-scrolls, pomegranates, geometrical scrolls, and inter-lacings of bands channelled with two or with three slant-cut grooves, all developed almost to the point at which Islam took them up to form polygonal designs, or, by constraining the vine-scroll to geometrical law, the so-called arabesque ; such places are the flat bands of arcading and sloping surfaces under the eaves, the arcading round the windows, and, later, the blind arcades covering the lower walls and the drums beneath the domes. Other countries of which stone is the natural building material have, like Armenia, preserved such motives by translating them into this durable substance. While elsewhere we have only sporadic examples, Armenia has imprinted a uniform national style on monuments distributed in comprehensive groups.

Armenia is not alone in furnishing us with data for the mental reconstruction of East Iranian art ; there exist also a number of widely scattered stone monuments which impress us as foreign to their environment, and permit us to infer their derivation from Iranian buildings of unburned brick lined with stucco, tiles, mosaic, metal, and wood. Two such buildings are extant in the country east of the Jordan, and one in India. Of the first two, one, of quatrefoil plan, is in Moab, in the citadel of Ammān ;[1] its interior is decorated with three tiers of the

[1] This building was unfortunately much damaged by bombs during the war.

blind arcades which were so common on the exterior of Armenian churches, and were no doubt originally filled with painted ornament. At Ammān they are filled with those formal tree designs which form one of the richest features of Iranian art. We may reasonably assume that the building was originally domed; but as the dome was supported on squinches it has collapsed without leaving a trace above the four walls from which it rose. The second of these buildings in Moab is Mshatta. The ornament of the entrance wall at the west end of this three-aisled trefoil-ended building, four piers supporting three arches linked by a ⌐-shaped moulding above them, and the decoration of the triumphal arch before the trefoil itself, are so many proofs of Persian influence. The Corinthian capitals of the entrance wall are of course Greek; but the continuous moulding framing the arch is Iranian, as are the six enclosed rosettes, the four ribs on the soffit of the triumphal arch and the impost capitals encased in vine-scrolls. On the other hand the arch's vine-leaf moulding surmounted by acanthus belongs to that mixture of Iranian and Graeco-Mesopotamian art which is the distinguishing feature of the colossal façade now preserved in Berlin.

The chronology of Mshatta would not be a matter of dispute if archaeologists and art students would only give full and careful consideration to my book on the subject. At the present time a comparison with the churches of Mesopotamia and Armenia dating from the fourth to the seventh centuries, and with the remains excavated at Samarra of the ninth century (all of which were still unknown at the time I wrote my *Mshatta* in 1904), enables us to conclude with certainty that Mshatta antedates all other Christian and Islamic monuments, and may even be regarded as perhaps of Parthian rather than Sassanian origin. The classical friezes (comprising base mouldings, cornice, and an intermediate band of zigzag) should be compared with those of Mesopotamia, where the oldest surviving example belongs to the year A.D. 359; the rosettes in the zigzag should also be compared with Armenian parallels; and the vine-scroll with enclosed animals not only with that which occurs on the so-called throne of Maximianus, but also with classical examples on the one hand and the pilasters of Acre and Zwarthnotz (A.D. 650) on the other. Such comparisons will clearly show that the Mshatta façade cannot be attributed to the early Islamic period. Indeed it reveals that fusion of Iranian and Greek art which succeeded the displacement of the latter in late Roman times, and led gradually to the development of Byzantine art on the Mediterranean, of ' Romanesque ' in the West, and to the complete triumph of Iranian art in the world of Islam.

The third stone structure with Iranian decoration is the Sarnath Stûpa near Benares (Fig. 32, opposite). It has borders of scroll-work, in which the vine is replaced by the lotus, while the intermediate zone is occupied by the same kind of swastika fret which occurs as a continuous pattern on the columns of the Amida façade and on the remains of numerous Christian churches in Egypt. Sarnath and Aswân (Assuan), both of them situated near the tropic, were probably the two most southerly points reached by Northern or mediaeval art.

Examples of Iranian decoration in wood and stucco from the eighth to the tenth centuries have gradually come to light in great profusion. A comparison of the stuccoes of the Church of El-Hadra in Deir es-Suryani in lower Egypt (inspired by North Mesopotamian art) with almost contemporaneous work in Afghanistan, which takes us back to Mahmud of Ghazna, clearly indicates the centre from which both were derived, and even suggests that the influence of Eastern Iran penetrated as far as Eastern Europe and Scandinavia along the paths followed by thousands of Samanid coins. The ornament of the wooden carts and sledges discovered in the Oseberg ship in Norway shows close affinities of style with East Iranian decoration.

The Samarra excavations and their bearing upon Islam have given us some idea of the light that excavations in Iran might reasonably be expected to throw on the relations between Mazdaism and Christianity.

Glazed wall tiles of Iranian style, dating from about the ninth century of our era, have been discovered at the monastery of Patleina near Preslav in Bulgaria. Their ornamentation presents a close parallel to that of certain capitals found in Iran (Figs. 45-47, facing p. 146) and of the silver pouch-shaped plaques with repoussé design excavated in Hungary, believed to date back to the original occupation of the country by the Hungarians.

Persian stucco-workers, like those of Italy at a later date, would appear to have traversed the whole of the late classical and Early Christian world. In Cividale I succeeded in finding examples in the style of Mshatta. In other materials, too, such as textiles and leatherwork, we find a constant recurrence of Iranian

32 Sarnath, stûpa ; zone of ornament ; photo., E. La Roche.
See pp. 114, 125.

33 Island of Achthamar, Lake Van, cruciform church ; South view.
See p. 159.

34 Mshatta, façade ; to left, end of the Hvarenah wall-facing. See p. 124

features throughout the Eurasian continent. To mention only a single instance, it is instructive to compare the ornamental capitals, illustrated in my book on the miniature-paintings of ' Lesser Armenia ', with the decorative art of the Amur region ; the common source from which both derive must be sought in the area between the two countries in Altai-Iran.

III. *Mazdaism*

It has already been pointed out that our total ignorance on the subject of Mazdean art is not a sufficient reason for denying the possibility of its existence. Equally inconclusive is the fact that the cult of Mithra, in its triumphant passage through the Roman world, borrowed Greek forms in the representation of the god at the bull sacrifice. The disposition of the, Mithräic temple and certain traces of its decoration should alone impose caution ; one may fairly assume that the reason why Mithraism borrowed from Greek art was that it had never itself depicted the figure of Mithras, and was indeed generally unacquainted with representational art. But that is no ground for proceeding to argue further that Mazdaism had no art. The apparent absence of concrete evidence is no reason for doing so.

On this analogy, if our knowledge of Christian art were limited to the Roman catacomb paintings—which belong to classical Christian art—we should be forced to conclude that the Christians had no distinctive art of their own, simply because they lacked a distinctive style of representation. In point of fact, the only pre-Constantinian examples of their art at present known to us are those at Rome, which are Alexandrian. But it is a fallacy to conclude, as is so often done, that other Christian monuments cannot have existed before the time of Constantine, simply because they have not survived to the present day. In the study of Christian architecture attention has hitherto, for some inexplicable reason, been confined to the Hellenistic timber-roofed basilica, which is structurally just an example of classical Christian art. The preceding chapters of this book will, I believe, bring about a clearer perception of the facts. There must assuredly have been some form of Christian art in the East during the first three centuries of our era, an art of Christian communities and their places of assembly. And similarly we may fairly assume that in Achaemenian, Parthian, late Hellenistic, and Sassanian times there existed some form of Mazdean popular art, the character of which we could certainly never deduce from a study of the grandiose art of the Sassanian court.

The question still remains whether this new province, into which I have opened up a path by the method of retrospective inference from the art of Islam, should be called ' Mazdean ', or whether we should not do better to retain the geographical term ' Altai-Iran '. Non-representational art is characteristic of the pastoral-nomadic and Northern peoples. It is present both in Islam and in Christian Armenia. Is it likely that Mazdaism, the oldest of the religions of Hither Asia established by a Founder, should not have preceded them on the same path? Mazdaism, while exceptionally rich in religious ideas, never strove in its popular art after realistic self-expression by means of the human figure. In Christian art we find representational subjects based upon Mazdean ideas ; but in Mazdean art itself we shall look in vain for scenes from the life of Zoroaster analogous to the figures of Christ or Buddha in Christian or Buddhist art. Nor need we expect to find Mazdaism dramatically expressing by means of the human figure those general ideas of the world and life, of death and a future state, in which the Avesta is so exceptionally rich.

It would therefore be wrong to place Mazdean art on the same footing as that of Buddhism or of Christianity. Nevertheless research should be able to define this art with some approach to accuracy. It is impossible as yet to distinguish in particular cases between religious and profane monuments. In this respect Mshatta, Ammān, and Bus-i-Hor present unsolved riddles. In the case of Islam, where proximity gives a clearer view, we know that religious art, though forming an important section of Islamic art as a whole, is nevertheless far from co-extensive with it. It is best to apply the term ' Mazdean ' to Iranian sacred art, because it comprises the religious expression common to Achaemenians, Arsacids, and Sassanians, whereas the term ' Persian ' suggests a Southern predominance non-existent in the case of formative art.

Concrete examples of Mazdean sacred buildings are entirely wanting. I do not propose to consider here whether this fact indicates that they were always few in number, or whether it simply results from the perishable nature of the unburned bricks

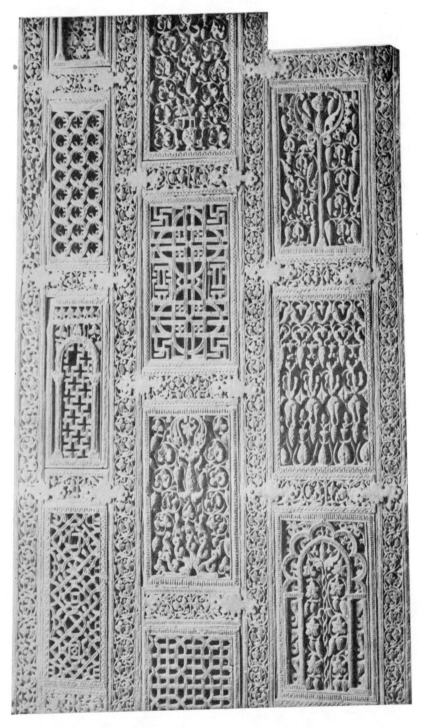

35   Kairwan, wooden mimbar ; pierced interlacing, niches, &c.
See pp. 117, 125, 241.

of which they were constructed. One fire-temple has been excavated at Šusa, and there is literary evidence for others of a later date. It is at least noteworthy that the deficiency is one which Mazdaism shares with the older Oriental cultures of Mesopotamia and of Iran ; in the latter case, evidence of temples has only been revealed by recent excavations carried to a great depth. Similar results will perhaps be achieved for Mazdaism in the future. At present our knowledge is in the main limited to its fire altars. And it is a fact of no small importance that the two oldest examples, the great altars of the rock-reliefs at Naksh-i-Rustam, already show the blind arcade, that commonest of motives in the decoration of Armenian churches (Fig. 2, facing p. 62), a feature which some authorities would derive from Iran, or from the galleries round early Aryan wooden buildings (Figs. 15–16, facing p. 80). Before considering this point more closely I may recall another trace of Eastern influence. An examination of the evidence clearly proves that orientation in Christian churches was indigenous to Armenia and Asia Minor, and spread from these regions, superseding the ancient classical practice, which made the important end of the building face the west. One cannot help wondering how far Mazdean influence may not have contributed to this result.

Mazdean decoration is purely formal ; that is, it entirely avoids expression by means of human figures. Instead of these it employs animal and bird forms, scenes from the chase, and the conventional landscapes common in mediaeval art. But it has a special preference for friezes of arcading, blind arches, interlaced bands—in fact just those features which are characteristic of Islamic art (Fig. 35, opposite) and of that Western art which we misname ' Romanesque '. It would thus seem incumbent upon students of art to give more attention to this forgotten province, if only for its bearing upon the decorative forms affected in mediaeval Europe.

Of the features properly belonging to Mazdean decorative art, only a portion can be traced to genuine Northern tradition. The blind arch, preferably of horseshoe shape, the cushion base, and its colonnette might be shown to derive from wooden architecture ; the same applies to the decoration of the walls beneath the eaves with arcading in low relief or the inclined surfaces with interlacings. I have treated this question in greater detail in my work on Armenia. At present I am more particularly concerned with the patterns used on the inner surfaces of vaults. They naturally owe their origin to those countries where bricks were used, namely, Iran proper, Irak, and Mesopotamia. I shall now analyse the designs employed, but only from the point of view of their religious content.

A. *The Hvarenah Landscape.*

At the very heart of Aryan piety on Iranian soil lay the idea of Hvarenah. Söderblom has shown in his work, *Das Werden des Gottesglaubens*, that it represents the crowning glory of Iran. A comprehensive description of its nature is given in a long hymn in the Avesta. It is connected with the cult of the dead, representing the might and majesty of departed spirits. Hvarenah is the power that makes running waters gush from springs, plants sprout from the soil, winds blow the clouds, and men come to birth. It governs the courses of sun, moon, and stars. Hvarenah therefore is that which permeates the whole countryside, and particularly the land of Seistan through which the river Helmand flows. To this country, alternately frozen and parched by drought, water forms the very pulse of life and is full of a mysterious beneficent potency. ' O water, to him who sacrifices to thee vouchsafe thy glory ! ' Hvarenah, created by Mazda, is the power that makes the waters rise from the world-ocean. From Hvarenah the sun derives his strength. If ' the mighty immortal Sun with swift steeds illuminates and warms ', if it purifies earth and water and banishes the evil demons of darkness, it is from Hvarenah that such magic influence comes. Even so are Moon and Stars endowed with power and fulfilled with majesty.

Were such ideas expressed in art, we should expect to see a barren landscape, above it the sun with his swift steeds, below it the world-ocean ; the land between would have its gushing springs, and its scattered plants springing from the earth ; over all would float clouds. ' With milk (cattle) have I created the ' glory of the Aryan people, rich in herds, rich in lands, rich ' in glory ; endowed with wisdom, endowed with possessions ; ' bringing gluttony to nought, bringing hostility (enemies) to ' nought.' In such a Mazdean landscape I should expect to see flocks and herds and symbolical presentation of attacks and conflicts of wild beasts.

Are there such landscapes ? If so, they would not be

representations in the strict sense, but compositions pieced together out of the elements enumerated above, mere symbols of nature, devoid of realism.   Other artistic treatment could hardly be looked for in Iran.   I thus find myself on the track of a kind of Asiatic landscape, originating, like the Chinese ' philosophical landscape ' of the Sung period, in religion, or rather in a philosophy of the universe, and based upon significance and form, not, like the landscapes of the Southern peoples, upon natural objects exactly reproduced.   It is quite possible that this type of landscape first passed from symbolism to true representation not in Iran, but in the regions of Hellenistic or Christian culture ; in the same way, Indian ideas appear to have found their earliest representational expression in the Taoism of China and the indigenous landscape paintings which it inspired. We shall see at a later stage whether the existence of such landscapes can be proved in Christian art.   I shall for the present exclude all mention of Hellenistic landscapes, although they offer a promising field for research.

Scenes from the Chase.   The chase was one of the pleasures of the Mazdean paradise and future world.   We should, therefore, expect to find it frequently depicted in Iranian art, and not exclusively in the traditional Assyro-Babylonian style.   The palaces of Persian kings were once filled with subjects of this kind. A single example of this Court art has been preserved, a rock relief at Tak-i Bostan, representing the chase of deer and of wild boars.   It consists of flat composition aiming at strict naturalism rather than at artistic values such as spatial unity ; in this quality, as well as in its concentration on the person of the ruler, it resembles the ancient oriental hunting-scene more closely than the Greek.   On Sassanian silver dishes we find similar scenes repeated in almost endless variety, depicting the chase of deer, ibex, and wild boar, with the aid of falcons or trained panthers. The decoration of the main hall in the small castle of Quseir 'Amra is executed entirely in the Iranian spirit, and shows the persistence of this ancient tradition in Ummayad times ; the walls are covered with scenes from the chase.   Even the Normans still decorated their interiors in Palermo with hunting-scenes of this type.   One of these, executed in mosaic, is preserved in the Palazzo Reale.   Later examples are to be seen in the Alhambra.   On the far side of Iran, in Turkestan, this kind of landscape encountered Chinese influence, and the product of their combination is seen in lozenge-diapers with characteristic conical mountains, sometimes containing animal figures, sometimes real hunting-scenes, or figures of Buddha. The Shosoin at Nara (A. D. 749–56) contains excellent examples of Iranian work in both the freer and the more conventional style.

River Landscapes. In the paintings of Chinese Turkestan the river landscape is a stock composition introduced on floors, walls, and ceilings ; numerous examples will be found in the pages of Grünwedel, Le Coq, and M. A. Stein, where illustrations are given of the cave of the Hippocamps at Ming-oï near Kyzyl, a fresco in Dandan-Uiliq, and in particular the roof of the Naga-cave at Sorčuq (Fig. 42, facing p. 137). Here again we can find parallels on the opposite side of Iran : river-landscapes with formal tree designs (candelabra motives) similar to those at Sorčuq occur in the church of S. Costanza and in two Roman apse-mosaics, of all of which I shall have more to say presently.

These river-scenes, probably Iranian in origin, afterwards formed a permanent foreground to Buddhist representations of ' The Western Paradise '. The Padmapani tree of Bäzäklik, which I shall presently discuss, is also depicted as growing out of waves (Fig. 37, opposite).

B. *Hvarenah Symbols.*

Mazdaism, like Buddhism, and Christianity at a later date, appears to have made full use in its symbolical art of that great stream of animal ornament which began in the North and East, poured in flood through the funnel-shaped gap between Altai and Iran, and finally issued in Hither Asia. The clue to the interpretation seems here again to be Hvarenah, the Majesty of God, the best possession of the home, averting evil, giving increase to prosperity. Animal figures are repeatedly named as vehicles of Hvarenah. ' In mythology and popular belief Hvarenah ' appears sometimes as a bird in flight, sometimes as a swimming ' or diving creature, sometimes in other animal forms, and ' follows the Elect (after the Karnamak and the Shanama the ' glory of the king came to Ardeshir in the likeness of a great ' ram and rode at his side). Sometimes it resides in the sedge ' at the lake-side, is eaten by the cows and passes into their milk. ' The high esteem in which the cow was held in Iran, as in ' India, rendered it an appropriate medium for the transmission

36 Brunswick Museum, ivory
carving; Yima. See p. 122.

37 Bäzäklik, Chinese Turkestan, temple group; painting;
Padmapani on scrolled stem;
after A. Grünwedel. See pp.
120, 123.

38   Spoleto, façade of S. Pietro ; photo., Alinari.   See p. 121.

' of divinity.' The bird, the ram, the sedge in the lake, the cow; are these really unfamiliar to us in art ? I think we have here the key to many riddles which have perplexed our minds but have always been left unsolved.

Let us examine a façade such as that of the Church of S. Pietro at Spoleto, a place full of interest for students of Early Christian and mediaeval art (Fig. 38, opposite). All periods, including recent centuries, have left their mark on the building. But there still remains a central core, represented above all by sculptured ornament which one critic ascribes to masters of the year *c.* 592, others to the Umbrian masons of the period of transition to Romanesque. Both the main entrance with its horseshoe arch and the pair of cows in the lower panels of the pediment impress us alike as foreign to their actual environment. Noteworthy, too, are the decoration of the blind arcades on either side of the main door, the animal scenes in the adjacent panels, and several other features into the significance of which I cannot at present enter. Are not these things echoes of a forgotten music audible here upon Italian soil ? I shall now consider the various Mazdean symbols individually.

Animals. A well-known ornament of the Sassanian royal crown is the pair of wings. Plastic art adopted them as an ornamental feature, for instance, in the entrance façade of Mshatta. That these may have been actual wings attached to the crown is suggested by the passage in which we read that the feathers of the bird Varegan are protective against the black magic of an enemy. No man carrying a single one of this bird's bones or feathers can be either killed or overcome : ' He first receives homage, first majesty.' Probably the disk between the wings of the Sassanian crown originally represented the sun ; it is sometimes placed above a crescent moon. The bird Varegan is the vehicle of Hvarenah. When Yima in the presence of the mighty of the empire ascribed to himself the creation and the happiness of the world, ' the glory flew forth in the likeness of a bird ' ; the bird Varegan forsook Yima in its three capacities successively as the glory of the priest, of the king, and of the peasant, as it is written in the Avesta :

> Yima, the radiant, the good shepherd,
> Wandered haplessly to and fro ;
> He hid from before his enemies,
> And concealed himself under the earth.

In many collections there are ivory carvings representing a good shepherd who sits dreaming on a hill. Among the rocks are depicted all manner of creatures on either side of a central spring or waterfall. A particularly fine old specimen in Brunswick (Fig. 36, facing p. 120), and the rich example at Naples, depict in addition the cavern below, in which Yima is seen reclining before a book doing penance like the Magdalen. Sometimes sheep are the only animals represented, but frequently we find various other species both wild and domesticated, as in a marble relief at Athens. Sometimes, too, they symbolize the triumph over evil, like the figure of the lion on the hare at Naples. It is by no means improbable that the Christian conception of the religious founder as the good shepherd fell upon peculiarly favourable soil in Iran.

Figures of single animals are distributed so widely and in such profusion alike in the art of Islam, on the Mshatta façade, at Amra, Amida, and as far afield as Korea (Fig. 31, facing p. 99), that a separate volume would be needed to do justice to the subject. Probably these figures were originally symbols of Hvarenah and of other Mazdean ideas ; in later times their purpose may often have been purely decorative. It is remarkable that these animals and birds are frequently depicted with a branch beside or underneath them.

Plants. The vine and the pomegranate are certainly to be included among the symbols of Hvarenah. Such at least is the inference I draw *a posteriori* from Armenian churches like that of Zwarthnotz (erected in A. D. 650), and its imitations. Vine and pomegranate are here used in combination to decorate the spandrels of the blind arcades on the exterior of the building ; in other churches both in Armenia and in Syria they are similarly treated but not together. I have pointed out in my *Mschatta* how frequent and striking a feature the vine forms in Islamic art ; coincidences between it and the art of Early Christianity in Hither Asia are probably due to their common debt to Iran, and I conclude that both vine and pomegranate were Mazdean symbols. These types are characteristically free from the familiar realism of Roman work, and it is not surprising to find the vine-leaf treated conventionally both at Mshatta and earlier at Hatra, the stem being placed on the top of the leaf and made to terminate in one or more buds. The branching of the vine is likewise arbitrarily planned with the sole object of filling a flat

39   Island of Achthamar, Lake Van, cruciform church, A.D. 915–21 ;
East side.   See pp. 123, 150, 159.

40   Lemberg, Armenian gospel of A.D. 1198 ; Eusebian canons.
See pp. 123, 241.

space ; the plant does not conform to the laws of natural growth. The hunting frieze of Achthamar, which is prima facie strangely inappropriate to a church, appears to be a pure echo of Mazdaism. It is particularly striking that the wood, in which the chase is depicted, is composed of vines and pomegranate stems or branches (Fig. 39, facing p. 122). I shall not recur to the ' arabesque ' (Fig. 31, facing p. 99) at this point.

The commonest motive is a kind of ' tree ', not less widely removed from nature than the landscapes, but like them composed of a number of elements, each of which, taken separately, is realistic. I call this a ' formal tree ' or Candelabrum. It occurs as a border on the outer rock-sculptures of Ṭaḳ-i Bostan ; from the thick stem and branches feathery leaves of Indian style grow upwards like palmettes. The branches terminate in buds curving to one side, such as are often depicted as pendants to the horse trappings of riders in early Persian representations. The distribution of this ' formal tree ' design throughout the Asiatic countries both East and West of Iran is so uniform as to prove its popularity in Iran proper, the centre of its distribution. At Bäzäklik in Turkestan a formal tree of this kind forms a support for a six-armed figure of Padmapani (Fig. 37, facing p. 120); it might equally well be used as a support for a cross in one of the countless miniatures of an Armenian manuscript (Fig. 40, opposite). In Mshatta it appears in the midst of the scrollwork filling the great zigzag, while at Ammān it is used in great variety to fill the blind arcades of the interior (Fig. 29, facing p. 99). It is an equally familiar feature of the interior decorations in Armenian and Georgian buildings, as well as of the south sides of Georgian churches. Even in modern works of industrial art, such as an Armenian embroidery from the Bukovina (Fig. 41, facing p. 124), it reappears in opulent growth on either side of a hunting-scene interspersed with flowers and animals, betraying unequivocal, if indirect, connexion with those formal tree-designs which occur at intervals along the walls of the nave in the Church of the Nativity at Bethlehem. Whether this design is to be identified with the ancient motive of the tree of life and the Mazdean Haoma is a question only to be decided by scholars better versed than myself in the archaeology of Mesopotamia and Iran.

C. *Decoration of the Mazdean House.*

'May holiness, strength and prosperity, excellence and 'happiness dwell within this house.' 'May the Excellence 'that brings fortune never fail within this house.'[1] Such passages show that Hvarenah was a virtue which men desired for the houses in which they lived. In the blessing invoked upon the hearth and home of the pious, the spirits were invited to enter with their manifold gifts, 'in order to further the reign of might and excellence.' When, remembering all this, I contemplate the rich decoration of monuments like Mshatta and Ammān, I begin to perceive that this decoration does not proceed from a mere delight in ornament, but that it has a symbolical foundation. Fragments of stucco ornament from a building in Mesopotamia recently brought to Berlin have, amid other motives, medallions with pearled borders (the pearling perhaps representing pomegranate stones, and enclosing for central subjects either the pair of wings with an inscription, or the figure of a ram or an ibex; there are also formal trees with birds and pomegranate (?) fruits. This seems to indicate that the interiors of houses were decorated with symbols of Hvarenah. I am inclined to apply the same interpretation to the Mshatta façade. The illustration (Fig. 34, facing p. 115) shows the walls on either side of the entrance covered with symbolical designs, the vine interspersed with birds and animals, especially with those flanking vases as symbols of blessing and protection. Similarly enriched with ornament, though belonging to a later period, is the apse-buttressed square building of Ammān; the inside walls have three tiers of blind arcades filled with Hvarenah symbols (Fig. 29, facing p. 99). The Korean tomb (Fig. 31, facing p. 99) should perhaps also be included in this category.

In this connexion I may mention another kind of interior decoration, familiar to students by its occurrence in Christian churches, although its origin has never yet been satisfactorily explained. I refer to decorative hangings without representational designs. I conjecture that it was largely by way of Iran that they made their fresh entry into the West. The influx of pastoral nomads, especially Turks from Inner Asia, makes intelligible the spread of influence from that quarter. Chinese Turkestan is permeated with it. Undoubtedly the tent, which served

---

[1] These are the terms used in the Zend Avesta.

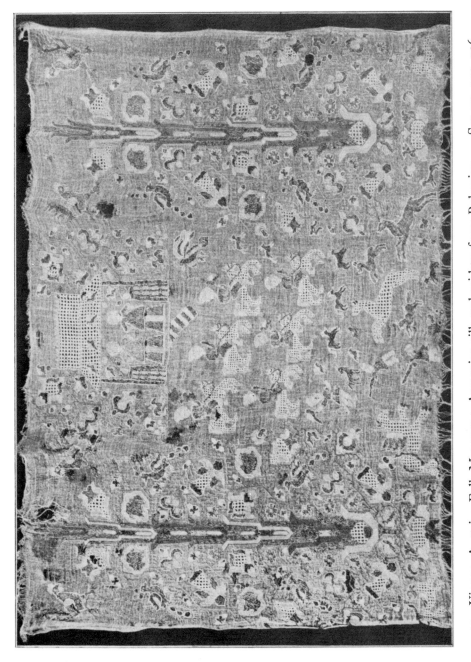

41 Vienna, Austrian Folk-Museum ; Armenian silk embroidery from Bukovina.   See pp. 123, 126.

these pastoral nomads for a dwelling, was important to the art of Iran during the Mazdean period long before the rise of Islam. I attribute to it the origin of the lambrequin pattern, perhaps also the use of folded hangings to decorate the lower parts of walls, a practice which spread rapidly, and of which we have evidence in the case of Early Christian churches. Painted imitations of it are legion. It appears in the mosaics crowning the dome in the Baptisteries at Naples and Ravenna, and is a constantly recurring feature in the roof-paintings of caves in Chinese Turkestan. We are not yet in a position to say whether it had any connexion with Hvarenah.

It is possible that the art of Iranian wall-linings may ultimately be connected with the designs of such coverings, varying with the materials of which these consisted. It undoubtedly derives its distinctive character from the qualities of woven and plaited fabrics, from wood and metal ornament with 'slant-cut' ornament, stucco openwork, &c. Among the designs, that of the swastika was a particular favourite, and reappears constantly in a variety of combinations. The finest of all examples of this kind of work are found on the wooden pulpit of the great mosque at Kairwan which originally came from Baghdad; it reveals an astounding variety of patterns in interlacing openwork (Fig. 35, facing p. 117). In stone we have the older parts of the Amida façade, sculpture in Coptic churches, and on the Buddhist stûpa of Sarnath (Fig. 32, facing p. 114). On Iranian soil there are similar designs on architectural and other remains from the time of Mahmud of Ghazna; we found them on the earliest Islamic remains discovered by us in Khorassan.

D. *Mazdean Costume.*

We have seen that houses were decorated with symbols to secure the protection of the divine might and majesty; costumes appear to have been similarly treated with a view to protecting the wearer. In the rock-reliefs of Taḵ-i Bostan one cannot help noticing that the garments are completely covered with symbols of Hvarenah. The commonest of these is the duck; and next to it the cock and the curious Persian dragon, viz. a winged lion with a peacock's (?) tail; with these symbols occur the formal tree and the rosette. Remains of silk fabrics have been preserved, which are true counterparts of these imitations in stone. The same designs recur in paintings in Chinese Turkestan. Moreover, a large number of stuffs have scenes from the chase resembling those on the well-known silver dishes. We are thus once more confronted with the art which we have already defined as Mazdean. Its later influence in Christian times, which will be discussed later, confirms the view that we have to deal here not with meaningless ornament, but with a form of decoration which originally possessed religious signifi-cance. I refer the reader once more to the seventeenth-century silk embroidery (Fig. 41, facing p. 124), acquired by the Austrian Folk Museum in Vienna from an Armenian private owner in Czernowitz. On either side is seen a formal tree with palmettes and birds ; in the centre, under a house with two female figures [1] is a hunting-scene disposed in two rows to be followed from left to right ; it consists of mounted figures holding falcons in their hands ; beneath them is a gryphon confronted by wild animals in the midst of which are seen a single figure with a falcon and a pair of others with guns. The latter give a contemporary note ; but the remaining portion of the design probably belongs in all essentials to an ancient Irano-Armenian folk-tradition.

IV. *Manichaean Art*

Manichaean illuminated manuscripts must have been the vehicle of a very rich form of decorative art. Mani, who suffered martyrdom at Gundeshapur in A. D. 274, was himself a painter, and therefore the only religious Founder from the outset aware of the importance of the formative arts as a means of influence. His teaching, comparable with that of Islam in its rapid expansion and its proselytizing power, soon made its way into the West also. The presence of this Babylonian religion can be attested in Rome and Gaul in the fourth century, and it continued to exert an influence for centuries after. The Albigensian move-ment in France was indirectly connected with it. Now this Manichaeanism, which was a forerunner of the Persian movement in Christian art, must itself have been a carrier of oriental art forms to the West. Augustine after his conversion bitterly demanded the burning of the numerous costly manuscripts, of which he specially notes the fine bindings, but he retains

[1] Compare the architecture of the Chinese temples in the reliefs illustrated by Chavannes in his *Mission archéologique dans la Chine Septentrionale.*

the words : *non in aliqua mole corporea inspicanda est pulchritudo*. Discoveries in Turkestan confirm this tendency to rich ornamentation, although here figure art predominates. The Manichaeans were also familiar with a kind of *Hetoimasia* (Preparation of the Throne) in the vacant decorated chair which at the feast in memory of their Founder they set up as his symbol.

It is probable that Iran was the source of those systems of decorative design occurring in early mediaeval manuscripts which cannot be referred to Hellenistic art. How far Hvarenah motives underlay these designs is at present a doubtful question. It is none the less a striking fact that in the art of illumination, which flowered so richly in Armenia and passed thence to the West and Byzantium, a prominent place is occupied by familiar Hvarenah motives, such as figures of birds sipping water and symbols of the divine majesty. The familiar fish-bird initials of Merovingian and Armenian manuscripts may also derive from the same source.

These indications suggest that non-representational art won for itself a serious religious basis in Iran. There is a kind of sentiment to which representational art is repugnant on account of its histrionic character. Let us call this feeling popular, and oppose it to that of the cultured upper classes, and we shall at once see what I mean when I contrast the harsh conditions of the North with the forcing-house atmosphere of the South. Students of Indogermanic art must start with certain well-defined presuppositions in so far as the North- and East-Aryans form the subject of their research, and Buddhism and Mazdaism, Christianity and Islam, stand out against a background of Asiatic migrations.

The ancient Aryan migrations are connected with a form of wooden architecture, which was carried by the Greeks to the Mediterranean and by Iranians and Indians to the Far East, and had a decisive influence upon the development of architecture both in these regions and in the North. It was accompanied by a decorative art originally devoid of figure subjects, but soon superseded in Greece and India by the representational style indigenous to those countries. It was otherwise in Iran. There the non-representational style became permanent through the influence of the national religion, and subsequently passed over to Islam without substantial change. We shall now have to consider whether things were not very much the same with Christianity.

Be this as it may, it shows a certain bias to derive the origin of Christian art exclusively from antiquity or so-called classical sources. This method confines attention to the forcing-houses of Southern culture, and ignores the pastoral nomads, with whom were linked those two small nations which gave birth respectively to Christ and Mohammed, the last two individual Founders of religions. It likewise excludes those branches of the Northern races which penetrated to the South without succumbing to classical culture, and interchanged ideas with the small nations inhabiting Palestine and Arabia. The religious art of both Jew and Moslem is steadily opposed to representation. The former only begins to waver after coming into closer contact with Hellenism and being thoroughly permeated with its influence, as for example in Alexandria. The artistic tendency of Islam was not due in the first instance to the prohibition of figure art by the Koran ; the really decisive factor was that the Beduins, like the Jews, were nomads at the time when their religion was founded. Moreover we know that the religion of Mohammed came with a rush across the desert to Iran, and only found its true intellectual foundation after contact with the pastoral peoples of the Altai-Iran region. When we seek the origin of Christian representational art we encounter the Hellenism of the Mediterranean ; similarly on our present path of research we are confronted by Mazdaism as the dominant religion. The appearance of Mazdaism in Armenia allows us to test the conclusions reached from the above evidence ; we can infer the Mazdean attitude towards representation from what occurred in that country during the Christian period. The Sassanian dynasty was hated in Armenia, and the Arsacids remained in power until the year 428. The Armenian Church, in so far as it remained national in character, eschewed representation ; may we not infer that Mazdaism originally did likewise ?

Clearly, Mohammedan art does not stand alone. There rises before us the possibility that Mazdaism and the earliest Christian art were pioneers of Islam, and closely akin to it in spirit : that we have in fact a whole group of non-representational religions forming an *enclave* between Buddhist and classical-Christian representational art. It is perhaps only on this hypothesis that we can rightly understand the beginnings of Christian Church art, the violence of the iconoclasts at a later time, and certain characteristic features of Christian art in the West.

It has long been recognized that Early Christian mosaics are throughout arranged according to a definite plan, the stamp of which is most definitely impressed upon the apse. In it the hand of the Almighty holding the wreath takes the place of the Hellenistic radiating bands of colour ; beneath is seen a conventional ' landscape ', in its powerful but rigid expression, equally far removed from Hellenistic ideas. At the bottom is a strip of green foreground decked with flowers, behind it other bands of colour ; are these really intended merely to give depth and perspective, as Sybel has maintained ? The figures of aquatic animals and birds which fill out the spaces are likewise ascribed to Hellenistic picture making. But may not the truth be that the *putti* form the only Hellenistic contribution to what is essentially a river Helmand, a feature of Hvarenah landscape, in Egypt called the Nile, and in later times christened the Jordan. The palms (' which Italian artists could see growing in their own country ') and the phoenix are symbolic of Paradise. What is this but a picture of the earth dominated by the might and majesty of God, whether in the guise of the sun, symbol of Ahuramazda, or in that of the cross, symbolic of Christ ? There were apses, such as that described by Paulinus of Nola, in which the sole decoration consisted of such composite symbolical landscapes. Can this be properly described as Hellenistic, as Christian classical art ?

VI

Non-representational Church Art, and the subsequent Anti-representational Movement

THE constant features in the religious art of the North and China during their earliest period of development, as well as in that of Mazdaism, Judaism, and Islam, appear to have formed the first stage of Christian art also in the inland regions East of the Mediterranean. From these regions there sprang, in despite of Hellenism, a form of non-representational art extending as far as Rome, Lower Italy, the two Gauls and the British Isles. This fact has hitherto escaped observation because the Catacombs with their paintings have been too exclusively regarded as the only starting-point. There are writers who assure us that they would gladly trace the course of Christian art from the East Westwards, but that the complete absence of earlier material in the East unhappily precludes any such attempt in the case of the Catacomb paintings. But if this be so we are faced with the question whether our whole attitude is not based upon a false assumption and mistaken premisses. Is it really necessary to place Hellenistic sepulchral art at the beginning of the series ? Should we not rather concede this place to the earliest forms of church architecture and its decoration, so far as these may be established by retrospective inference ? How is it possible to believe that painting came first, to be followed only at a later stage by sculpture, and finally by the earliest Christian architectural monuments ? Is it because the view as seen from Rome wears this aspect, and because in Rome monuments happen to be preserved only in this chronological sequence ? The classical archaeologist who proceeds in this manner makes himself entirely dependent upon the few monuments which happen to have been preserved. Critical training and method, however perfect, will avail him little while he persists in this attitude ; and he will incur the reproach of deliberately relying upon chance survivals.

The specialist will not let himself be blinded in this manner by the fortuitous.

We have already seen that Islam spread like wild-fire over the East and attained its second creative centre in the distant north-eastern corner of Iran. Mecca indeed remained the religious centre, but apart from this the region of Altai-Iran became the source of moral and intellectual life. Is it conceivable that Christianity, which at an earlier date took its origin at no great distance from Mecca and Medina, can have failed to make its way eastwards along the same natural path from the Syro-Egyptian end? Why does it never occur to archaeologists to include the east in their survey? and why, inspired by the holy fire of the twin orthodoxies of classical learning and the Church, must they needs go on to attack the disturber of their peace, who dares, for example, to ascribe to Mesopotamia a leading rôle in the rise of Christian vaulted architecture? Will they now show a like hostility to the idea that domed architecture originated in Iran and travelled by way of Armenia? Arabs and Jews were alike connected with Iran, the former through the caravan route across the desert, the latter as a result of the dispersion of the twelve tribes. The Jew, like the Beduin, found in Iran an atmosphere more suited to his genius and the pure expression of his non-representational form of religion than in the Mediterranean region. It was therefore probably due in the first instance to the Christians of Jewish birth, as in Islam to the Arabs, that Christian art at its very commencement acquired a non-representational character, and subsequently found, like Islam, that its true and natural support lay in the East. Evidence of this relationship is still clearly perceptible in Armenia, owing to the twofold circumstance that the Parthian Arsacids adopted Christianity as the state religion, and that the most distinguished of the succeeding dynasties, that of the Bagratids, endeavoured to prove itself of Jewish descent.[1]

[1] As regards the relations of the Jews with Armenia and Iran, Leo Meyer writes as follows, with a reference to D. H. Müller, *Semitica II*, and V. Aptowitzer, *Die mosaische Rezeption im armenischen Recht* : ' The Jewish population of Armenia was numerous and anciently established, as recorded by Schürer, *Jüdische Geschichte*, and Ritter in *Erdkunde*, x. The Talmud also mentions Jewish-Armenian learning ; a Jews' high school existed in Nisibis ; *doctores iudaei* are mentioned, and were not without influence, as is shown by the code of the Meckitar Gosh and others. Felix Lazarus, in Brüks *Jahrbücher*, x, tries to prove that the legend of the Bagratids is not devoid of an historical

We have seen that as early as the eighth century, when the seat of Mohammedan power shifted from the Syrian capital of the Ummayads to the Abbasid capital of Baghdad, the Iranian spirit became dominant in wall decoration, and the expansion of its peculiar style can be traced as far as Egypt. Iran in fact possessed an indigenous art, quite independent of Greece and Rome, and more closely related to the genius of Islam and of the Christians of Armenia than to the art of the Mediterranean area. Is it conceivable that this art should have failed to manifest itself in the architecture or ornamentation of Christian churches in the Mediterranean area in the same degree as the various forms of the vault, viz. the apse, the barrel vault, and the dome?

Having once established the fact that Christianity developed on a wide basis on Persian soil and created indigenous forms of architecture uninfluenced by the Mediterranean, ought we not to consider the probability that the Eastern spirit had no less influence in Church-decoration as well? We shall therefore inquire whether it is not possible to detect in the barrel-vaults, domes, and vaulted apses of Early Christian buildings a new tendency, the mediaeval, foreign to Greece and Rome, and first borne into the Mediterranean upon the tide of Christianity. The permanent basis of its strength lay in its markedly Iranian origin; it was the same source which ultimately controlled the art of Islam. This faith, after its brief interlude in Syria, attached itself to Iran and its culture even as the Christianity of Greece and Rome embraced a Hellenism already in decline. Between these two cultural regions were the theological school of Nisibis and its sphere of influence, both under Aramaean direction, and Armenia, of which the art was permeated by the spirit of Iran. Originally all Christian communities maintained constant relations with each other. It was the conflicting influences set up by the Church, and especially by the Councils of the fifth century, which first produced schism and separation, the rise of race against race and nation against nation, despite the common bond of their Christian faith. The Council of Ephesus in A. D. 431, insisting upon the divine motherhood of Mary, provoked the counter-movement of the Nestorians in Mesopotamia. The Council of Chalcedon in A. D. 451 was the ultimate cause of the final defection of Egypt and of the

background; it appears in fact that the names of the Bagratids occur identically in the lists of the Jews of the house of David who led their countrymen during their exile.'

Armenian Church, which had by artful devices been brought almost to a state of unity in the service of pictures. But while the Semites reverted to representational art, the Armenian people entered upon a fierce struggle in defence of their ancient non-representational style. This internal enmity of the various national churches increased the existing antagonism of Byzantium and Rome, and had the effect not only of impeding their own political development but also of ensuring the subsequent triumph of Islam.

In order to demonstrate the original non-representational character of Christian art, I shall begin with the decoration of such vaulted buildings as have survived on Italian soil and are therefore best known. I shall deal first with the dome, then with the barrel-vault, and finally with the apse.

I. *Italian Mosaics*

The method of covering interiors with small glass cubes probably originated on curved surfaces, to which it is admirably adapted. In any case it is a fact that strong and creative work has survived only on vaults, whereas on flat surfaces we find imitation of well-known forms borrowed from other arts, more especially from that of manuscript illumination, whether on papyrus or parchment ; an excellent example may be seen on the nave walls of S. Maria Maggiore. In seeking examples of forms adapted to the peculiar character of mosaic it will be well to confine our attention for the moment to vaulted surfaces.

A. *The Decoration of the Dome*. The mosaics of S. Costanza, in spite of certain Hellenistic intrusive elements, afford good early examples of the Iranian style. We find here the characteristic difference between dome and barrel-vault decoration ; I shall begin with a comparative examination of the former. The dome was divided radially by richly branching formal tree designs springing from a river with rocky banks ; a middle zone was filled with a series of figure subjects. Were we to substitute Buddhist figures, we should have the decoration of the Naga cave of Sorčuq in Chinese Turkestan (Fig. 42, facing p. 137) ; if we eliminate the representational element we are left with the Iranian decorative style, which was the origin of both Christian and Buddhist roof paintings, though each of these made the additions natural to its own genius. We find Constantine Porphyrogennetos still employing the same style of decoration for the Chrysotriclinion in the palace at Constantinople. In Armenia the radial division of dome decoration became a permanent feature. At Mastara, in the Hripsimeh, at Thalin, and in other places, we find eight ribs meeting at the top in a medallion. In some cases the effect was possibly enhanced by painting. This disposition was carried by the Goths as far as Spain.

More than a century elapsed between the building of this church under Constantine and that of the Baptistery at Ravenna. The Hellenistic modification had by now disappeared, not so the Syrian; the Aramaean theologians perceived the value of the radial division of the dome and used it to further their didactic system. The general scheme of decoration both in mosaic and stucco remains purely Iranian in form. The interior of the dome is divided radially into compartments by formal tree-designs, purely geometrical in structure, and connected at the top by a border of ' lambrequins '. The middle zone below is filled by a blind arcade in stucco with the peculiar crowning with which the East-Iranian buildings of Kashmir have rendered us familiar. The spaces of the arcading round the octagon at the base are filled with a scroll-design enclosing central motives, which correspond to the rosettes of the Mshatta façade.

S. Giovanni in fonte in Naples occupies an intermediate position between S. Costanza and the Baptistery of Ravenna. Its Iranian character is at once betrayed by its square ground-plan and by the use of squinches to effect the transition from square plan to dome. The interior of the dome is once more radially divided by formal trees connected at the top by ' lambrequins '; in the compartments formed by this ornament and in the spandrels above the squinches are characteristic Hvarenah motives in the form of a vase between birds, or of whole landscapes with sheep or stags by the side of a shepherd and flanked by palms.

A special group is formed by the domes of the two cruciform churches with a single nave, namely, the tomb of Galla Placidia and Casaranello. Here we see the cross depicted on a starry sky as background. These features seem to indicate an Eastern origin, and the supposition is confirmed by the decoration of the adjacent barrel-vaults. I shall revert to this question when discussing the apses.

B. *Barrel-vault Decoration.* In this group too we can begin with the mosaics of S. Costanza, though now with those of the circular aisle. The barrel-vaulting of this aisle is divided into twelve distinct panels, which are not homogeneously treated ; each is filled independently with a continuous pattern, but the arrangement is such that opposite pairs have identical designs, of which there are thus only six. One of them consists of a vine-scroll formally treated, though certain Hellenistic features show that it is intended to suggest the vintage. Another shows a familiar Iranian motive introduced through Syria, detached branches of pomegranate type, with a bird or a vase to almost every branch. One of the barrel-vaults of Quseir 'Amra has the same motive, but in a lozenge-diaper. It is very common in the Eusebian canons of Syrian and early Armenian Gospels, and reappears in the Mesopotamian Gospels of Rabula (A. D. 586) as a decorative detail near the base of the arcades. Two other corresponding vaults in S. Costanza are decorated with inter-connected circles ; in one case these are triple-banded with contrasting colour. The last two pairs have a four-rayed and a six-rayed pattern of the kind which reappears in Amida and Egypt. The six-rayed variety was afterwards very popular in Islamic polygonal designs.

Equally rich examples of barrel-vault decoration have been preserved in Salonika. In the Church of S. George remains of mosaics were saved from destruction by Rosi in 1889 ; with the exception of one piece, these might quite well be imitations of Persian silk fabrics, as might be those of S. Sophia in Constanti-nople. In front of the apse in the Church of S. Sophia in Salonika there is a barrel-vault decorated with a cross within a circle on a gold ground, and bordered with a textile repeat-pattern com-posed of vine-leaves and crosses. In the West similar barrel-vaults occur in the nave of the mausoleum of Galla Placidia at Ravenna. There the transept is decorated with gold vine-scrolls enclosing the sacred monogram on a blue ground, while the window is surrounded by acanthus scrolls and figures of stags at watersprings. The latter designs are enriched with colours suggested by bird's plumage, and differ from those of S. Costanza, which have a white background. I shall return to this subject later.

Another type of barrel-vault decoration is described by Agnellus as occurring in the Basilica Ursiana at Ravenna. The Syrian Bishop Ursus had the *testudo* of this church decorated with mosaics before the year 400, the work on the women's side being executed by the mosaicists Eusebius and Paulus, that on the men's side by Satius and Stephanus. The passage almost certainly refers to vault decoration : *et hinc atque illinc gipseis metallis diversa hominum, animaliumque et quadrupedum enigmata inciserunt et valde optime composuerunt.* In a letter written by Nilus of Sinai a few years later there is a reference to the use of stucco in church decoration as a means of pleasing the eye with figures of creatures flying, walking, and creeping, and of every kind of plant. We are reminded of the use of Hvarenah symbols in the decoration of Mazdean interiors ; there we find a combination of similar motives in stucco, the function of which is not to please the eye or serve as *aenigmata*, but rather to encompass the room with the glory of God. A good example of this type of decoration, modified of course by Christian influence, is preserved on the chancel roof in the Church of S. Vitale at Ravenna. It consists of four formal tree-designs converging from the corners to a crowning circle, the intermediate spaces being filled with continuous scrolls enclosing a large number of birds and animals.

C. *Apse Decoration.* There are two apses in Rome which have always attracted notice on account of the river-landscapes on their lower borders. Unhappily they were both altered about A. D. 1300 ; but there is little doubt that in one of these buildings, S. Giovanni in Laterano, the existing decoration has preserved the original cross above the hill with the rivers of Paradise ; in the other building, the Church of S. Maria Maggiore, the lateral scroll-work with its figures of birds and animals is almost certainly part of the original decoration. Thus a combination of the features exhibited by these two apses would show a river landscape, surmounted in the middle by a cross, and bordered by continuous scrolls enclosing animal figures as a surface decoration. Whence could so curious a composition have originated ?

Other similar apses exist in a fairly good state of preservation, but in these the river-landscape at the lower border is no longer to be seen. Thus in the vestibule of the Lateran Baptistery (SS. Seconda and Rufina) we find a purely formal perpendicular treatment of the middle portion ; in S. Clemente, a building of later date, the cross has been superseded by the crucifixion, although the design of birds and animals retains its full luxuriance to delight the worshippers' eyes. These examples suggest that the cross was not originally an integral part of river landscape and scroll designs.

42   Sorčuq, Chinese Turkestan ;   fresco in the Naga
     Cave ;   after A. Grünwedel.   See pp. 120, 133.

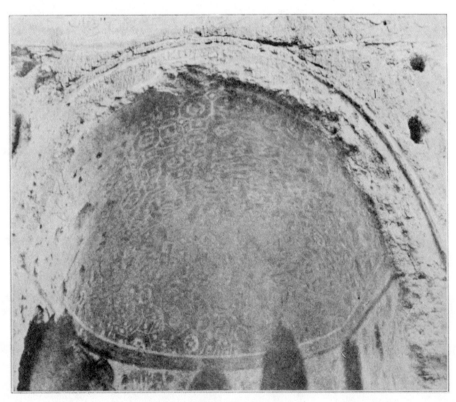

43   Oasis of El-Khargeh ; apse decoration of a funerary chapel ;
     after V. de Bock.   See p. 137.

In the Church of S. Apollinare in Classe another type of apse decoration has survived from the sixth century ; its existence as early as the years A. D. 401–3 is attested by Paulinus of Nola. It consists of a landscape into which symbolical figures of a lamb and a dove are introduced, and over which a cross is suspended. It is important to remember that such landscapes are placed in the apse, the point on which the eye of the spectator is focussed ; we have therefore to deal with art on a monumental scale. The most important remaining example is the apse of S. Apollinare in Classe, the lateness of which is always felt to be an anachronism. In type it really belongs to the fourth century ; thus the way in which the sun's disk, here transformed into the cross of Golgotha, floats large over the landscape, almost makes us forget to read the symbolism of the Transfiguration. Examples of such landscape also occur in other churches in all the various parts of the nave. Thus we find the Good Shepherd represented over the western door of the mausoleum of Galla Placidia, and as a recurrent motive on the nave-walls of S. Maria Maggiore ; a pastoral landscape recurs again and again in the scenes from the Old Testament. In the same position in the Church of S. Sergius at Gaza was a representation, praised by Chorikios, of waters enlivened by birds among flowering meadows, and S. Nilus even alludes to hunting and fishing scenes. Evidently these scenes form a distinct group, in which the two river landscapes of the above-mentioned apses should be included. The importance of this kind of landscape decoration in the earliest churches is strongly emphasized by the fact that the iconoclasts revived it, a circumstance which seems to indicate that it can hardly have been confined to the surviving examples in Italy, but must have had its original area of distribution in the East.

There are isolated examples of apses which make no attempt at representation ; instead they contain purely geometrical ornament, or, at most, rows of symbolical devices. One of these still exists in the oasis of El Khargeh (Fig. 43, opposite); here eight-pointed stars connect octagons each filled by four hearts, and these form a repeat-pattern. Similar designs are commonly used to fill the arches of doors.

In this survey of evidence for an Early Christian art of a non-representational character, we are immediately struck by its wide distribution in the fourth century ; whereas only a few straggling examples can be adduced for the later period, until its subsequent revival on a large scale by iconoclastic movements. It appears in fact to have béen completely ousted by representational art. All the examples quoted belong to the Mediterranean sphere of influence. What then was the attitude of the Christian East ? It might seem obvious to make responsible for the non-representational style the people among whom the Christian religion had its origin. We are naturally tempted to think of so-called ' Christian Art ' as directly inspired by the Founder. But do we in fact find the slightest evidence for associating Christ with an artistic movement of this nature ? Christ resembled Buddha, Zarathustra, and Mohammed in excluding art from the activities indispensable to the religious life. The attitude of Buddha and Zarathustra towards representational art is sufficiently explained by their Aryan origin ; Christ and Mohammed belonged to branches of the Semitic race which, unlike the Mesopotamian Semites of the Great Monarchies, never represented in art. The explanation must be sought in the fact that they were pastoral nomads at the time when their religions were founded.

If, then, the Founders ignored representational art as a means of furthering their aims, who was the first to make use of it ? Certainly neither the apostles nor their immediate successors. Moreover, the satisfaction of definite individual needs led at first to forms dictated less by art than by utility. I cannot but conclude that the character of Christian art, as of architecture, was determined in the first instance by the several nations among which Christianity struck root, and in the next by those great regions of East-Aryan and West-Aryan culture into which it subsequently expanded. Such is the path of inquiry I shall pursue, commencing with the middle regions.

II. *The Eastern ' Hinterlands ' of the Mediterranean*

The origin of a certain kind of non-representational symbolism can perhaps be attributed to the Jews. I refer to the embodiment of the divine in the form of a lamb. ' Lamb of God ' (John i. 29) would be a metaphorical expression natural enough to a people of shepherds like the Jews. Equally natural would be the representation of the apostles as lambs, after the fashion of the apse-mosaics already cited, and of many other examples. The same origin is perhaps even more definitely suggested by the introduction of whole scenes in the spandrels of the blind arcades on the sarcophagus of Junius Bassus or on the Ravenna sarcophagi.   Even a decree of the Council of 692 was unable to suppress this deeply-rooted symbol.   It was not indeed employed in Jewish synagogues ; but in them we do at least find an instance of plant symbolism in the palm.

Other examples from Jerusalem and the Syrian, coast are certainly not indigenous, but belong to the hybrid art of the Mediterranean, though showing in part an increase of oriental influence, as will appear below.

In the church architecture of East-Syria, the period of which certainly falls between the fourth and the beginning of the seventh centuries, representation of the human figure is entirely absent.   In this region, curiously enough, the earliest representational paintings known to exist are those of Quseir 'Amra, belonging to the Ummayad period.   In the main part of the building are hunting and other scenes which may be classed with landscapes, while the roof decoration recalls the Indian paintings of Ajanta.   The ornamentation of the Baths in this desert palace is rather Indo-hellenistic in style, with the exception of a diaper enclosing animal figures on one of the barrel-vaults.   In Christian East-Syria we shall search in vain for anything beyond symbols on doorposts, such as the cross, or stars enclosed in circles, and a few other very modest ornaments.

In Mesopotamia, again, paintings have not been discovered as yet in wide distribution.   This country is the home of the barrel-vaulted church with transverse nave, and of the single long nave with barrel-vault ; on its borders we also find the type with barrel-vaulted nave and aisles, the best examples of which have survived in Armenia and in the interior of Asia Minor. As in the case of the dome, we are confronted with the question whether these barrel-vaults and apses were, or were not, originally destitute of ornament.   In the *Tur 'Abdin* the apses of a number of churches have a cross in low relief, and the apse of the Basilica of Resafa still contains original stucco-decoration, with radiating bands connected at their bases by arches.   Might we not reasonably expect to find similar ornament elsewhere in stucco, mosaic, or painting ?

Quite distinctive, in this region, is the decoration of the architectural members adjoining the curved surfaces.   Our knowledge is at present limited to the triangle of towns in the

North: Edessa, Nisibis, and Amida. There we find that the Greek architectural members, designed for organic construction, have been adapted to a system in which decorative lining was all-important. The transition can hardly have originated in stone churches, such as those which have survived; it probably first occurred on buildings of unburned brick, and therefore in Iran or South Mesopotamia. Gandhara, like Armenia, shows no trace of it. I should, therefore, be inclined to rule out Eastern Iran as a possible source. There the simple interlacings and repeat-patterns of the kind proper to wall-lining are indigenous, and entirely unaffected by classical influence. But on the lower Tigris and Euphrates, such a transition from the constructional to the decorative may quite well have occurred. In the present state of our knowledge we can only infer back from the stone buildings which have survived; and these have in all probability been affected by Iranian as well as Mesopotamian influences. The monuments are mentioned in my work on Amida. The chronicle of Söört allows us to conclude that there was a connexion with Antioch.

In addition to the general spread of Hellenism under the Seleucids, there was a special circumstance affecting South Mesopotamia which cannot be left out of account. I refer to the transportation of the inhabitants of Antioch after it had been twice conquered by Shapur in A.D. 256 and A.D. 260. The captives were settled in certain towns in Babylonia, Susiana, and Persis. 'They were given allotments of land to cultivate and houses to 'dwell in. In consequence Christians became numerous in the 'Persian Empire, and monasteries and churches were erected. 'There were priests among them, who had been carried off as 'captives from Antioch; they dwelt in Gundišabur, and elected 'Ardak of Antioch bishop, since Demetrius, the patriarch, had 'fallen sick and died of grief.... The Christians spread throughout 'the empire, and their numbers multiplied in the East. In 'Rašahr, the seat of the Archbishop of Persis, two churches 'were built, one of which was named the Church of the Romans, 'the other the Church of the Syrians. The service in them was 'conducted in the Greek and the Syrian tongues.'[1]

In my opinion it was this current of Antiochene influence coming from South Persia which in the North brought about

[1] I have taken these passages of the Söört Chronicle from the translation of Sachau.

the obvious transition in stone buildings, from the Greek to the Perso-Mesopotamian style. This would appear to have been the result of a return migration from the South and not of any direct impulse from Antioch. This is borne out by the appearance of Assyro-Babylonian features in Greek forms of ornament, an instance of which is the breaking-up of the frieze. On the other hand the shapes of individual capitals and their decoration are Iranian.

Armenia was the only point at which the West- and East-Aryans of the South came into direct contact ; and there Christianity, adopted as the official religion about A. D. 300, preferred Mazdean to Hellenistic forms. The oldest surviving Armenian churches date back to the fifth century ; inscriptions prove their existence in the sixth century, and their wide distribution in the seventh. In the matter of exterior decoration a number of churches show a rich and homogeneous style ; examples occur in the case of the Cathedral of Artik (an apse-buttressed square), and that of Thalin (a trefoil-ended church with three aisles), at Zwarthnotz (a quatrefoil with ambulatory), and Irind, which has an eight-foil plan. The decoration consists of blind arcading with cushion capitals, the arches themselves being ornamented with interlacing of three-grooved bands, or with vine and pomegranate foliage. In addition there are arcaded fillets or slant surfaces with interlacing under the roof, and decorated bands following the curves of the window heads. Of the interior decoration nothing remains ; but documentary evidence goes to prove that Armenia, so far from being an original home of representational art, received it first from the Greeks, while it became one of the chief centres of hostility to pictures.

The question now arises whether the vaulting of Armenian domed buildings was devoid of all coloured decoration. I have already mentioned that in the domes we often find eight ribs radiating downwards from the Crown and terminating in disks. This would seem to imply the absence of figure art ; but does it justify us in ruling out every other kind of decoration in painting, mosaic, stucco, or other material ?

In Armenia we find ourselves surrounded by one of the main groups of vaulted buildings, the unit with a single central dome ; this in its early development is accompanied by apsidal buttresses ; soon afterwards, barrel-vaults are interposed between these buttresses and the central bay. Are we to suppose that all

these vaulted surfaces were entirely destitute of ornament?
In the oldest surviving buildings in Armenia, dating from the
fifth to the seventh centuries, we now find no contemporary
figure-paintings; for the original decoration we can at present
only adduce documentary evidence. Peculiar importance attaches
to a statement occurring in Moses of Kaghankatuk's history of
the Albanians, which dates from the seventh century. He
narrates that, while the Armenians and Byzantines were engaged
in disputes and rivalry, peace reigned among the Albanians
until news reached them of a movement hostile to pictures.
Thereupon Bishop David referred the question of paintings
and drawings to John Mairagomier and received the following
instruction: ' This sect (those in favour of ikons) arose after
' the time of the apostles, first appearing among the East-Romans;
' wherefore a great Synod was held in Caesarea, and the painting
' of pictures in the House of God was sanctioned. Hence the
' painters grew arrogant, and wished to place their art above
' all the other church arts.' They said: ' Our art is light, since
' it is the means of enlightening old and young alike; whereas
' but few can read the holy scriptures.' Hence arose that controversy which spread to Albania, and involved not only painters
and writers, but whole sects of iconoclasts and ikon-worshippers
in conflict.

In Armenia the defeat of the painters was a foregone conclusion, both on account of the ingrained opposition to representational art in that country and because the Armenians had
a script of their own in addition to the ecclesiastical language.
A further reason was the embittered conflict with Byzantium,
and the separation of the Armenian church, which repudiated
the decrees of the Council of Chalcedon. This Council (A. D. 451)
had far-reaching effects upon the history of art. The mono-
physites, and with them the Armenians, adopted a hostile attitude,
and soon regarded all who accepted the decrees as their bitterest
enemies. At the Council held at Vagharshapat in 491 the
decrees of Chalcedon were formally condemned; as Topdschian
justly observes: ' The Armenians sacrificed everything in order
' to protect the foundations of their national Church, which
' has to the present day proved an important religious and
' political factor in the preservation of their nationality.' It is
hardly possible that an entry into Armenia could have been
effected before the Byzantine period (i. e. before the tenth to

the eleventh centuries), by any iconography expressing the decrees of the Council of Chalcedon as described by Corippus, presumably in connexion with the confirmatory Council of A. D. 553 in the Church of S. Sophia. True, there was a period of eighty-nine years—between the Council of Karin in A. D. 630 and that of Manazkert in A. D. 719—during which six patriarchs (including Nerses III the constructor) followed the 'shameful doctrine of Chalcedon', until John the philosopher (A. D. 717–28) re-established monophysitism. But as he simultaneously opposed the Paulician sect, his period is one of considerable unsettlement in this matter. Did the remains of mosaics and representational paintings found in ruins, together with isolated mention by historians, convince us that decoration with cycles of representational paintings was habitual in these early Christian churches, then we should have to place Armenia in the same class as the Mediterranean area and the West. But it is precisely here, I believe, that one of the characteristic contrasts between Armenia and that more familiar culture of the West is most conspicuously displayed. Ter-Mkrttchian points out that in the twelfth and thirteenth centuries the Armenian patriarchs defended themselves against the reproaches of the Byzantine Emperor for refusing to accept sacred painting, while in the tenth patriarch Wahan (A. D. 968–70) was dismissed and condemned for introducing them and for banishing the glory of the cross from all the altars by substitution of 'ikons'. It is not likely, he argues, that Armenia's attitude towards sacred painting in the sixth and seventh centuries was any more favourable than in these later periods. ' They probably ' never had them in their church and had no particular reason ' for discussing the matter. The question was first brought to ' a head through the attacks of the Greeks ; and among the ' iconoclasts of the time of Moses (A. D. 574–604) arose a party ' which opposed the veneration of pictures as an unchristian ' innovation, and, perhaps influenced by existing sects, extended ' their hostility to all forms of religious expression. This hostility ' inevitably gathered strength and intensity in proportion as ' hatred of the Byzantine Greeks increased with the growth ' and spread of their cult of pictures. It may be laid down as ' a general rule that figure representation in church interiors is ' a sign of Aramaean or Greek influence.' In Armenia we can see clearly enough the positions taken up in the struggle by the parties which arose at the change from the nationalism of the

fourth, to the ecclesiasticism of the fifth century. But supplementary evidence of great value is furnished by a document actually written during the transitional period; this was the letter sent by Nilus of Sinai to the prefect Olympiodorus at the beginning of the fifth century. It commences as follows : ' Having under-
' taken to erect a large temple in honour of the holy martyrs,
' you ask me whether it be proper and fitting, in the first place,
' to introduce figures of them in the choir illustrating the toils
' and sufferings wherewith they testified to their Christian faith
' in the agony of death ; and secondly whether it be proper to
' cover the walls with all manner of hunting scenes both upon
' the right hand and upon the left, depicting snares spread out
' upon the land, and likewise hares, deer, and other creatures in
' flight, also figures of men pursuing them breathlessly with their
' dogs, desiring to slay them ; or again, nets let down into
' the sea and filled with all kinds of fish, or drawn up on the dry
' land by the hands of the fishermen. Further, whether it be
' right to introduce all manner of stucco ornament, a pleasure to
' behold in the Lord's house ; and yet again whether you should
' decorate the part used for the congregation (accessible to all the
' laity) with thousands of crosses, and representations of flying,
' walking, and creeping beasts and every kind of plant.'

In the continuation of this letter Nilus denounces this kind of ornamentation with such vigour that he is obviously dealing with a wider question than that raised by the prefect. In point of fact the kind of decoration referred to here is identical with that which reappears later both in Byzantium and farther East during the iconoclastic period, so that we are justified in speaking of it as a kind of reversion to the original East-Christian art. I shall now pursue its traces in the region which lies beyond the interior region east of the Mediterranean, bounded, roughly speaking, by the river Tigris.

III. *The East-Aryan Province.* In this section I shall be compelled to depend on presupposition, first derived from the evidence of Armenia, and secondly from monuments both in East and West, which have preserved in a durable material the perishable decoration of original Iranian buildings. Armenia was at first very poor in architectural ornament ; it borrowed from Iran the blind arcade and the manner of filling the spandrels with geometric forms of vine foliage, pomegranates, animals, and birds. Zwarthnotz (A. D. 650) and the Church of Gregory

of Honentz in Ani (A. D. 1215) represent the average type ;
Achthamar (A. D. 915–21) with its rows of animal figures and its
frieze depicting the chase shows the pure unmodified Iranian
style. I shall now give a systematic review of this group of
buildings according to their different styles of decoration.

A. *Structural Members*. In Mesopotamia we found merely
a modified form of classicism in the structural members ; the
evidence relating to Iran is altogether different in character.

(*a*) *The Support*. The evolution of this member is most
important both in a geographical and a chronological sense ;
it serves as a criterion by which to test the progressive fusion
in Early Christian architecture of the ' organic ' Greek style
and the decorative style of Iran. Assuming that classical antiquity
was acquainted only with the support and the architrave, and
Iran only with the wall and the arch, we find the first attempt at
fusion in the combination of the column or the pier with the arch.
Whether this first occurred in Christian times or earlier is irrele-
vant. The combination was certainly effected at an early date
in isolated examples. In the indigenous art of East Syria it was
confined to pier and arch. In the palace of Diocletian (*c*. A. D. 300),
which bears clear traces of Syrian influence, and in Syria itself
after the fourth and fifth centuries, the process was freely extended
to the column and arch.

The migration of the vault and the arch from East to West
was accompanied by quite new forms of decoration. We have
already observed these in their Mazdean garb and have now to
inquire how Christian architects gradually adapted themselves
to the new style. This can best be done by examining the
motives of engaged shaft and column.

The national art of Iran, if we exclude imperial palaces,
was unacquainted with the column, which in classical architecture
was used in definite proportions of diameter and height as a
detached perpendicular support for a pressure horizontally
distributed. The vaulted architecture of Iran was only acquainted
with the engaged shaft, a projection running up the wall and
dividing it perpendicularly into compartments. The engaged
shaft quickly became acclimatized in Christian Armenia and in the
last quarter of the first millennium it coalesced with the pilaster to
produce the clustered column (Figs. 21 and 23, facing pp. 94 and
95), which is so familiar and typical a feature of Western, and more
especially of Gothic architecture at the beginning of the second

millennium. Judging by its distribution in Armenia, India, and the Islamic countries, the engaged shaft in Iran must have had two forms of termination, the ' knob ' and the cushion capital, both of them probably derived from Aryan wooden architecture. That explains how it is that we find the cushion capital, which entered Lombardy probably under Armenian influence (Figs. 2 and 24, facing pp. 62 and 95), appearing simultaneously as an indigenous feature in the North. The columns of the Norwegian wooden Church of Urnäs, if pre-Romanesque, illustrate its wooden origin. The ' knob ' termination was adopted by preference in Islam as soon as it began to develop an individual, i. e. Iranian, style, distinct from that of the Mediterranean.

The decoration of the ' knob ' and cushion capitals is never derived from plant life ; or, if so, it is purely a surface pattern, and never suggests the freedom of organic growth. On the contrary the shaped sides of the ' cushion ', which occurs both in Armenia and the West, suggest something hanging down. And in point of fact they probably have some connexion with textile hangings.

More important than Islam or the North for our present purpose is the district surrounding the islands of Marmara at the gates of Constantinople. The ancient marble quarries of Cyzicus acquired a new value when Constantine designedly founded his new city in their vicinity and collected his workmen from every corner of the Empire. The presence of Armenians and Iranians among them is proved by the line of development followed by the capital.

At first its old composite form is retained, and only the acanthus is modified in the direction, apparently, of Anatolian style. As we know from the Sarcophagi—of which the ' Christ ' relief in Berlin is a good example—a favourite practice in the ' Cilician corner ' was the production of deep shadow effects by drilling ; the same device appears in the Theodosian capitals, which were sold and exported in all directions from Constantinople. This modification of the leaf was followed by another affecting both the shape and decoration of the capital, which, if it came from the Mediterranean, would be quite unintelligible. This new type, which is intermediate between the cushion and the knob, I have called the impost capital ; in it the square sides are gradually rounded off for purely technical reasons. Even if there were any doubt as to the origin of its form, the decoration

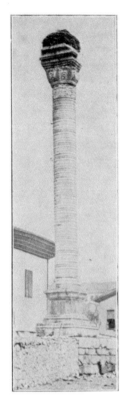

44 Angora, Asia Minor ;
so-called column of Augus-
tus. See p. 147.

45–47 Bisutun and Ispahan ;
capitals. See pp. 114, 147.

48 Edessa ; impost capital.
See p. 147.

49 Baghdad ; impost capital.
See p. 147.

50   Meiafarqin, Church of the Virgin ; interior from West door ;
photo., G. L. Bell.   See p. 147.

51   Mshatta, capital from the trefoil-ended hall,
Trikonchos ; left half.   See p. 147.

52   Dara ;   basket capital.
See p. 147.

of this capital stamps it beyond question as distinctively Iranian. Each side is as far as possible treated as an independent panel, and filled with geometric interlaced or scrollwork patterns. I have collected a few examples from Angora, Bisutun, Ispahan, Edessa, and Baghdad (Figs. 44-9, facing p. 146), and assume that the reader is familiar with those from Constantinople. The space between the square abacus and the springing of the arch is frequently filled by an impost block, which like the capital itself is covered with sacred monograms or unequivocal symbols of the glory of God. The 'knob' is transformed at times into the representation of a basket after the Greek manner, a change suggested both by its rounded form and interlaced ornament. Again I may quote a few examples from the East (Figs. 50-2, opposite), viz. the Church of S. Mary at Meiafarqin, Mshatta, and Dara. This 'basket' is sometimes wreathed with a design of vine-leaves and bordered with the Hvarenah animals of ancient Iran, rams, or goats, birds, and lions. In Armenia capitals with rams' heads called *chojak* were known in the fourth century, reminding us of the Achaemenian bull capitals; in the Cathedral of Zwarthnotz we still find the basket form of capital with Ionic volutes. The usual type was the knob surmounted by interlacings and by circles bearing symbolic emblems.

(*b*) *Door and Gate.* The East-Aryan treatment of the door differs from the West-Aryan. Its distinguishing features are the trilateral or round termination above and the porch, both of which are derived from timber buildings. The wooden churches of the Ukraine contain examples in the original material; older still are the stone imitations in Kashmir of the second half of the first millennium, while the churches of Armenia illustrate its full development in rubble concrete. There, too, we can clearly trace how the fusion of the round door and the porch produced the recessed door, which later became acclimatized in the West, and developed on so magnificent a scale. This fusion was effected by a series of recessed colonnettes; the idea, achieved only by degrees, was to make those who entered feel that they were being drawn through a kind of funnel into the interior of the building. In Armenia, where this development is well illustrated, it is carried to further lengths than in the West, where possibly it had a more or less independent origin in wooden architecture. The method adopted was to amplify the arch by surmounting the original semicircle with others rising progressively higher in the centre, until finally the largest assumed the shape of a horseshoe (Fig. 53, facing p. 152). In the West the addition of human figures, which were naturally absent in Armenia, led to that richness of effect which eclipsed even the 'High Gate' of Seljuk mosques. Nevertheless comparison between the two is not unprofitable. In both cases the more showy side of church architecture was concentrated exclusively upon this member with its accessories; the latter took the form of lateral porches in the one case and walls with fountains in the other, to which were added towers serving respectively for bells or for the muezzin. Observations of this kind may ultimately stimulate comparative research in art, which can hardly fail to produce better results than the existing historical and aesthetic classical schools with the local limitations of their narrow horizon.

B. *Decoration of flat surfaces*. This subject has already been discussed in part. Here I shall deal only with a particular type. It has been shown that a form of symbolical landscape, strikingly similar to that found in the earliest Christian apses, was also a feature of Mazdean art. But there is a school of thought which regards this same landscape-decoration as a survival of Greek naturalism, and attributes the appearance of 'stiffness' to the introduction of a gold background. In opposition to this view I would tentatively put forward the hypothesis that this estrangement from nature has absolutely no connexion with the use of the gold background to produce an effect of unlimited space; nor can it be regarded as a last degenerate stage of classical art; rather it is connected with the spread of influences from Altai-Iran in the late-Roman period. This landscape is not based upon observation of nature, but must be regarded as a congeries of Mazdean symbols forming a composite whole. Clouds, water, and earth, together with certain symbolical animals and plants, constitute the main subject-matter, the terrestrial section being supplemented by the sun, moon, and stars. It is admittedly impossible at present to point to a single extant Mazdean work of this kind; but the art student cannot afford to ignore this hypothesis as lightly as the dilettante, despite the rule of reckoning only with concrete evidence and disregarding the notorious gaps in our record of existing monuments.

In the course of this inquiry I have been led to assume the

existence of a counterpart to ' Christian classical art ' in ' Christian Mazdean art ' ; by this I mean the form of Church art existing in the fourth century, which even in the Hellenistic area borrowed not only the vault but also its form of decoration from Mazdaism. The most important examples are dome and apse mosaics at Rome, so far as they can be assigned with certainty to the fourth century. These are supplemented by contemporaneous and later examples in Milan, Naples, and Ravenna, while there are a few isolated traces in the East. I shall take the various types and forms of decoration in their order, commencing with the cross, on account of the way in which it was frequently made to dominate the whole landscape (see the letter of Paulinus of Stola).

(*a*) *Crosses*. India originally had no representations of Buddha; so too in Iran the figure of Christ was not represented. Mazdaism made use of religious symbols ; similarly the Aryans in India regarded as emblems of divinity the wheel, the tree, and later the stûpa, but not originally the human form. In the East-Aryan region the Christians universally adopted the cross as their favourite symbol of Christ ; in fact we might regard it as one of the three means of depicting the religious Founder, the Iranian ; the other two were the Greek unbearded type of Christ, and the Semitic bearded type. We cannot here discuss the origin of the cross itself ; the vision of Constantine gives food for reflection. There is no need to quote evidence for its existence in the most varied forms, more especially in that of the swastika, in pre-Christian times. Characteristic of the Iranian cross are its various kinds of terminal additions, e. g. single disks or pairs of loops. There is no ground for asserting that in the oldest Roman mosaics its place was taken by actual representations of our Lord.

(*b*) *Landscapes*. I regard the apse of S. Aquilino in Milan, which has survived from the fourth century, as an example of a Christian landscape of the Mazdean type. It was actually possible to discover vestiges of the sun-god depicted as riding in his chariot above the figures of the shepherds below. He may also have been accompanied by the moon and stars. Beneath are those conventional rocks from which on either side water is seen flowing towards the foreground. To the left are sheep, to the right cattle with their herdsmen. Here we have a definite Hvarenah landscape partly modified by Hellenism. We can still observe on late-Armenian tombstones the manner in which the sun and moon were depicted in Iran, as disks made to resemble faces above running animals. The mosaic of S. Aquilino did not originally stand alone. In the porch of Constantine's Baptistery at the Lateran, opposite the apse decorated with scrollwork (p. 136), was a second apse with a landscape, in which the Avesta symbol of the sun had been supplanted by the cross. The 'inappropriate decoration' of this mosaic was inexplicable to the classical Christian school. Unfortunately it is now completely lost ; but records and partial imitations establish beyond doubt that the subjects depicted were herdsmen with their herds, others with birds, aviaries, and cleverly executed emblems, together with trees and flowers.[1]

(c) *Scenes from the Chase.* Running round the exterior of the cruciform church of Achthamar, built on an island of Lake Van between the years A.D. 915 and 921, there is a median frieze in low broken relief (Figs. 39 and 57, facing pp. 122 and 159) depicting archers and animals of various kinds in a remarkable forest consisting of scrolled vines and pomegranates. On the same frieze also occur figures, not of vintagers at work as on Roman sarcophagi, but represented frontally in a squatting attitude after the Persian manner, embracing the vines and grasping at the clusters or raising their cups. Thus we have here a combined representation of the joys of the chase and the pleasures of wine. All this is as little connected with the Christian church as the hunting and fishing scenes depicted on the interiors of the fourth-century churches mentioned by Nilus, or the remarkable river-landscapes which make their appearance in the Roman mosaics.

(d) *Vine Scrolls.* The origin of the vine scroll and the remarkable richness of its employment in Christian art is customarily accepted without question as adequately explained by its symbolical and allegorical character. But the student of art is gradually beginning to take a wider view. He perceives that, originating in India and Iran, it spread to other countries as a purely decorative design, being transformed beyond recognition in Rome by fusion with the acanthus, converted into the palmette in Islam, and into the lotus in Buddhist countries. The Hvarenah façade of Mshatta is a comparatively late specimen of this type

[1] Compare the well-known miniatures of the Vatican Virgil and those of the Christian Topography of Cosmas Indicopleustes (*Repertorium für Kunstwissenschaft*, xxxix [1916], p. 243 f.).

of decoration, but unless its early existence is assumed, the scroll decoration of the Ara Pacis at Rome and certain variant forms of the so-called Arabesque are not easily to be explained.

The principal example of Early Christian treatment of vine scrolls in the Mazdean style is the well-known episcopal chair of Maximianus at Ravenna. The upper and lower borders of the front are decorated with handsome vine scrolls interspersed with various animals, including stags, peacocks, and humped oxen. This design extends over the uprights in a continuous pattern. Only the panels are adorned with figure subjects; we shall have occasion to refer to these below. The question now confronting us is whether this form of decorative scrollwork is really Christian in origin, as has hitherto been generally assumed, or whether it should not be ascribed to Mazdean influences accompanying the import of ivory from India by way of Persia. Conclusive evidence is not at present available, but the constant recurrence of this motive on vault mosaics suggests its ultimate derivation from a common source. The vine scrolls in barrel-vaults and apses are constantly associated with the life-giving water, although the latter is supplanted by the cross with gradually increasing frequency. A striking example of its modification for Christian purposes is the symbolic picture of Psalm xli, viz. a pair of stags drinking from a single spring, which occurs in the Baptistery at Naples, in the mausoleum of Galla Placidia, and in several other places. This spring is depicted issuing from a rock in the manner already described in the landscape of S. Aquilino.

The best example of the symbolic treatment of vine scrolls and palms in mosaic is the roof of the Matrona chapel of S. Prisco at Capua. Not very different, we may suppose, was the original appearance in colour of the Mshatta façade, making due allowance for the difference between the mediocre craftsmanship of a stagnant art and the brilliant powers of execution possessed by a culture to which that building is the sole surviving testimony.

(e) *Dawn clouds.* One of the most remarkable intrusive elements in Christian mosaics consists in the highly conventional clouds which appear as a number of wavy lines in colour superimposed on a blue ground. They are purely symbolic in character, and can in most cases hardly be recognized as pictorial features. The best example is in the two lateral arches of the Matrona chapel of S. Prisco, where the Glory of God arises in the centre on the prepared throne, flanked on either side by the symbols of the Evangelists placed respectively above and below these horizontally stratified clouds. Contiguous bands of red and yellow indicate the dawn; at least that was probably the suggestion which they were intended to convey. The selection of the colours is in itself significant.

C. *Woven and embroidered Stuffs*. Among the most surprising discoveries resulting from careful excavation are the silk and woollen stuffs, to the preservation of which the sand of Egypt has conduced even better than the care lavished upon them in museums. They agree in every respect with those Western examples with which we have long been familiar through examples in mediaeval reliquary-shrines. The monuments recently discovered (in Central Asia) in Chinese Turkestan, especially in Khotan and as far as Tunhuang, which have been similarly preserved by absolutely dry conditions, confirm us in the belief that we have to deal here with an industry and form of decoration not peculiar to Egypt,[1] but having a perfectly homogeneous distribution round about the central area of Iran. These textiles rarely deal with Christian subjects, but for the most part distinctively retain that spirit which I have already tried to describe in the section on Mazdean costume. The large majority of the silk stuffs depict with mirror-like fidelity Persian horsemen engaged in the chase, or, as a substitute, a formal tree of palmettes; these are invariably disposed in a system of interlacing circles. The woollen textiles are geometrically divided by interlaced bands into panels filled with figures of animals and birds in the varying combinations usual to Hvarenah symbols. It has often been conjectured that these textiles may have suggested the predominant style of architectural decoration as well in Lombardy as in Scandinavia. But in point of fact—quite apart from what

---

[1] At this point brief reference may be made to Otto v. Falke's *Kunstgeschichte der Seidenweberei*, a work of great value through the amount of comparative material which it brings together, and its wealth of illustration. I have stated my position with regard to it in *Altai-Iran* (see Index under *Falke*). The author had not a sufficiently wide range to be a sound judge in questions of development, and he makes untenable assertions as to origins, which continue to distort the facts for students (cf. *Amtliche Berichte der preussischen Kunstsammlungen*, xl [1919], pp. 143 ff.). A work of my Institute (Dimand, *Die Verzierung der koptischen Wollwirkereien, Strömungen des Weltverkehres im Kreise der Mittelmeerkunst*) might help to restore some sort of order amid the prevalent confusion, but present conditions make an early publication impossible.

53   Armenia, Ketcharus monastery ; South door of Church of S. Gregory
See p. 148.

54   Dashlūt, Egypt ; door of Court of Mosque ; the mounted saint,
half destroyed.   See p. 175.

55 Vienna, in private possession ; woollen fabric from Egypt.   See p. 153.

56 Urnäs, wooden church ; door with interlaced beasts ; after A. Haupt.
See pp. 153, 215.

was indigenous in the North—this obvious affinity is adequately explained by the connexion of Iran with the extreme North as well as with Egypt and upper Italy ; and in this matter the agency of workers in mosaic and stucco was no less effective than the trade in the textiles themselves. I have given an illustration of a woollen fabric from Egypt (Fig. 55, opposite), showing the Iranian vase with scrolls in the centre, flanked by a double row of formal trees, animal figures, and medallions.

IV. *The European North.* The path pursued here was essentially similar to that of the East Aryans. True, it is hardly possible for us now to imagine this area as having ever been devoid of representational art; and yet at the end of the first millennium it was still devoted to a purely decorative style.

Let us consider the Scandinavian wooden churches such as Urnäs. The gable decoration reveals an almost hypersensitive delight in expressive line : the Greeks filled this triangular space with human figures. Or again, consider the oldest surviving woodwork on the exterior of the same church (Fig. 56, opposite), which is among the most delicate memorials bequeathed to us by the soul of the North. In such a spiritual revelation the human figure would have a crude effect. Salin has solved the riddle of certain ancient Germanic bronze ornaments which betray a similar delight in the play of line, the inspiration coming here too from animal forms. We do indeed find on the portals of wooden churches isolated examples of scenes from the myth of Siegfried depicted in combination with scroll patterns. But instances of this kind are rare and late ; moreover, it is necessary to distinguish between realistic and imaginative figures. Imagination will be found to be the basis of every work of art both in Iran and the North, as well as in all artistic movements connected with them and uncontaminated by Southern influence. The human figure may be sporadically introduced in conjunction with animal and plant motives. But, like these, it is never treated objectively with continual reference to a natural form ; it is simply an intelligible sign written in a readable hand.

The point to remember is that the North, like the East, employed in the decoration of its buildings a system which excluded the human figure. The style of the finds made in the Oseberg ship, finds of unprecedented richness, differs from that of the prehistoric bronze ornaments and that introduced by the Goths and Lombards into Italy ; these Oseberg objects are decorated not with interlaced patterns purely geometric in character like the Armenian, but with that luxuriant riot of animal forms, with which the important publications of Sophus Müller and Salin have made us acquainted. The East was as unable to follow the North on this path as in later mediaeval times it was unable to share the vigorous contribution made by the Northern spirit to the decoration of Gothic cathedrals. In these cathedrals the dominant quality is the feeling for organic structure possibly carried over from earlier architecture in wood ; it makes itself felt in the smallest details ; the ever urging impulse lends every point and edge the luxuriance of plant growth, just as, long before, the same ferment in the Northern nature had covered every inch of space with expressive animal forms. In Armenia, which took half a step in the direction of ' Gothic ', we find no trace of this more recent movement in decoration.

I shall refrain here from pointing out evolutionary affinities in the decoration (as I attempted to do in the architecture) of the ' Romanesque ' churches in the West, which I call oriental. Such an attempt would carry me beyond the scope of this volume.

VII

The Triumph of Representational Art.
Hellenism, Semitism, Mazdaism

FORMATIVE art employs visible signs as intermediaries
between the direct effect of mass, space, light, and colour,
and particular meaning and purpose. Religious art, more
especially, has a predilection for the most familiar of all symbols,
the human figure, which seems, like the actor, to bridge the gap
between life and art. At the same time we have observed that
religious areas of considerable extent renounce this mediation;
they rely solely upon structural form, and adorn their buildings
with decorative designs which are often of a symbolical character.
In Christian art the practice of representation appears to have
been introduced as a result of contact with Hellenism and
Buddhism. To depict Christ as a human figure was not such an
obvious idea to Jews, Armenians, Arabs, or Iranians, as it was
either to men inheriting the traditions of the great Semitic
empires, or to Greeks and Romans. As late as the tenth century
the Armenian historian Thomas Artsruni, in referring to a picture
representing Christ in a manner quite familiar to us, thought it
necessary expressly to state that it was the Saviour thus depicted
in human form. It is significant that we in the North require
to have our attention deliberately drawn to the fact, before we
can see anything surprising in the use of the human figure, in
which our religious art of the present day finds almost its sole
expression.

We distinguish between realistic and conventional representations. Down to the thirteenth century Christian, as opposed to
ancient Semitic and Graeco-Roman art, practised only conventional representation. In its infancy the representational art of
the Christians in West-Aryan regions was admittedly much
influenced by good Hellenistic models. Hence originated a
classical-Christian style, of which the Anatolian type of Christ
is an example; in this type the head might be the work of a

Praxiteles.   The figure of the Teacher on the Berlin sarcophagus
reproduces the antique type of the orator; the familiar marble
statue of Sophocles reminds us what the original was like.   In
the flourishing city-life of Northern Mesopotamia, in Edessa
and Nisibis, more remote from the heart and pulse of Hellenism,
we find a very different form of expression.   There the national
type of Christ early assumed Aramaean features ; the straight
hair was parted in the middle, and the beard was long.   The
influence of the powerful Semitic states led to this kind of realism,
which was accompanied by an historical conception of art.   The
reduction of naturalism in Christian-Semitic representations was
principally the work of the third great source of artistic influence,
the Mazdean.

It has been asserted that a diminishing fidelity to nature and
its wholesale reduction to geometrical forms, a process already
observable in late-Roman art, is neither more nor less than a
confession of artistic bankruptcy.   This is a mistake.   Roman
powers of observation were slow to weaken ; but Eastern Iran
had introduced a new taste, which completely reversed the ancient
trend of art.   The tendency to ' geometrize ', in the East-Aryan
manner, might almost be described as convalescence in art.
Art began to develop afresh from within, and to use new imaginative forms of expression ; these were applied exclusively to the
surfaces of buildings and designed to impress the spectator from
a distance, differing in this from figure sculpture, which is
calculated for a closer view.   For this reason alone, if for no other,
it is necessary for any one approaching the subject of Christian
art to begin with the Churches and not with the Catacombs and
the Sarcophagi.

Eastern Iran had always secured its effects chiefly by the
combination of mass, space, light, and colour, at the same time
supplementing these with a non-representational form of art.
The Jews among whom Christianity arose themselves inclined
to this form of art less on account of their Semitic origin than
because they were pastoral nomads at the time when their own
religion was founded, and they retained the mode of expression
inspired by a desert life.   The Semites of the empires holding
the great river-valleys became uncompromising exponents of
representational art ; in fact it was probably among them that the
tendency towards portraiture originated.   This was a natural consequence of their compact organization and their approximation of

the ideas of God and king ; they depict not only their rulers but even God with individual features ; while in scenes depicting life, they show a tendency towards naked realism. The origin of historical scenes must also in all probability be ascribed to them. They played an important part in the growth of Hellenistic, Buddhist, and Christian art by bringing about the transition from symbolism to representation, whether of the king's own life or of biblical events. It is, therefore, hard to understand how any one can assert of Hellenistic culture that it was oriental only in its political and monarchic basis while artistically it remained Greek. Not only is it misleading to make ' representation ' stand for art as a whole, but it is a mistake to regard as inherently Greek an art based on monarchical conceptions and only temporarily clothed in a Hellenistic garb. Christianity re-introduced the ancient oriental flat treatment with its ' primitive ' handling of space, mass, light, and colour ; and in particular it revived the continuous arrangement of subjects in rows, the object of which was to represent the hero (whether ruler or religious Founder) with overpowering effect as the perpetual centre in a long and varied sequence of illustrations.

In this respect art must have been decisively affected by that focus of ecclesiastical influence which must be placed some-where midway between the East Mediterranean littoral and India, because Buddhism passes from symbolism to historical representation in the same way as Christianity. This transition was consummated in the period between the purely Indian art of the stûpas of Barahat and Sanchi and that of the Gandhâra sculptures, the style of which stamps their origin as Hellenistic beyond question. But they are so only in outward appearance ; their underlying spirit remains no less Semitic than that of the Christian art of the Mediterranean in its transitional period as seen during the fifth century. The experiences of the last few years incline me to assume that it was masters from northern Mesopotamia who introduced the practice of representing a series of events in the life of a hero alike into late classical, Buddhist, and Christian art. Whether we consider the spiral reliefs of triumphal columns at Rome and Constantinople, illuminated rolls of papyrus or parchment, or the sculptures of the Indo-Afghan frontier ; whether the subject be emperor, Christ, or Buddha, we invariably find the same blending of Semitic ideas with a Greek or Indian style. I shall first examine the features which distinguish symbolic from realistic representations, in so far as their traces are still discernible in the East ; I shall then attempt to locate the point at which the transition was effected, so far as the present state of our knowledge permits.

I. *Symbolic representation of the West-Aryans*

Wherever the Aryans came into contact with the art of the South and adopted the representational style without losing their spiritual predominance, we find the human figure treated less as the embodiment than as the symbol of divinity.   The greatest reserve in this matter was practised by the Indo-Aryans, who originally avoided representing God or the Founder in human form, but employed suggestive symbols such as the wheel, the Bodhi-tree, or the stûpa. Such symbols are indeed ubiquitous ; the peculiarity of Indian art consists not so much in the symbols themselves as in the attitudes of the groups of human figures surrounding them, which indirectly suggest the divine presence. Max Klinger has recently adopted a similar method, though in a somewhat different sense, in his sketches illustrating the Sermon on the Mount ; here the meaning is not directly expressed by the figure of Christ in the act of preaching, but suggested by the contrast between what went before and what followed. The Greek generally agrees with the Semite in getting into direct contact with his subject, only differing in his conception of God ; the Semite views Him as the embodiment of power, the Greek as the perfection of manhood. A change indeed occurred in Hellenistic times. Nevertheless, in those Greek regions which were not actually imperial residences, such as Alexandria and, later, Asia Minor, the ancient beauty of the human figure in some degree survived and was transmitted to Christian art. The persistence of this Hellenistic current of symbolic representation may be seen in the Joshua Roll, the Psalter 139 in Paris, the reliefs of the Sidamara Sarcophagus at Berlin, depicting Christ as an orator, the *Lipsanothek* in Brescia, and the statuettes of the Good Shepherd. An example of the Hellenistic treatment of a Mazdean idea is, in my opinion, also to be seen in the ivory carvings of Yima, the good shepherd [1] (*supra*, p. 122) ; and in this connexion we should also remember the Mithraic reliefs.

[1] For further information on this school of art the reader is referred to the appendix of a short work by O. Kern entitled *Orpheus, und verwandte iranische Bilder*.

57   Island of Achthamar, Lake Van, cruciform church ; West side.
See pp. 150, 159.

This Hellenistic character is dominant in Early Christian sepulchral art at Rome, permeated though it is with the ideas of intercession and redemption. Both in the Catacombs and on the Sarcophagi human figures alone convey the symbolic meaning, and, on the latter, they are crowded together in a most inartistic manner. Despite the obviously Greek treatment of forms and drapery, the influence of another school of art is apparent, a school which knows nothing of individual values, and seems in a fair way to treat human figures as no more than light pattern diffused on a black ground. Representation is in fact retained only by the imperative demand for a significance in which the mere object and the endless mechanical repetition of symbols count for more than content.

That this art was not unconnected with the East in its origin and growth[1] is proved by a monument hitherto ignored by Christian archaeologists, but of exceptional importance, in spite of its late date. I refer to the exterior decoration of the Armenian cruciform church of Achthamar on Lake Van, to which allusion has already been made. This building, erected between the years A. D. 904 and A. D. 938 by King Gagik of Waspurakan, has the lower part of its exterior entirely covered with reliefs, which are probably not to be connected with the Iranian animal frieze discussed above. On the West side (Fig. 57, opposite) the king himself is represented standing before Christ and holding a model of the church. On the East side (Fig. 39, facing p. 122) are the evangelists (?) and saints. But the reliefs which concern us here are those on the North and South sides. They too breathe the same spirit as the animal friezes ; interspersed between the biblical scenes are whole rows of Hvarenah animals one above the other, but in the present place I shall discuss the figure scenes alone. They are inspired by the same group of ideas as the paintings in the Roman catacombs, the ideas conveyed in the Easter prayers, or the prayers for the dead, and the instances of redemption enumerated therein, more especially those from the Old Testament. At the West end of the South side (Fig. 33, facing p. 114) the story of Jonah is depicted at considerable length, but not in the classical Christian style. In the scene of Jonah addressing the Ninevites, the king is seen full face, seated with crossed legs ; but the arrangement of

[1] Jewish prayers for the dead and the thoughts proper to the Easter festival are often held to have influenced this art. Alexandria with its large Jewish population is assumed as the point of departure

the figures is still the old familiar one of the Catacombs and
Sarcophagi. The same applies to the scene of David and Goliath,
in which Saul stands on one side in caftan and turban. Scenes
from the story of Samson lead round the Church to two pictures
of Adam and Eve and the Fall. The Western corner of the North
wall opposite the Jonah pictures completes the circuit with
figures of the three children in the fiery furnace and Daniel in
the lions' den. Circular panels containing figures of prophets,
saints, some of them contemporary, and of Christ and the Virgin
enthroned side by side, are inserted between these biblical scenes.
The richness of these sculptures is quite un-Armenian in character.
Achthamar is evidently an example of the blending in a frontier
region of Mazdean Hvarenah ornament with that style of
sepulchral art which reached Rome from the Syro-Egyptian
region in the first centuries of our era. When we remember that
the national form of Armenian church was emphatically of the
memorial type, and stood in the midst of a large courtyard, we
can understand why the exterior of the cruciform church of
Achthamar gives expression to the hope of redemption. Here
we may assume a new artistic province, for which few proofs
are elsewhere available. My theory is that it was the custom to
decorate the exterior surfaces of churches built of unburned
brick with flat reliefs in stucco, as well as with painting. Examples
of both these styles exist in the geographical area covered by the
Orthodox Church. They are not actually built of unburned
brick faced with stucco, but, like Achthamar, imitations in stone.
I refer to the churches of Vladimir and Yuriyeff Polskiy in Central
Russia. Their outer walls, dating in the latter case from the
years A. D. 1230 to A. D. 1234, are covered with a profusion of
flat reliefs, disposed in zones under blind arcades, and illustrating,
though in a much less rigorous sequence, the same group of
ideas expressed at Achthamar. The Church of S. Sophia in
Trebizond affords another example. Here on the south side is
a band of reliefs with scenes from Genesis. Examples of the second
or painted type of decoration may still be seen in the Rumanian
monastic churches of the Bukovina, dating from the sixteenth
and seventeenth centuries (Fig. 58, opposite). In these buildings
we invariably find the Last Judgement on the West wall ; while
the North and South walls are decorated with a large series of
pictures illustrating the Tree of Jesse, the Akathistic Hymn, the
Ladder of John Klimakos, scenes from Genesis, and other

58 Voronetz, Bukovina, monastery church; South-West view. See p. 160.

subjects. On the trefoiled East end we find figures of saints in superimposed zones, in the uppermost a band of angelic choirs; all these figures are grouped about the Trinity.

We have here apparently the monastic version of an old tradition. This type of art has no connexion with the West, but it occurs in the monasteries of the South, for example at Mount Athos, in the porches and refectories. It brings before the eyes of the monk that which should form the subject of the day's reflection. The only affinity between these and Early Christian pictures lies in the manner of their application; we may recall their absence in the account of Neon's refectory at Ravenna. Unhappily these things have never been brought into their true relations. My only reason for introducing these examples here is to illustrate their connexion with the monumental art of churches and monasteries and that fundamental love of symbolism which marks the Early Christian period. Nevertheless they are characterized not so much by the ideas of intercession and redemption as by a didactic spirit, for the origin of which I am inclined to look in another direction.

II. *Semitic Realism*

The idea of God among the Semites living under the empires in the great river valleys appears to have been directly inspired by the ruler's lust after power. The divine figure is furnished with all the attributes of the despot; he receives the marks of homage for which the earthly monarch longed. In Christian times the true carriers of Semitic culture were the Aramaeans of Mesopotamia, who played a part similar to that of the Arabs and Nabataeans in Islam. These Semites were indeed subjected successively to Roman and Persian rule, but their old love of the royal title, conferred in ancient times upon every little princeling, now found its expression in the field of religion. It was no doubt in this cultural area that the great type of Christ Pantokrator developed from the Hellenistic figure of the judge. This manner of representing the Almighty seemed so natural to Semitic Hellenism that theologians found no difficulty in applying it to the person of the Founder. This figure gained general acceptance, since it avoided all controversy as to his human or divine nature. Compare with it the type of Buddha seated cross-legged and sunk in inward meditation.

In India Buddha is never depicted with the ruler's attributes ;
he is never enthroned, nor does he wear the severe aspect of the
judge holding the Law in his hand. How different the type of
Christ.

The type prevalent even among ourselves to-day, that with
beard and long smooth hair, is a Semitic creation. The Founder
bears the physical characters of his race, like the first portrait
heads of Peter and Paul, which in the same way have never
changed. The two Hellenistic unbearded types of Christ, the
long-haired of Asia Minor and the short-haired of Alexandria,
have been completely superseded in the West. The Aryans, in
fact, abandoned the Greek figure of the Founder in favour of the
Semitic type of God personified as the Ruler. The true originators of this change were the Aramaeans, and they were closely
followed by the Byzantine Court. As far as origin is concerned,
this remarkable sequence of development is proved by the fact
that the Pantokrator, who embodies the popular idea of the Judge
of the World, assumes this Syrian type ; as far as distribution
is concerned, by the fact that Christ is early surrounded with
the emblems of royalty.

The Aramaeans were not only settled in northern Syria ;
they migrated to Mesopotamia also ; and it was precisely in
ancient Assyria, bordering on Armenia, that the moral and
intellectual influence of this people was at its strongest. Their
significance for Christianity is due partly to this central position
between the Mediterranean and Persia, but even more to the fact
that, when the Persians overran the Near East, Aramaic became
the official and commercial language of the western half of their
empire. Thus cultural unity was established throughout the
southern territories of Persia, extending from the Indian frontier
over the Sassanian middle region to hellenized Asia Minor ;
we understand why Edessa and Nisibis reached the paramount
position which made their territory the very heart of Christianity
in the East, why it actually became the starting-point of western
monastic activity, through Cassiodorus' foundation of his monasteries in Southern Italy.

Christian Semitic art derives its spirit, indeed, from Semitic
tradition, but its outward form in great part from Hellenism.
Its root-idea is to instruct, and its use of the human figure is
classical only in so far as the ancient oriental world allies
itself with the Hellenistic East. This current appeared in Chris-

tian art at a later date than the non-representational art of the East-Aryans, and combined with the latter to form that whole which we call 'mediaeval' art. In this mediaeval art, an art far from nature, the symbolism of the West-Aryans of the South only reappears sporadically in genuine Renaissance movements, which occurred in Byzantium as well as in the West. I shall now examine first the meaning and subsequently the outward form of this Semitic-Hellenistic province of art.

A. *The Didactic Element.* The first change in Christian Hellenistic art, the true home of which in the first three centuries lay in Western Asia Minor rather than Alexandria, took place in Antioch, the great port of Asiatic commerce, and thence was transmitted to the Mediterranean. Symbolism was displaced by a didactic tendency, the purpose of which was to teach the faithful by the help of graphic art how the teaching of Christ and the prophets was handed down through the apostles and evangelists to the Church. This purpose is clearly expressed in fifth-century mosaics such as those of the Mausoleum of Galla Placidia and of the orthodox Baptistery at Ravenna. In the former the cross is shown at the crown of the dome, and the illustration is completed with the figure of the Good Shepherd bearing the cross, and the burning of the writings condemned by the Church ; in the latter, the Baptism of Christ is appropriately represented in the dome ; this is succeeded by the Church and the prophets, while the scheme was formerly completed by the four subjects in the lower corner-niches ; the division into compartments by formal trees may be compared with that in the Church of S. George in Salonika and that in the Church of the Nativity in Bethlehem. The conception of this purely ecclesiastical system is most characteristically expressed in the scenes representing the Giving of the Law and the Keys, as they appear both in mosaics at Rome and in the sculptures of the Sarcophagi at Rome and Ravenna.

This influence from Antioch must be distinguished from another, to which the reader may best be introduced through that letter of Nilus, the first part of which has already been quoted on p. 144. In reference to the Iranian non-representational style, which we discussed above (pp. 111 ff.), he continues :
' To this communication I can only reply that no one but a babe
' or a suckling would wish to pervert the eyes of the faithful
' with such trivialities as those which you describe. It beseems

' a manful and firm mind to place in the apse, at the East end of
' the house of God, nothing but the cross alone ; for by the single
' cross of salvation mankind is saved and hope universally
' proclaimed to the hopeless ; but it is not unfitting to decorate
' both sides of the holy temple by the hand of the finest painters,
' with scenes from the Old and New Testaments, that the man
' who is ignorant of writing and unable to read the holy scriptures,
' may gaze upon the painting and gain knowledge of the fathers
' of all virtue, who served the true God ; and that he may thus
' be roused to emulate them in the great and celebrated deeds
' of heroism, through which they won heaven in exchange for
' earth, setting the things which are unseen above those which the
' eye perceives. But in the nave with its various chapels, each
' chapel should display the sublime cross alone. Anything beyond
' this should in my opinion be excluded.'

It will be observed that the letter consists of two sections :
the first is a restatement of the question asked by the eparch
Olympiodorus. The second is a violent attack on the proposal,
quite ingenuously made, for Iranian forms of ornament, to which
is appended a reasoned counter-proposal for a decoration after
the Semitic manner. Nilus is thus a living witness of the
transition from an individual and freely developed religious art
to an art under ecclesiastical control. The time at which he
wrote seems to have been an ideal moment for some such
change. Christianity, which had begun by making its way in
small communities, and had then been raised to the position of
a state religion, was now devoting all its energies to the struggle
for power and the complete subordination of the peoples to the
authority of Church and Empire. The artist was degraded by
them to the position of a mere instrument. He was no longer
permitted to decorate freely, but forced to depict what the Church,
and subsequently the Court or the combination of Court and
Church, prescribed. Thus the character of religious art was
changed ; the talent of the artist was exploited by authority ;
his personal freedom was destroyed.

The most important demand formulated by Nilus, which
finds its parallel in similar utterances by the Fathers of the
Western Church, was for a form of mural decoration in churches
which should serve to teach the illiterate believer. The struggles
and sufferings of the martyrs had been depicted in apses before
A. D. 400 ; now the Church demanded that the opposite walls of

the nave should be decorated with parallel scenes from the Old
and New Testaments. The Semitic historical sense was beginning
to triumph over East-Aryan non-representational feeling and
West-Aryan love of symbolism by means of the human figure.
For the purpose of determining the date, place, and culture in
which this tendency originated, it is worth noting, as has already
been pointed out, that it is also to be traced in the Buddhist art
of Gandhâra. In studying this didactic manner we may best
begin with ivory carvings, the very material of which points
towards the East.

The chief work of this class, the chair of Maximianus, has
already been mentioned (p. 151) in the section dealing with the
earliest phase of Christian art in the East, as an illustration of
rich decoration with scrolls and animals. But even more important, perhaps, than these are the figure-subjects which fill
its panels. Like Achthamar, but earlier by four centuries, it
illustrates in a most instructive way the fusion of Iranian ornament not so much with the purely symbolic as with the Aramaean
didactic style. On the front of the chair, enclosed between
borders of scrollwork containing animals, are figures of those
who spread the faith, grouped on either side of John the Baptist,
last of the prophets, represented bearing the lamb. In their
treatment these figures resemble those of the sarcophagi from
Asia Minor, which stand between the columns of arcades with
scalloped canopies, and reveal the dearth of contemporary models;
for though one sarcophagus belongs to the Christian period,
all betray imitation of Greek sculpture dating from the fourth
century before Christ. A related ivory panel, now in the British
Museum, with the figure of an archangel and a Greek inscription,
points more definitely to Antioch as the source of inspiration;
the figure is placed in front of the proscenium in a manner
resembling the priest before the altar-screen at a later date
(cf. the Pola casket). We are carried a stage further by the panels
on the back of the chair, carved with low reliefs illustrating
the life of the youthful Christ. Both in their limitations and their
freedom these carvings closely resemble the five-panelled diptychs.

These very diptychs show the same remarkable arrangement
of a single central figure surrounded by scenes from Christ's
childhood on the upper, lower, and lateral panels. They resemble
the front of the Ravenna chair in almost every point except that
the scrollwork is replaced in the upper panel by a figure of Christ,

or by a triumphal cross borne by hovering angels, and in the lower by an Adoration. They clearly belong to the same school of art. We can no more ascribe their origin to Ravenna than we can regard the two in the Ravenna library as Coptic. I agreed with these attributions until my eyes were opened by Mshatta and Amida ; I see yet more clearly now that I have been able to study Altai-Iran and Armenia. The ivory of which the diptychs are composed suggests a connexion with India ; moreover the arrangement of the scenes in vertical and horizontal bands grouped about a central figure finds such a marked analogy in the Gand-hâra reliefs that it can hardly be explained by independent invention consequent on the inevitable likeness between two such kindred subjects as the lives of Christ and Buddha. Hitherto I had always regarded Jerusalem as the centre of distribution for this type of sculpture, without perceiving its affinities with India ; I now recognize that it was probably a posthumous influence from the Graeco-Semitic centre of Edessa–Nisibis, which here affected Christian art as, at an earlier period, it had affected that of Northern Buddhism. It would take me too long in the present place to demonstrate the similarity, hardly yet noticed, between the Gandhâra sculptures and the didactic school of Mesopotamia and, later, of Byzantium and Europe. The relationship of their subject-matter has already been pointed out by Metzger-Milloué.[1] My immediate purpose is to give a fresh and somewhat fuller account of the iconographic cycle ; and in doing so I shall treat the types of sculpture and their arrangement separately.

B. *Aramaean Cycle.* Since no example of an Early Christian, or, in particular, of a Nestorian church with its original paintings has yet been discovered in Mesopotamia, we have to rely on the evidence of rock caverns, though these are only of secondary value. For paintings we shall begin with the Catacombs of Palmyra and Edessa ; for sculpture with those of Dara. In the latter place the entrance to the rock-cut tombs is decorated with an arch enclosed by a ⊓-shaped moulding, a form of ornament the Iranian origin of which is repeatedly impressed upon our minds. In one instance (Fig. 59, opposite) the spandrels between the arch and the moulding are filled with sculptures in relief, among which is an undoubted representation of Christ in

[1] *Les quatre évangiles. Matériaux pour servir à l'histoire des origines orientales du christianisme*, 1906.

59   Dara, rock cave ; exterior.   See p. 166.

60   Berlin, Kaiser Friedrich Museum ; mounted Christ from Upper Egypt.
See pp. 174, 175.

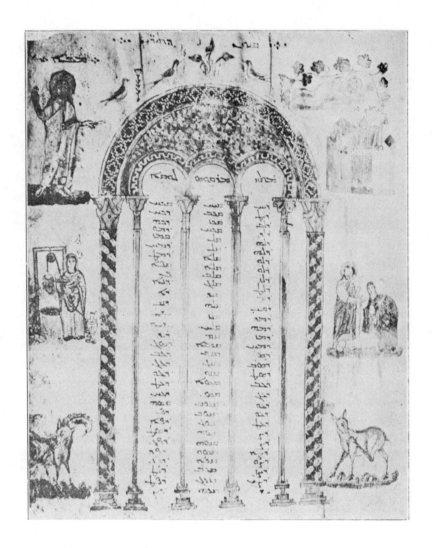

61, 62 Florence, Laurentian Library ; MS. of Rabula, A.D. 586 ; Eusebian Canons ; photo., G. Millet. See p. 167.

Limbus. He is depicted striding rapidly towards small naked figures of Adam and Eve, which appear above a mound of skulls. In the corner above and behind Christ is the hand of the Almighty. This is probably one of the earliest surviving representations of this subject, which later became so popular in Byzantine art, and was frequently associated with the scene of the Last Judgement.[1] The subject in the opposite corner is no longer recognizable, but its chief feature is a large cypress. The arch beneath is ornamented in the regular Graeco-Persian style of the Christian period in Northern Mesopotamia. May not these Mesopotamian sculptures have been the prototypes of the Achthamar cycle ?

Another important monument from this region is the Laurentian manuscript in the Laurentian Library at Florence, written by Rabula in A. D. 586, and originally in the monastery of Zagba. The Eusebian Canons of the Evangeliary are famous (Figs. 61, 62, opposite). The arches are enriched with geometric ornament ; flanking them at the top are figures of the prophets ; below these are scenes from the New Testament arranged in series, and at the base Iranian animals and plants, including vines and pomegranates. It is the richest decoration of its kind surviving from so early a period ; and, taken in conjunction with the *ampullae* from Jerusalem at Monza, in which the treatment of the figure-subjects is similar, it is very important evidence for the derivation of later Byzantine iconographic motives from the religious centre of Northern Mesopotamia : it was there that this special type of art was devised for the instruction of those who could not read. Other Syrian manuscripts of the same type exist, for instance, in Paris ; there are also Armenian and Greek manuscripts which follow the same lines. But the arrangement of the figures about the arcades is not retained. They are generally placed after the Canons at the beginning of the separate gospels, and often take the form of whole-page miniatures. To any one familiar with the mass of illustrations in the Oktateuch, the derivation of which is known, the extraordinary profusion of miniatures in the Gospels with illustration in zones or friezes will hardly come as a surprise. On some pages two or three superimposed zones interrupt the text. The important points to notice are that the composition of individual scenes is always the same, and that the scenes illustrating the childhood of Christ, as in the diptychs and on the episcopal chair, are based upon the apocryphal

[1] e. g. in the Torcello Mosaic.

gospels. Most striking of all is the arrangement of the Nativity scene, including the figures of ox and ass, Joseph in an attitude of meditation, and frequently the bathing of the Infant. It is impossible for me here to enter into the details of even a few of these innumerable illustrations. For points of detail, published studies in iconography should be consulted.

I am thus driven to assume the existence in Northern Mesopotamia of a school of representational art, in which early streams of Eastern-Semitic and Greek culture met and intermingled. Its influence extended first to India and later to the Mediterranean, and is readily distinguishable from the East-Persian non-representational type of art which I have already discussed. Its style is that of a continuous narrative, in which the central figure is consistently thrown into relief, whether in the character of Christ, the Virgin or Joseph, saint or martyr in Old or New Testament.

This was the centre which initiated the parallel arrangement of Old and New Testament scenes on opposite walls demanded by Nilus. Its place of origin was possibly the same as that of the Eusebian Canons, in which the parallel passages in the gospel are arranged opposite each other. In the surviving monuments of Early Christian art we cannot indeed point to any example of such an arrangement of parallels from the Old and the New Testaments ; but the story of Joseph on the sides of the episcopal chair is depicted with as much detail as that of Christ and the Virgin.

The proper place in churches for this arrangement of parallel subjects was on the walls of the nave, a fact attested by others besides Nilus. No example has been preserved, unless we count the Church of S. Maria Maggiore, where scenes from the Old Testament are placed in the nave, scenes from the New Testament on the triumphal arch. It is noteworthy that the latter breathe the same spirit of the apocryphal gospels, from which the reliefs of the ivory diptychs and the chair of Maximianus derive their peculiar charm. If my interpretation is the right one, and the oldest and most important of the five-panelled diptychs in the Louvre represents Constantine in the centre as the champion of the Faith with the Caesars on the lateral panels, the conception of the rider triumphing over evil indicates an eastern origin and contact with Mazdean ideas : I shall revert to this matter below. On the other hand, the treatment of the reliefs on the rest of these diptychs is distinctively Semitic. In the mosaics of S. Maria Maggiore yet another influence is apparent, particularly in the figures of Christ and the Virgin, which are invariably accompanied by angels and a splendour of costume obviously derived from the pageantry of court life.

C. *Sequence of Didactic Subjects.* I have pointed out how necessary it is to distinguish between type and composition. The latter is as variable in church decoration as in the manuscripts; and I believe that the Early Christian subjects of the Catacombs and the Sarcophagi, where all centres on the idea of redemption, were modified under Aramaean influence. I base this conclusion upon a study of the reliefs and paintings on the exterior of the churches discussed in connexion with Achthamar. They do not introduce any new set of ideas, but merely serve to transmit the old symbolism of the Catacombs and Sarcophagi to later times. Second in point of time comes that province of art which I discussed in connexion with S. Nilus; it is associated with the architectural form of the basilica, in which not only the apse but also the walls of the nave above the arcades were decorated with scenes from the Old and New Testaments. In the arrangement of subjects, a leading part was played by the theological school of Edessa and Nisibis. Whether the introduction of the concordance between the two Testaments may be attributed to its influence is a question on which I must reserve judgement. But there is no doubt that it created the cycles familiar to us from innumerable domed churches, and from the instructions in the ' Painter's Manual ' of Mount Athos. It was first designed for the single-domed church, and probably originated, like the domed basilica, on the Armenian frontier. This iconographical scheme received general recognition as an integral part of every domed church, but Jerusalem was the starting-point of the individual figure types, which reached Western Europe through Byzantine channels and Eastern Asia through the missionary activity of the Nestorians, thus acquiring world-wide significance. The essential point remains the association of Aramaean iconography with domed architecture, and its achievement in these churches of a decorative system so logical and perfect that in its quality of immovable persistence it stands without a rival. The first traces of the system are characteristically found in Ephraim the Syrian's picture of the Last

Judgement. We do not, indeed, meet with a full union of this iconography with domical architecture before the *Nea*, the palace church, built by Basil I in A. D. 885 ; this emperor was the first of the Armenian dynasty to ascend the throne of Byzantium, and may well have employed an Armenian architect in the construction of this church, which is of the characteristic cruciform domed type. Its decoration may likewise have reached Byzantium from a foreign source. It is well known that there was a figure of Christ Pantokrator in the apex of the dome and of the Virgin as *Orans* in the apse, accompanied by rows of apostles, martyrs, prophets, and patriarchs together with angelic choirs. The much later 'Painter's Manual' from Mount Athos prescribes in detail the exact position of all these figures, adding instructions for five superimposed zones of paintings for connexion with these subjects. I shall not pursue this subject further, only remarking that the 'Painter's Manual' also distinguishes the types of figures from their arrangement.

This rapid survey must suffice for the didactic iconography of Edessa–Nisibis. It triumphed in Constantinople and in the whole of the Mediterranean area, as well as in Armenia and the Orthodox Greek Church. In the latter it survives unchanged to the present day as the ideal both of type and arrangement ; but in the West it was superseded as early as the fourteenth century. A counter-movement started in the North and thence spread into Italy. It is interesting to notice how Duccio, Cimabue, and the elder Pisano were forced into the background by their own pupils under Northern influence.

Reviewing the course which I have followed since the publication of *Cimabue und Rom* in 1888, I am struck by the need for a work dealing with the penetration of the South by the North of Europe and the subsequent rise of the so-called Renaissance. Burckhardt was mistaken in claiming that the artistic emancipation of the individual took place in the South : on the contrary, it is Northern. Even if we maintain that the Renaissance was a purely Southern movement, in Italy it only matured by slow degrees, at first under the artists employed by the Hohenstaufen, then through the adoption of classical ornament in architecture, and finally by the imitation of statues and the study of the orders. Between Cimabue and Giotto, the elder and the younger Pisano, intruded the North. It began with wooden architecture and pure decoration. The Teutonic beast-ornament, discussed above, can in no sense be regarded as representational art. The latter grew independently out of the organic impulse of Northern church-art (Gothic), first in opposition to plant motives, in the form of animal finials and gargoyles ; of this development Achthamar may be regarded as an enigmatical forerunner. The human figure also appears as an organic part of the structure ; but its characteristic quality is subordinated to its function as an invisible support for drapery. Naturalism, as a deliberate aim in art, became a disease in the South, when, like decadent Greece, it began to think in terms of science.

III. *Mazdean Ideas in Christian Representation*

Up to this point my treatment of representational art has been based upon known facts ; only my interpretation of the links in its development rests upon impressions formed by the experience of many years. But there is one province, the most important in the whole range of church-art, which I have so far left untouched. Its peculiar and dominating feature has never been adequately emphasized or defined. I refer to the mosaic-decoration of the apse. In this vaulted ending of the church towards the East, invariably present in the wooden-roofed basilica, a form of decoration was developed which, if I am not mistaken, has had an extraordinarily widespread influence on art. Rome and Ravenna are the only places in which examples of this style have survived ; we shall therefore begin by considering the well-known monuments on the Tiber and the Adriatic.

The mosaics of Rome and Ravenna show clear traces of a non-representational substratum, which was gradually super-seded by representation. The apses of S. Maria Maggiore and S. Giovanni in Laterano, the last great survivors of their kind, suffered much damage at the hands of Torriti about A. D. 1300, but not so much as to preclude us from reconstructing their original features. There is no need to discuss this subject again. But we must give our attention to the gradual rise of representation, which can best be observed in Rome and Ravenna, and in apses extant elsewhere. The oldest of these mosaics, that of S. Pudenziana, built under Innocent I (A. D. 402–17), is an excellent example of the ecclesiastical style ; it is the most important outcome of the representational stream which flowed from Nisibis–Edessa–Antioch for the diffusion of Christian doctrine. In Rome, as in Ravenna, it was probably not before the fifth century that the full force of this Eastern influence made itself felt. I question the recent theory to the effect that S. Pudenziana shows indisputable influence from Jerusalem. The cross in the apse conforms to the general Eastern usage. Here, as in the mosaic of S. Giovanni in Laterano, it stands upon a hill. The scene depicted below, including the figures of Christ and the Apostles, is merely an elaboration of the Heavenly City, which, in the Lateran mosaic, is seen on a miniature scale in the hill under the cross. The resemblance in the grouping of the figures of Christ and the Apostles in S. Pudenziana and the Antiochene Pyxis in Berlin can hardly be accidental. The architectural background is modified to suit the requirements of a monumental art, and opens out in semicircular form, as opposed to the type seen in S. Prassede, where the Heavenly City is enclosed by a wall.

Hitherto we have divided the representational art of the Christian Church into two distinct provinces : one, the purely Hellenistic province of Asia Minor, the symbolism of which, in Alexandria, admits a partly Jewish strain ; the other, the province of Antioch, the emporium of the Semitic centre of Edessa–Nisibis, where symbolism is replaced by didactic purpose. The latter had an ever-increasing range of influence in the West, Jerusalem and Constantinople acting as agents of diffusion. It still remains to call attention, in the representational art of Italian mosaics, to an older influence which, in my opinion, must be connected with Iran, and more particularly with Mazdean ideas. It is a striking fact that mosaic, the decorative covering of vaulted surfaces, should be the chosen medium for the transmission of this influence ; its use may perhaps be regarded as a clue pointing to Northern Iran, just as ivory, in another field, gives a clue with regard to India. Before entering upon a discussion of these mosaics, it may be well to repeat certain pertinent observations which I have already made in my work on Armenia.

By way of a general preface we should note that Zoroastrianism adopted an attitude antagonistic to the ancient classical world, developing along thoroughly East-Aryan lines ; later, at the time of the Reformation, it strove for recognition also in the North within the pale of the Southern religion. Mazdaism preaches in its purity a moral conception of the world as divided between Good and Evil. The protagonists of Classical Christian

Art have paid too little attention to this fundamental characteristic.
It was left to the Sassanian dynasty to make the almost Christian
teaching of Mazdaism subserve the interests of property and power
in the spirit of the older Semitic and Mediterranean cultures.
Before Sassanian times Mazdaism had no need of ' representation';
this fact in itself, quite apart from the perishable nature of
unburned bricks and stucco, is sufficient to account for the
absence of permanent monuments, and the unhampered con-
tinuance of the decorative art characteristic of Northern and
nomadic peoples.   Two other Aryan religions, the Buddhist and
the Greek, in like manner created forms of art untrammelled
by ideas of power and property, though in their case the human
figure was included ; only after the death of Asoka and Alexander
respectively did they lose their essentially Aryan character
through their adoption by imperialist religions.   Ancient Iranian
art, in this perhaps following in the footsteps of old Aryan
religious ideas, made no representation of God ; even in later
times it only did so rarely, and then, probably, under foreign
inspiration.   Attempts to represent God in Achaemenian times
may be fairly ignored, since they had no influence upon the later
popular art, with which we are here concerned.   How it was
that Zoroastrianism failed to obtain any influence over the
Achaemenian court is a question which we are not yet in a position
to answer.   The motive of the mounted God will be examined
presently.   The hypothetical figures of God and Zoroaster on
one of the reliefs of Ṭak-i Bostan belong to Sassanian Court art,
and are not here in point.   There can be no question of a popular
religious representation.   It is the art of a royal court that has
need of visible figures, in order to make manifest a power conferred by the grace of God.   First Assyrian-Babylonian, subsequently Hellenistic art supplied Persia with figures for that
purpose.   Indian and East Asiatic influences only intruded into
Early Christian art in so far as they accompanied raw materials
such as ivory and silk.

A. *The Mounted Saint.*   The contest between Good and
Evil is a subject familiar to students of Christian art in the East
through representations of the Mounted Saint.   The two problems which it is our present purpose to investigate are, first,
the date and place at which the God was originally depicted as
an equestrian figure, and, secondly, the date at which this figure
developed into a champion of Good against Evil.

In the earliest times the Aryans were not horsemen, but drivers of carts. But we already find them mounted in the Rigveda ; and the game of chess has preserved ocular proof of this up to the present day in the figure of the ' knight ', just as the ' castle ' recalls the elephant and the ' bishop ' the wheeled vehicle. In the religious ideas of Mazdaism the six great good spirits, the *Amesha Spenta*, are represented as mounted figures. This conception runs through the whole Avesta ; I will give only a single instance. In the Zarathusht-Nameh (a work written for Parsis in New Persian, and completed in A. D. 1278) we read how two of these *Amesha Spenta* (good spirits or perhaps angels) appeared, with two holy fires, before King Gushtasp in the form of mounted figures (*Suvaran*), carrying weapons of war. Each was like a walking mountain, clad in warlike dress and coat of mail. . . . All of them wore the sacred colour of green, the colour of angels, and were equipped with weapons : ' they ' brandished their lances before the King . . . each sitting thus ' upon his horse.'

Concrete evidence for the mounted figure of God in art may be seen in the Sassanian rock-cut reliefs which depict the investiture of the ruler by means of two confronted figures on horseback, representing Ahuramazda and the prince. The horse was so integral a feature of Aryan life that it is inseparable from the Aryan idea of God.

But there is a much more convincing piece of evidence which I have had in mind for years. In Egypt in 1901 I first discovered that not only S. George, but every Saint, even Christ Himself, was represented as a mounted figure (Fig. 60, facing p. 166). Even at that time I assumed that for the origin of the type ' all the ' signs pointed in one direction, towards Iran, whence the horse ' itself was introduced into the West '. The equestrian relief from Suweida in Syria gave me the opportunity of expanding this hypothesis, for which so much evidence has since accumulated that it has gradually developed into a certainty. First of all a whole series of such figures of mounted saints was discovered in Christian Mesopotamia ; later I found them widely distributed in Armenia, one such figure representing the Founder, and others as at Achthamar a large variety of saints. The fundamental idea is clearly that of the saint as horseman, an idea demonstrably known to Mazdaism. Whether the popular religion of Iran actually translated the idea into representational form, or whether this was first done through the medium of Hellenism on Persian soil, as in the case of Court art, is another question.

So far we have only considered the horseman and his equipment. But I am inclined also to attribute to Mazdaism the conception of this figure as a champion against evil. Formative art carries us farther than legend in this matter. It is significant that the Alexander of the Pompeii mosaics, the Heracles Maximianus of Suweida, and the Horus of the Louvre are all depicted as armed and carrying the lance in the manner of the *Amesha Spenta*. Like these they should properly be shown striking down an enemy. There seems to be evidence to prove that this was a favourite subject in the symbolic decoration of church gates in post-Constantinian times. In my published work I have often had occasion to discuss the mosque gate of Dashlūt (Fig. 54, facing p. 152), where the tympanum has apparently been transferred from a Christian church. Actual church gates of this type, with representations of God as a mounted warrior, may not exist, but they are attested to by Syrian literature. An Arab tradition ascribed by older commentators on the Koran to Mohammed himself relates the fact in the case of Lydda. Even Christ is there said to have been depicted mounted on a mare and slaying Anti-Christ. The same commentators render it probable that the slaying of a wild boar adorned in like manner a gateway in Jerusalem. The practice is also corroborated by the narrative of Eusebius, who relates that Constantine had his own figure painted over the entrance to the imperial palace, with the cross over his head and a dragon under his feet. Eusebius explains this as another method of suggesting the victory of the Faith— a favourite subject in the Egypt of the fourth century.[1] In this particular case, where the victory is symbolized by a mounted figure slaying a beast, the type may well go back to the Mazdean conception of the triumph of Good over Evil.

The same subject reappears constantly in Armenia. An exhaustive search commencing in that region would lead us straight back to Iran. In the representation of the mounted saint, Egypt has as usual retained the original Irano-Armenian character in its purest form, as is the case with the mounted figure of Christ, which I brought to the Berlin Museum (Fig. 60, facing p. 166). In the West the same idea survives in the form of S. George, and attains a lofty artistic expression in Dürer's ' Knight, Death, and

[1] Cf. the wood-carving in the Kaiser Friedrich Museum at Berlin.

the Devil '. In this arresting picture the German master almost seems to have had intuitive knowledge of the ancient Aryan conception, and to have applied it at the time of the Reformation to the idea of the Christian knight.

B. *The Last Things.* In treating of the miniatures of the Serbian Psalter in the National Library at Munich, I had occasion to discuss three unusual subjects, ' The Cup of Death ', ' The Tree of Life ', and ' The Uncovering of the Bones '. The second of these subjects derives from the legend of Barlaam and Joasaph, and ultimately from Indian sources ; a similar pedigree recurs in the ' Physiologus '. The struggle for the soul is a thoroughly Mazdean idea. The best incentive to a closer study of this subject is afforded by the motive which our familiarity with the Campo Santo fresco at Pisa has led us to describe as the Triumph of Death. Other students must have been impressed by the Oriental derivation of certain features in these pictures. The apocalyptic cycle likewise suggests a Mazdean background.

C. *The Last Judgement.* The setting of the Last Judgement scene at Pisa closely approximates to Mazdean Christian ideas. It is the consummation of those Last Things which are among the oldest traditions of the Avesta. It accords so perfectly in every part with Iranian and Jewish conceptions, that by turning to the work of Ephraim the Syrian (*d.* A. D. 373), a pupil of Jacob of Nisibis, we can find a summary of all these subjects, and follow their development in an unbroken sequence down to the time of Dante. These relations must be realized, if we would understand how such a profusion of detail came to exist as early as the fourth century, and how both the converted Bulgarians and Mohammed were able to make such full and efficient use of them. All this mass of details was already present in Mazdean conceptions before the appearance of Christian art, which merely added the representational element. To illustrate the importance of Mazdean influence in the apse mosaics of Rome and Ravenna, I shall examine one example in each of these places. For the study of the subject of the Last Judgement in general the reader is referred to the large representations on the west walls of church interiors, such as the mosaic at Torcello and countless other examples in orthodox churches. I would suggest a comparison of these with the text of Ephraim and with the ideas of Iranian and Jewish eschatology. My present purpose is to trace the pure symbolism of fourth-century art to its source, and to show that the idea of the Last Judgement already dominated the art of mosaic, in a form not yet recognized, before its transmission from East to West. The artistic influence of Antioch is relatively of minor importance.

In the preceding chapter I showed that Early Christian art made use of a kind of landscape with fishing and hunting scenes, scrolls of vine and pomegranate, and a rich symbolism based on animal and plant life ; and that certain remarkable features of this art point to Iran as the source from which its underlying ideas were derived. I shall now attempt to supply the key to its interpretation, in so far as what has been said about Hvarenah has not already done so.

We may begin by examining one of the smaller and more unassuming mosaics in S. Apollinare Nuovo, along the top of the wall above the windows. The reader is probably aware that their subjects are arranged with figures of the prophets as we find them in the Syrian Bible from the Mesopotamian monastery of Zagba, and that the choice and sequence of the biblical scenes agree in general with Syrian liturgy. An Easter lection from the Gospels akin to that used by the Jacobites has here been pictorially translated. Let us take the mosaic depicting the judgement of the sheep and goats. Christ is there shown sitting amidst a rocky landscape accompanied by a red and a blue angel and stretching forth His right hand towards three white sheep, opposite which are three black-spotted goats. Paulinus of Nola, who also refers to the Hvarenah landscape, describes the subject of the goats and sheep in an apse mosaic of the Basilica at Fundi. It depicted a broad landscape, in the centre of which stood the solitary figure of Christ on the rock ; it thus differed somewhat from the well-known mosaic over the entrance to the Mausoleum of Galla Placidia, which belongs to the same class. The Shepherd was shown caressing four sheep at his right hand, and motioning four goats away at his left. Above the figure of Christ were the symbols of the Trinity.

The allegory of the sheep is also used by Ephraim the Syrian in his Last Judgement, and appears, contemporaneously perhaps, on the lid of a Roman sarcophagus in reference to S. Matthew xxv. 32. The idea in itself was very probably Mazdean in origin, and is described in the Avesta. At the resurrection of the body, we read, every one will see his good and his evil deeds. ' Then shall be held the assembly of Catvaçtran

' and the Evil shall be separated from the Good as the black sheep
' from the white.' I have already pointed out that the figure of
Christ as the Good Shepherd is a Mazdean conception (Yima) ;
the mosaic in the Mausoleum depicts Him in a landscape of the
Hvarenah type, and the sheep in Early Christian mosaics indicate
a similar origin.

D. *The mosaic of SS. Cosmas and Damian* (Fig. 63, facing
p. 180). I shall now consider in some detail the mosaic of
SS. Cosmas and Damian, artistically the finest of the Roman
mosaics; it holds a unique position, outside the ordinary lines of
development on Roman soil, and similar to that occupied in the
architectural field by the ' Minerva Medica '. The mosaic depicts
red clouds sinking towards a band of water behind the land in the
foreground, and filling the whole central portion of the semicircle.
Palms on either side, a phoenix in one on the left, carry the eye
upwards to other clouds floating at the summit of the apse. This
' landscape ' on a dark blue ground reveals the same composite
symbolism of clouds, water and earth, phoenix and palm, which
I have already explained as typically Mazdean. In the midst of
this setting appear Christian figures ; in the centre the Saviour,
with large gesture, standing high up on the clouds ; on either
side smaller figures of the saints led in by Peter and Paul ;
finally the ' Founders ' ; the whole somewhat theatrical composition showing a calculated effort to impress the spectator.

When I consult published works on Roman mosaics with
a view to discovering what is meant by this creation of Pope
Felix IV (526–30), I fail to find any appreciation of the landscape
as such, but, at most, only a passing reference. Wilpert is of the
opinion that the ' Jordan ', flowing behind the figures, is rather
meaningless in this position and might equally well have been
omitted. He frankly describes the mosaic as the Abode of the
Blessed or the Heavenly Paradise, and considers that in the
figure of Christ the artist intended to emphasize the divine
nature. That is why the artist has depicted Him standing upon
clouds as though He had just appeared, and the light which
radiates from His form reddens the clouds like the rising sun.
The apostles, he goes on to say, are intended to draw attention
to His presence ; the martyrs are in the act of turning towards
Him. The blue ground heightens the mystic character of the
whole scene, while the gold of the lower zone with the sheep
accords better with the more joyous character of Christian

symbolism. That is all that the Roman specialist is able to say
about this work of art. Other authorities have succeeded in
advancing a stage farther. Zimmermann is right in laying stress
on its essentially representational character, and on its solemnity,
which inspires in the beholder an involuntary feeling of awe and
silent reverence. Let us go more closely into the matter.

This mosaic stands outside the series of fourth-century
mosaics, whether decorative or depicting only landscape ; nor
can it be included among those of the fifth century, which
represent Christ as the Teacher among the apostles. Yet Wilpert
considers that we should be mistaken in regarding it as a wholly
independent work of art and the first successful attempt at apse-
decoration. There is evidence, he says, that earlier models were
available ; this is shown by the account of the apse-mosaic of
S. Lorenzo in Lucina, which was at least a century older and
showed a strong resemblance to it. Wherein lay this resemblance ? In the landscape ? That cannot be ; for it depicted
wreaths and foliations, as in S. Maria Maggiore, and single
figures. Are the figures of Christ, with Peter and Paul, the
protomartyrs and the founders, really an original part of the
composition ? And are the human figures really of primary
importance from the artistic point of view ? Clearly, the great
feature in SS. Cosmas and Damian is the boldly conceived
landscape consisting of earth, water, and clouds arranged in
a series of distinct masses. The scroll designs of S. Lorenzo in
Lucina have not the remotest connexion with this form of landscape ; they are more nearly related to the mosaics of S. Maria
Maggiore and the Lateran. But it is precisely the landscape
which distinguishes the mosaic. I am not concerned to trace
the figures of ' founders ' to the Church of S. Peter and the time
of Constantine, or to show that the figure of the summoning
Christ is derived from some pre-Constantinian Roman church
art, imitated in the Catacomb of Domitilla. My object is to
grasp the full significance of the pregnant form of art employed
by Pope Felix, and to probe it to its source.

We may learn from inscriptions on Armenian churches that
they were sometimes founded for an intercessional purpose; this
is corroborated by inscriptions on tombstones. One of these
runs as follows : ' Mayest Thou (Christ), when thou appearest in
majesty, intercede for me, an unworthy servant of Christ.' The
inscriptions of SS. Cosmas and Damian run similarly: *Aula Dī*

*claris radiat speciosa metallis | in qua plus fidei lux pretiosa micat |
martyribus medicis populo spes certa salutis | venit et ex sacro crevit
honore locus.* This is followed by the dedicatory inscription :
*optulit hoc D̄no Felix antistite dignum | munus ut aetheria vivat in
arce poli.* ('Felix offered unto the Lord a gift worthy of a Pope,
in order that he might dwell in the Heavenly citadel'.)

The event depicted in this mosaic is the great Epiphany of
Christ, of which Ephraim the Syrian in his description of the Last
Judgement says : ' Behold, the day of the Lord breaks suddenly
' upon Creation and the righteous draw near to him with burning
' lamps (represented in this particular case by the crowns of
' the Martyrs). But I am in utter darkness and have no oil in
' my lamp, wherewith to go and meet the bridegroom when
' he comes.' This is the true explanation of the mosaic. The
conception is reminiscent of the Avesta and that belief in im-
mortality and eternal judgement which was a chief dogma of
Mazdaism from the earliest times. The twenty-second Yasht
describes the fate of souls after death ; it also contains a passage
which supplies the key to the landscape of SS. Cosmas and
Damian in words that almost literally describe it : ' At the
' breaking of the fourth day, and the rising of the rosy flames
' of dawn, when the gates of Heaven are opened ' the soul goes to
judgement. And at the Last Judgement, according to Yasht 19,
the Redeemer of the World is supposed to rise from the water
Kansu, ' from far away out of the East, the original source and
' dwelling place of the light. It is his task to accomplish the
' renewal of the world. He maketh the living immortal, and the
' dead he awakeneth out of their sleep. He putteth an end to
' age, death, and decay. To the godly man he giveth everlasting
' life, everlasting happiness and the fulfilment of all his desires.'

This is the Iranian conception, to which the mosaic of Pope
Felix gives visible expression ; the treatment of the figures is
its only Graeco-Semitic element. The introduction of the
figures of the ' founders ' is alone sufficient to indicate an eastern
origin. But the landscape, which would be more effective without
the human figures, is clearly derived from Iran. The ' Jordan '
is not a negligible element ; it is precisely the water, the ocean
of the world, which, in conjunction with earth and clouds,
forms the decisive factor. The religious landscape transcends in
importance the human figures with their calculated dramatic
effect, and gives to the picture that air of simple and sublime

63 Rome, SS. Cosmas and Damian ; apse-mosaic ; after Wilpert. See pp. 178, 218.

64   Kioto, Zenrinji temple ; figured silk ; after the *Kokka*.   See p. 181.

repose, which characterizes not Greek art alone, but also, in its distinctive fashion, the art of Eastern Iran.

It was my intention in this volume to deal exclusively with Christian art ; but I should like to make an exception at this point in order to point out how great and alluring is the goal that awaits those who apply the comparative method to art. Phenomena very similar to those which we have noticed in Roman mosaics occur in a Buddhist silk picture of the Zenrinji temple at Kioto in Japan (fig. 64, opposite). In this picture the figure of Buddha, the religious founder, represents the dawn, and is accompanied, in place of Peter and Paul, by his Bodhisattvas Kwannon and Seishi, beneath whom are smaller figures of the four Deva kings and two Founders. The essential point is the use of landscape to introduce cosmic ideas. Buddhism, in its passage from India to China through the Mazdean culture area, seems to have had its ideas modified much in the same way as Christian art. For if I am not mistaken, the picture in question is a reproduction by a Japanese in the thirteenth century of an original work by the great T'ang master artist Wu-Tao-tse who lived in the eighth. Curiously enough, the Zenrinji picture has been eulogized in practically the same words as the mosaic in SS. Cosmas and Damian, though less with reference to its subject-matter than to its artistic worth. I quote the words of Otto Fischer, which run as follows : ' The Amida of the Zenrinji picture, rising like the ' moon from behind the hills, is one of the most wonderful con- ' ceptions in the whole range of religious art. The theme is treated ' in a spirit infinitely serene like that of autumn, and permeated ' with such an atmosphere of celestial peace, that the sight of it is ' one of the most impressive of all experiences. Yet here again ' this unique effect is the result of an abstract composition and ' partition of space, which depend upon conditions admitting of ' calculation, symmetry and gold contours, pyramidal construction, ' the balance of curves, and the skilful variation of scale ; such were ' the means which the painter employed. They give the picture, ' notwithstanding its inspiration, a sense of destiny detached from ' the emotions of the human kind. Even the wave-like outlines ' of the hills fringed with trees do not resemble those of experience ' or sight, but are disposed as decoration according to the laws of ' ascending and descending curves, so as to form an effective setting ' for the symmetrically inclined figures of the attendants, and the ' supreme repose of the facing Buddha.' If we apply this subtle analysis to the Christian mosaic at Rome, bearing in mind my repeated opposition throughout this work of Iranian form to Hellenistic–Semitic objectivity, we shall perhaps get some idea of the purifying influence of Mazdaism upon art. The truth is indeed as little recognized in Japan as in Europe. The picture at Kioto is generally supposed to be connected with a vision of the priest Eshin Sozu.[1]

With our horizon enlarged by comparison, we are in a better position to appreciate the narrowness of the classicists, whose attitude is well illustrated by such a statement as the following : ' If there still exists anything in Christian art for which we cannot ' point to a pagan, that is a classical analogy, we should remember ' that this may at any moment be supplied by a new discovery or ' excavation.' We know that the Greek spirit, in its earliest period, was far too robust to think of explaining this world by reference to a future state. The change of view began with Plato, and was probably not wholly uninfluenced by the East, where an Aryan religion centring round this dream had arisen two centuries before. In the origin of Christian art, Mazdean influence upon Graeco-Roman ideas was not merely indirect ; unless I am mistaken, Zoroastrianism, which at the birth of Christianity was still at the height of its power, exercised a direct and not inconsiderable influence on Western thought. One-sided insistence on the essentially classical character of Early Christian art is bound to provoke counter-movements with such watchwords as ' Christian Semitism ' and ' Christian Mazdaism '. Classical Christian art dies out in the course of the centuries ; Christian Semitism remains triumphant in the field of representation, and Christian Mazdaism in that of architecture. With these West-Aryan classicalism intermingled in Byzantium, and later also in the West, but only at sporadic moments of revival.

IV. *Influence of the Court*

The object of Edessa-Nisibis was didactic. Byzantium, on the other hand, made church and religion subservient to its imperialist policy and, like the Sassanians, transfused all things with

[1] The subject here represented is Yamagoshi-Amida. H. Schmidt kindly informs me that he is inclined to connect the type with the Taema-Mendara of the eighth century, and with Eshin's studies of Amida, but that up to the present no evidence is forthcoming for the earlier treatment of Yamagoshi-Amida or the influence which it had on later art.

the spirit of the court. Tangible proof of this is afforded by
the manner of depicting the Virgin and her life. The most
characteristic examples preserved are the apse-mosaic of Parenzo
and the Adoration by two processions of Saints (male and female)
in S. Apollinare Nuovo at Ravenna, in both of which examples
the royal treatment of the Virgin is derived from the church of
the Nativity in Bethlehem. In both cases she appears as an
empress enthroned, and separated from the Saints and founders
by attendant angels. This spirit and the source whence it sprang
are clearly shown in the dogmatic mosaics on the triumphal
arch of S. Maria Maggiore, and still more in the choir of S. Vitale,
where, appropriately enough, a representation of the court with
all its pageantry is bodily introduced. This court style subsequently gives way in some degree to the purely ecclesiastical
treatment of Edessa-Nisibis, although a special change takes
place in apse-decoration by the substitution of the Virgin for the
Cross.

In conclusion I must clearly repeat that I have ignored the
view of Christianity as a faith which created an art out of its own
resources, except in so far as an art relying on intellectual content
was encouraged by the theologians, or, to come down to matters
of detail, church architecture was made to conform more closely
to the new liturgy by the introduction of the apse and the connexion with it of a longitudinal axis, and other changes of this
kind. But, to be candid, we are only at the threshold of serious
research. I therefore feel it necessary at the outset to dissociate
myself from any standpoint restricted by a confessional point of
view or by a narrow horizon such as that which ascribes all
initiative to Rome. There are some who can see nothing but the
Church and ' representation ', and imagine both essential to
religious experience in the field of art. Yet it is important, even
in considering the Early Christian art of the large Hellenistic towns,
and among them Rome and Byzantium, to have a clear idea how
the Church began, and when representation first arose. It must
be definitely realized that neither Christianity nor representation
originally had the slightest connexion with Rome or its church
architecture, pregnant though that was with possibilities of development ; we should further remember that the Hellenistic timber-
roofed basilica to which Rome, once the home of a most brilliant
vaulted architecture, clung with a strange persistence, began in
course of time to yield to the pressure of Eastern communities,

while the vault, gradually advancing westwards, first profoundly modified the long church, and ultimately, after a thousand years, sealed its triumph with the dome of S. Peter's. Meanwhile both court and church vigorously collaborated in the destruction of the peculiarly Northern style known as Gothic.

V. *The West*

Representation established itself in Western church art mainly in the regions dominated by the South; the retreat of representation is in itself the proof of a strong indigenous feeling for art. The Goths and Lombards had no representational art at the time of their invasion of Italy. The crude figures which they subsequently produced bear in iconography the sign-manual of Byzantium, but in their form are Northern; they also show an East-Aryan strain, particularly in their use of symbols, which at times are quite reminiscent of Hvarenah decoration. This is perhaps even more marked in the Balkan peninsula, in contemporary Greece, and the old Croatian empire, where the dislike of representation manifests itself either in the modification of classical forms or in a faithful adherence to Byzantine, that is, Aramaean types; these, however, retain the treatment of figure-surface with triple-grooved bands after the manner favoured in Armenia and in Ireland.

The contact of the Frankish empire with the East is clearly revealed in illuminations of manuscripts, but Charlemagne employed the services of the Greeks and Syrians for other purposes besides that of editing the gospels. Architecture reveals, both in structure and decoration, connexion both with contemporary Eastern forms and with the old Hellenistic basilica. The occasional use of classical models and a certain hesitancy between the representational and non-representational styles is observable throughout the whole range of art, including illumination. Decorative and representational art go hand in hand, and it is rare to find even a tentative effort at something truly indigenous. Both subjects and figures were borrowed from the most diverse sources; it is in the treatment of form that the resistance of the North to the victorious church comes out most strongly. As in Armenia, there is a tendency more or less marked to modify the lines of the newly adopted subjects; at times they receive the suggestion of unrestrained movement and become true vehicles of expression. The same tendency appears in the best period of Romanesque ; we may compare the sculpture of Moissac with that of Armenia.

This formal tendency reached the highest level of accomplishment as soon as the North began to manipulate the forms evolved independently in the South-West. A logical development ensued, which for vitality of form can only be compared with the achievements of Greece and of Armenia. The result was a lofty expressionist art, unspoiled by scientific naturalism and in harmony with the spirit informing the structure as an organic whole. It is thus entitled to be called great art in the best sense of the term. Herein the Northern (Gothic) cathedrals attained a height hardly surpassed by Donatello, in whom, indeed, we mark an attempt to study classical sculpture and natural forms together. This was an unfortunate attempt repeated by many painters, by Raphael not least ; to it we owe in no small degree the subsequent confusion between art and science which has since but too often characterized the work of masters with individuality and of the unoriginal herd. Only the greatest were able to avoid the pitfalls of naturalism, intent on its near objective ; only they could make representation express their own souls and those of their peoples in a manner so exalted that even in the strait limits of the pictorial they remained great artists. Leonardo, Michelangelo, Giorgione, Dürer, and Rembrandt can never be surpassed in this kind.

The North preserved its own genius in representational art, as the East-Aryans of Asia theirs in landscape and in the expression which they achieved by abandoning imitation of Nature. In the end the South too was swept away in its turn by this Northern torrent. The spiritual quality which Dürer infused into a hackneyed subject in his picture of ' All Saints ', with its rosy dawn and the clouds sinking low over the seascape, was also profoundly felt by Goethe. When he says that the sun setting over the sea will always be the most sublime of symbols, we are reminded of the Hvarenah landscape in Mazdean art. The classic becomes a romantic when he adds : ' Even in its setting it abides the same.'

The origin of Christian Church art is much more definitely interlinked with geographical, racial, and national characters than people have hitherto been led to suppose ; they have underestimated the importance of the list of peoples mentioned in the Acts of the Apostles as present in Jerusalem at the first Pentecost.

Spiritual movements are superficial in comparison with the fixity of geographical factors ; they may modify this or that, embrace foreign influences, and even end by losing their identity ; but they can never produce new or decisive values. Christianity and its art had no true roots of its own ; wherever it went it stayed itself upon the local and national foundations which it found in existence during the first four centuries of our era. By following the list in Acts ii. 9–11 we can observe how the Jewish nation spun the threads of its distribution not, at first, in the direction of Asia Minor or Rome, but towards the lands of the Parthians, Medes, Elamites, and Mesopotamians, the very peoples, in fact, who created vaulted buildings and gave their walls that decorative lining, the object of which was not to represent but to adorn.

The Jews, who had no representational art, delivered infant Christianity to Mazdaism at a time when the Persian people had won control of their art and the Sassanian dynasty had not yet perverted it into a state religion. The mosaics of Rome and Ravenna afford the clearest proof in a style of decorative lining specially designed for the vault. In historical interest the churches of Armenia are almost surpassed by this species of art, which was particularly applied to the decoration of the apse in the timber-roofed basilica. The purely ornamental and landscape forms of decoration introduced from Iran still formed an attractive substratum in the art of Rome and Ravenna at a time when Semitic figure-subjects began to predominate. The mosaics of SS. Cosmas and Damian and of S. Apollinare in Classe are admittedly anachronisms in the sixth century. At that time Semitism and Hellenism had already contracted the alliance which remained their fixed policy, an alliance to which Iran, for all the efforts of the iconoclasts, offered an ever-weakening resistance.

In considering all this interaction between countries, races, peoples, and spiritual forces, we cannot leave India outside our range of vision. In the province of formative art we find links which show Gandhâra in its treatment of Buddha and his story so nearly related to Asia Minor and the home of Semitic Christianity that the discovery of similar affinities in ivory carvings no longer excites any surprise. This connexion explains the transition from Indian symbolism to the historical style of Gandhâra. The connexion of Christian art with India was especially strong in Egypt, where it is perceptible even at the present day.

It will therefore be necessary to broaden the old lines of

research : the new school can no longer confine its view of Christianity to Greece and Rome, but will extend its horizon so as to include Hellenistic Asia, the Semitic countries and Iran. As a general observation it is true to say that the proper creative period of Christian art terminates with the end of the fourth century ; the letter of Nilus clearly indicates the change from the unsophisticated style of Eastern communities to one according with the strict demands of the church in the Mediterranean area. It was only in the north of Europe that fresh creative energy survived, to produce, in the twelfth century, that flower of Christian art which we call Gothic. This art developed in the north of France out of a lost wooden architecture, just as Armenian construction was derived from vanished Iranian buildings of unburned brick, though in either case a considerable previous development in stone or in rubble building must be presumed. It will require generations of research to guide these streams from their first sources, which I have been able to indicate, into their broad and true channels, and to follow up all those divergences and creative innovations which lend such richness to the total picture. But the mere ascertainment of such historical facts is not our ultimate object ; these facts, critically examined and sifted, must themselves serve, after their kinds, as a basis for comparative research. It is only at this point that the task of the specialist can be taken up, and a systematic history of development begun.

In the present volume I have repeated the attempt, so frequently made in the last decades, to fill up one of those gaps which have hitherto made it impossible to carry out any work on Early Christian art or on the emergence of the Middle Ages from the evolutionary point of view. First Byzantium and the great Hellenistic cities, then Asia Minor, Armenia, and the group formed by Edessa, Amida, and Nisibis in Northern Mesopotamia, and now finally Iran,—all in turn claimed our whole attention. But do they really complete the circle ? Are no gaps still left to fill ? On the borders of this enlarged horizon lie India and Eastern Asia. The country beyond the Oxus, between Altai and Iran, was as it were the clearing-house whence routes led northwards as far as Scandinavia, and southwards to the great emporia of Syria. The Indian origin of the fish-symbol has formed a subject of dispute ; Buddhist temples in Turkestan have been claimed as intermediaries by those in favour of the theory, and rejected by its opponents. But such trifling details lead nowhere. Mazdaism and Buddhism already existed in a high state of development when Christianity forced its way into their territory. This is a fact which can no longer be ignored in the reckoning with Hellenism as now represented by classical philologists and archaeologists. But what do we know about the remains beyond the Oxus ? Or indeed about those of China ? Strange surprises await us in these regions, more especially in connexion with the Italian Quattrocento. This investigation into the origin of Christian Church art (from which sepulchral art has been purposely omitted) has led me, in the preceding historical section, to what has been called a complete transvaluation of all existing values. The reason is that I have not, like a philologist, been confined to a single language, or pursued research in the interest of a single and sharply defined province. It has been my advantage to employ a tongue universally understood, the *lingua franca* of formative art ; I have thus been able to roam freely throughout the territories of Hither Asia and so to comprehend the whole. In the old days special weight was given to Latin sources, more recently to the Greek and the Syrian as well. To-day the student can bridge the gap left by Pehlevi, and profit by the documents of Chinese Turkestan which are now being deciphered. But the most important advance of all came from the discovery that Armenia and the country of the Arsacid dynasty which gave it Christianity belong to the North, and may be held to have effected a penetration of Southern Hither Asia and its culture almost without a parallel.

The Arabs would never have raised Islam, nor the Jews Christianity, to those spiritual heights which they attained at any rate in the realm of art, had not the Iranians, living under similar economic conditions, supplied both movements with the vigorous style created by their national Mazdaism. The problem of the origin of Christian art cannot be solved by assuming spontaneous evolution from within, and accepting in a general way the significance of Hegel's ' content '. Rightly to appreciate the development of art in Early Christian times, the student must embrace in a comprehensive view peoples and races, the material used and the purpose conceived ; he must know how clearly to distinguish the essential values of formative art. I shall therefore round off this essay in development by a formal survey of the results yielded by this wide outlook in the purely artistic field.

VIII

Systematic Investigation of Essential Character and Application of the Comparative Method

IN the preceding chapters we frequently had occasion to allude to a certain method in the study of the history of art, a method which seeks not merely to describe and sift monuments and sources, but also to ascertain and interpret the course of their development. This method of study, which I may describe as research into essential character, is fundamental to our subject. While historical investigation precedes it and helps to prepare its material, its own scope is limited to the work of art itself. It thus forms a necessary preliminary to a third kind of research, which deals with the history of development in art, and is closely associated with the study of various other aspects of life, including not merely music and literature, but such matters as power and property, law and custom, economy and technology. These are the aspects and activities of life with which formative art comes into contact ; and scientific workers in these fields would readily open up relations with the art student were they not precluded from fruitful co-operation by the narrow horizon of contemporary officials and professors of art, who are too comfortably involved in their own small European field to be capable of devoting serious attention to things over its frontier. Some one place there should be where the whole range of problems concerning formative art might be conscientiously kept under review ; but so long as there are no institutes of research served by trained experts with adequate remuneration, the gap must be filled by the institutes of art at our universities, attracting audiences from all the various ‘ faculties ’ and striving to inspire in them an interest that shall outlast student days.

What I call the investigation of ‘ essential character ’ builds on a groundwork of historical fact and has no connexion with aesthetics or more general artistic studies, from which it is distinguished by the limitation of its subject-matter to the art known as 'formative', and to the works which this creates. It is not concerned with the psychology of the artist or spectator; it seeks nothing but experience from works of art, the period, provenance, and cultural background of which are definitely known. As a science it follows a course distinct from history, philology, psychology and aesthetics, studies which can only be regarded as supplementary to it. But it stands in close touch with similar investigations, based like itself upon historical data, in other spheres of art such as poetry and music, or those fundamental departments of life, which I have partly enumerated above. Even with these it cannot co-operate until it is firmly established on an independent basis.

This book has demonstrated how closely all these different spheres of life are interconnected and how largely they determine the fate of the formative arts. Religion itself, and particularly Christianity, which we took as our guide, is seen on a closer inspection to recede far into the background. All the growth and unfolding of the first millennium and a half were made intelligible in the first instance only by an examination of geographical and racial factors. Despotism of Church and State over communities came afterwards. We have seen how an attempt was made during the fifth and sixth centuries to weld the collateral national units of the fourth century into larger groups, and how the individual nations of the East resisted this movement and found a support in Persia, the second great state of the time, which, though not itself Christian, favoured the Christians so long as they were opposed to Rome. Thus local forms of art managed to persist, and subsequently to break through the restrictions imposed by Church and Court. This led, in the West, to the creation of 'styles', modified at their source by the influence of migrations and the intercourse of peoples, and reinforced in the North by indigenous movements. In this evolutionary process the North and South, the East and West, proved stronger than Church and State, but differed among themselves in age, economic conditions, and individual character.

The preceding chapters have, I hope, made it sufficiently clear that in early Christian church construction there were originally three distinct manifestations of art, which first developed side by side, then formed alliance, though lacking any close natural affinities. These manifestations were : the type of building ; its originally non-representational form of ornament ; and finally, representation. The long church is imposed upon that with transverse axis, and the dome upon both ; the church with decorated vaults triumphs over the wooden-roofed basilica, while representation supersedes the earlier non-representational style, and effects a gradual but inevitable compromise with every kind of structure and its decoration. I have already attempted to show how these conflicting groups are to be defined in regard to provenance, period, and social background ; my present purpose is to give a comprehensive view of Christian art resulting from their combined influence. I am assuming that Vignola's Gesù marks the close of its career, and that the most important turning-point in its development was the passing of the leadership from East to West, where the fusion of elements once geographically distinct appears to have been finally consummated about the year 1600. It is no part of the purpose of this volume to follow the course of subsequent history. My present concern is with the original geographical distribution of types, their later succession, and the manner in which the ruling powers strove to subordinate all the arts to their aims. In the first half of the seventeenth century the forces of Court, Church, and humanistic science generally were united, almost without distinction, in their efforts to suppress every kind of individualist movement, especially in so far as religion or art were concerned.

It was hardly possible until quite recent times to view objec-tively the complex movements preceding the year 1600 : heirs of that age, we were still too near it to see things in proportion. Moreover, systematic research in the history of art has hardly yet begun, at least not in an organized form. I hope therefore, as one who has made a lifelong study of the subject, to meet with a certain degree of indulgence, and to be spared instant and un-measured rebuke for presuming in this concluding chapter to attempt so difficult a task. It is a task to which I have addressed myself in a practical way in all my writings, and lastly in my *Armenia* ; in my belief, it is one which the specialist is bound to undertake, and its avoidance betrays the comfortable evasiveness of the dilettante. To make mistakes is human ; to evade difficulties is not merely lazy, but shows lack of courage or incompetence. Science is ill served by irresolution and resort to catchwords ; the abuse of vague generalizations, the exclusive concentration upon facts of space and colour, with a view to what are called objective standards, these are the subterfuges of those who will not make the effort to think out the whole subject for themselves. A scheme for the systematic investigation of essentials can only grow out of actual experience ; it can be no fruit of a one-sided or idly speculative mind.

The present book contains an examination into the origins of Christian church art by one who has specialized in the study of formative art. In the course of this examination certain lines of thought have developed, foreign to those which art-history and archaeology have been accustomed to pursue. Most important, perhaps, is my rejection of the old view that surviving monuments can be relied on for decisive results, either *per se* or as factors determining date ; this is a view which would place history at the mercy of chance. I hold that monuments are merely determinants of their inherent values and consequently of their composite nature to which these values contribute. Such is the method of what I call comparative research in essential character. In this kind of research we are concerned not with the monument itself, but with the units of artistic values to be discerned in it ; and our retrospective inferences relate less to the combined effect of these values at any particular monument than to the values themselves as units conditioning its essential character, and suggesting comparison with other monuments in which they may be quite differently combined. It is necessary at the outset to formulate some sort of arrangement as to the essential character of formative art, the values of which it is composed, and the manner of their investigation. This arrangement cannot be regarded as anything more than an expedient, but its aim is purely scientific.

Formative art, like every spiritual compromise between man and his environment, is confined to a definite vital activity, above all to happy craftsmanship aiming at visible effects. In order to get a clear idea of this elemental factor in art we must first study the conditions governing the effective use of new material and handicraft in varying kinds of physical environment. Next we must study the spiritual values which result from man's compromise. In the present case it is the ' mediaeval ' world which demands our attention. We have surveyed the inhabitants of those countries which bear upon the origins of Christian art, in the first instance from the racial point of view. It proved that the nominal originators of this art were the Jews, a small branch of the Semitic race, but that the true agents of its transmission were a greater

Semitic group, and two Aryan groups, the European and the Iranian, of which the latter, together with its country, has been completely neglected in the past. We then examined separately two distinct forms of artistic creation, architecture and its decoration; finally we divided the latter into two sections, decorative and representational, corresponding with the divergent tendencies of the two Aryan groups. It remains, in conclusion, to introduce into this inquiry the order and system befitting the character of formative art, since it is our express purpose to fill a gap which has seriously impaired the value of all previous theories. The new point of view, which I thus introduce, has the merit not only of independence but of freedom from all the violence which has prejudiced hitherto the systematic treatment of our study. Wickhoff sought to explain its origin in West-Roman, Riegl in East-Roman imperial art; Sybel derived it from Hellenistic lands, Rivoira from Rome and Italy, while Schmarsow rejected the historical in favour of an aesthetic interpretation. But the problem is one which can only be solved objectively and without personal bias by comparative study on a wide geographical basis; it is for this reason that we must begin with a classification of artistic values. Problems such as this cannot be solved by limiting our view to sculpture and painting, or by putting on blinkers which prevent us from seeing anything except representation, idealizing or realistic. I shall follow a scheme, the value of which I have proved during the work of a lifetime. I tabulate it here in its most condensed form :

	I. Handicraft.		II. Spiritual Values.	
			World.	
			Significance	Appearance
	1. Material and workmanship			
Man (artist)	Objective limitation		2. Subject	3. Shape
	Personal freedom		5. Content	4. Form

I. *Handicraft*

It is generally supposed that in a period of advanced civilization, like that in which Christian art arose, local conditions of material and work are a negligible factor. The best example of this theory is that a uniform artistic taste, call it Hellenistic, Roman, late-Roman, mediaeval or what you will, was able to impose a uniform architectural type, the timber-roofed basilica.

This is a superficial point of view and has had the deplorable results which we have already observed. It is true that in large towns artistic taste can be controlled, because craftsmen from all quarters of the earth congregate there, and because authority wields the necessary economic power. But the really decisive influences must be sought not in the towns but in the wide provincial regions. Here art long remains the natural and unaffected expression of humanity, serving the interests of the community and not the arbitrary will of autocracy ; here handicraft is determined by local conditions. A general consideration of this question in so far as it affects architecture will not be out of place.

1. *Material and Work*. These are stubborn factors, of which no great town with all its economic resources can make itself permanently independent. Our proper course would be to begin with a map showing the distribution of the indigenous building materials available. in those regions of the earth which bear upon the origins of Christian art.

A. *Building Material*. Any one who makes a comparative study of art on a geographical basis is practically driven to the conclusion that in the vast majority of countries wood was the original building material. Even the early history of Christian art bears out this hypothesis. The important point is not the introduction of the timber-roofed basilica, but rather the contrast between Mesopotamia and Iran ; at that time both of these countries were included in the Persian empire ; one of them introduced the barrel vault into church architecture, and the other, as Armenia proves, the dome. This contrast is surprising because in both countries the national building material consisted of unburned brick. The different manner in which it was employed is explained by the fact that in Iran Aryan wooden construction naturally led to the dome, because short beams had to be laid across the corners of a square to support the roof, while in Mesopotamia, on the other hand, there was no such necessity.

It is remarkable that in this significant matter Mesopotamia has received as little attention as Iran. This is presumably because wooden architecture was forgotten at an early date except in a few countries such as China, where it maintains its predominance to the present day. In India and Greece the earlier style of woodwork was at first retained unaltered in stone, and only subsequently underwent modification in conformity with the character of the new material. In Iran and Mesopotamia the use of unburned brick prevented the introduction of stone architecture on a wide scale; these countries thus became, each in its own way, the home whence the vaulted architecture of Christian times was derived. This was the type which ultimately prevailed, and it was for this reason that we have paid less attention to the long timber-roofed building introduced through Christian Hellenistic influences from the Mediterranean coast. There are two reasons why this hypothesis, of so cardinal an importance for the origin of Christian art, has never been advanced. The first, though perhaps not the principal, is the deplorable narrowness with which students concentrate their gaze upon Rome and the Mediterranean. They do not think it worth their while to search the East for traces of Christian art, and indeed meet my pioneer work with a hostility which is the measure of their prejudice. The second reason is that no monuments of early Christian art have or could have survived in some of the important regions, simply because the only building material was unburned brick. In these regions the remains of early churches, or at any rate of their upper structures, would long ago, even under the most favourable conditions, have been reduced to mere heaps of dust, though their foundations may still in some cases be discoverable by excavation. But who has ever thought of excavating for Christian churches in Mesopotamia or Iran? Unburned brick is as perishable as wood. Only in the dry atmosphere of Egypt, Seistan, or Chinese Turkestan could it survive to present times. Extant remains in rubble concrete (Palaces of Fars), burned brick (Tak̤-i Kisra), or stone facing (Armenia) are the only evidence from which we can infer the previous existence of such buildings. Such remains suggest that there must once have been a widespread form of national architecture East of the Tigris and Euphrates, which has been most unfairly ignored by students of art.

Art is conditioned at the outset by the soil and by the flora from which it springs; but its diffusion depends upon a system of centres and follows commercial currents and counter-currents, which are, in turn, determined by political forces. Constantine created such centres of Christian art in Rome, Constantinople, and Jerusalem, his successors in Milan and Ravenna. It is questionable whether these towns were situated in the line of natural trade-routes. They are outliers; their true area of distribution is sometimes very far away. The main lines of diffusion are independent of such artificial nuclei; they are the natural lines of commerce, though in a lesser degree migrations, pilgrimages, and other factors are also effective in determining their direction. Instances of the adaptation of an alien technique to a new environment may be observed in the *manus gotica* in Gaul, the *magistri commacini* in Upper Italy, the Crusaders with their ' Gothic ' huts in Palestine, and ancient Persian as well as modern Italian masters in stucco. Moreover artisans were themselves at times forcibly transplanted, notably in the case of luxury trades. All these are factors which at various times influenced the growth of Christian art.

B. *Work.* Such were the conditions affecting material and its manipulation, out of which the various types of work examined in this book were evolved. These were, in architecture, the wooden roof, the barrel vault or dome, and the column, the pier, or the wall ; in decorative art, the organic style of wooden architecture in classical and Gothic times, or the wall-linings employed in the countries of unburned brick. Here we can only indicate in a few words the profusion of forms from the very outset open to Christian art, growing up as it did on the borderland between East and West. Religion itself became the agency through which the different indigenous styles were exchanged and diffused. Our ideas on this subject have hitherto been far from clear ; the extraordinarily fascinating art of the first millennium and the subsequent development of ' styles ' in the West have always been regarded as a purely European affair, which is by no means the case. The court art of the ancient East, or, later, of Rome and Byzantium, never exercised so decisive an influence as the various national styles of architecture ; these were of wood in the North, of varying material in the South, of brick in Mesopotamia and Iran, accompanied, in the latter case, by an almost unimaginable variety of decorative linings. Just as the constructional basis of development is best inferred from Christian vaulted building, so is the decorative foundation inferred in the most convincing manner possible from the art of Armenia and Islam. Historians have hitherto regarded Christianity and Islam, the last two religions with historical founders, as embodying two diametrically opposed tendencies in art. That they might both have sprung, to some extent, from a common source was suspected by nobody, except in so far as the traditional reference was made to classical influence. The development of Christian art was determined by the fact that it chose the interior of buildings for decoration, and that it lived out its allotted time in the Mediterranean area; Islam chose the open court, and in the field of decoration entered upon the inheritance of Iran. In Europe, curiously enough, the ancient timbered style was again revived for roof construction under Southern influence at the end of the Roman period. Of the purely wooden architecture characteristic of the Northern peoples nothing has survived from the first millennium, and its artistic qualities are practically unknown. But Scandinavian wooden churches of more recent date plainly indicate whence 'Gothic' derived much of its organic character; the Oseberg ship, Urnäs and early Teutonic antiquities suggest that the birth of 'Gothic' did not so much imply a complete change arising out of stone construction as the logical development of the feeling for organic growth. Its original non-representational style was sacrificed to an increasing luxuriance of figures. Italy borrowed the idea from the North, taking the figures out of their architectural setting and adapting them to a nearer view. I shall not refer to painting again at this point.

The introduction of the decorative wall-linings of the East into the Roman basilica, and particularly into the vaulted apse, led to a completely new orientation in the art of the Western Mediterranean as well as in that which succeeded it in Europe. The Eastern ideas which accompanied vaulting were incorporated in the wooden-roofed basilica; we thus have the most surprising of alliances, that between an effete organic architecture and decorative wall-lining. The combination at a later time found approval in the North, where in wooden buildings decoration is confined to the covering of surfaces with design.

Whether I set out from East or from North, I invariably find confirmation of the conclusion reached by Gottfried Semper, though by a wrong use of historical evidence, that material and work are prime factors in the development of art. And again, if I consider that modern as distinct from classical art in Europe begins with the period of the great migrations, I still find it necessary to place the influence of craftsmanship at the head, whether it finds expression in plaited or woven materials, or in carved or incised work in wood, metal, or leather. At the beginning of the Christian era the Germanic peoples pressing down towards the South still maintained that intimate feeling for craftsmanship, which goes back, apparently, to neolithic times, and served as a foundation for their whole sense of artistic values. The need of the subject or the figure was rarely felt by them ; they were interested only in things and their decoration.

II. *Spiritual Values*

The religious man sees the world through spectacles, only removable when he is free from the dictates of the Church, or of State and Church acting together. Both of these forces victimize ; artists, nations, and cultures are all sacrificed to the lust after expansion of power. We have observed how communities originally created their own art, and how at a later time Church and State intervened with fatal effect. Freedom is essential to the artist ; his individuality shrinks at the tyrannical infliction of restraint ; serving the artistic ends of power, which makes him its tool, he degenerates only too often into the journeyman of art. The result is seen in a monotonous repetition of subjects and figures ; form loses its content, and development runs on to the worn-out rails of ' style '. It is the task of research to reveal a flowering-time of art only possible through religious freedom and often only attained at the price of bitter conflict ; it was a time so fruitful that it may inspire us even to-day. On the other hand so-called ' styles ' may be of service to modern craftsmen, and in some degree, though less directly, to the artist. Research clears vision only when it interprets, not when it merely classifies and describes ; only so can it reveal the origin of determinant values. Thoughtful artists even more than the educated public of the day have the right to demand such interpretation from research.

The general historian may find his account in giving special prominence to communities of artificial origin, in this particular case Church and State ; but for the specialist, soil, nationality, and the individual artist are the obvious foundations of research. Personality, in the sense of a natural unit, whether of the mass or the individual, is the only creative power, and not the artificial community. A history of art which attributes greater importance to the exploiting will than to original creative impulse may comprehend a fettered imitation, an art which is no art ; it is helpless to explain that which casts into the stream of development new and fruitful ideas. The recurrence of the same artistic values throughout Europe in the sixteenth and seventeenth centuries is due partly to the infectious influence of fashion, which accompanied the northward march of Court, Church, and Humanism, and was only resisted by a Rembrandt at the cost of poverty; partly also to a counteracting assertion of Northern influence in the South. In early Christian times the growing power and wealth of Church and State produced the same results.

Religious movements have rarely confined themselves to the lands of their origin and growth; ecumenical religions, in particular, spread their conquests far and wide. Christianity did not expand at a stroke like Islam; it knew centuries of freedom. It was not until about A.D. 300 that it became a militant power spreading in every direction. But it was during the earlier centuries of freedom that those forms of art arose which were to determine the course of its later development. We must not be misled by the fact that Rome in the fourth and fifth centuries, Byzantium in the fifth and sixth, each found its own direction within the compass of the wider currents. It was not the arbitrary welding of artistic values in these places which counted, but the units which were welded, the values which, in despite of Church and State, brought their native quality in all its freedom to peoples always, or at least for periods, unswayed either by Byzantium or Rome.

Significance. The opinion has been held that the essential character of Christian art may be inferred from the deeper meanings by which it is penetrated. This view involves contradictions, since there is obviously present a simultaneous and very powerful influence acting immediately upon the senses. One need only call to mind the recognition, not to say the admiration, bestowed upon mosaics by contemporary art critics; in this result the chief part is played by mere colour; remoteness from nature comes second, seeming pure expression. The juxtaposition presents a problem which can only be solved if we remember that Christian art combines within itself a number of distinct artistic currents, not to be confused, and springing from the most diverse sources, historical, geographical, racial, national. The gradual discovery of the East was a necessary preliminary to its solution. Byzantium was the first to be revealed; then came Asia Minor, Syria, and Egypt; finally, Mesopotamia, Armenia, and Iran; for me, it is now the turn of Northern Europe—so many names, so many distinct streams of influence, or transformations due to the blending in varying measure of such currents. These complex values are very different from those of Mazdaism or Hellenism which preceded, or those of Islam which succeeded them. But taken singly, they yet have their points of resemblance. It would be easier to define the character of each of these religious units by its negative than by its positive qualities. But the crucial factor in Christian art is not, as might appear, an arbitrary and enslaving will, but rather the vital impulse which reached it from the East and inspired it to fresh creative effort. This is especially apparent under various forms in the transitional period, when it passed from the East and South to Europe and the North.

2. *Subject* (Purpose). The form of the church was not at first everywhere or exclusively determined by its function as a place of assembly for the community. In Armenia, for example, that is to say in the ancient Mazdean culture area, it appears to have been permanently influenced by the form of the founder's tomb, although nothing is actually known of the tomb of Zarathustra. The same influence, albeit in an indirect and borrowed form, was possibly stronger even in Byzantium than is at present recognized. In Nisibis a church and a tomb-like baptistery still stand side by side in their original form except for their roofs, which have been partially restored ; the baptistery, together with the porch, is built on the South side of the church. The kind of building which followed the death of Saint James (A.D. 338) does not seem to have become the general rule. In Armenia the actual founder's tomb was enlarged for use as an assembly hall, the single building performing a double function, like the church of S. Peter in later times. In the fifth century, when the Church wished to introduce the vaulted long building as the type, it found an obstacle in this firmly-rooted style ; the result was the fusion of the domed with the long-naved building.

It was otherwise in the Mediterranean area. There the timber-roofed long building was the prevailing form of assembly hall from the earliest times. In Jerusalem, Constantine placed it next to the tomb, from which it was separated by an atrium on an axis running from West to East. It would be a task in itself to make a thorough study of the relations between these two practical types ; but we may note at once that at the tomb of S. Vitale in Ravenna, as well as in that of Charles the Great at Aix-la-Chapelle, the domed building served the second purpose of an assembly hall ; on the other hand, the tombs of Constantine in Constantinople and of Galla Placidia were domed structures, built from the first adjoining a cruciform church. Is not this a clear case of the partial influence of Eastern usage in the relationship between the form and function of a building ? This is a question which naturally does not arise in the case of the timber-roofed basilica of the West. The building with a main axis existed there from the very first ; but it is foreign to the church of Armenia in its earliest period. In that country the central square bay has four apsidal buttresses, of which that on the Eastern side appears by an afterthought to have been converted into an apse when a dais for the altar was introduced. Discoveries in Carinthia also indicate that the altar space and the hemicycle where the clergy sat were probably quite distinct in origin.

The fact is that the method of orientating churches varies in the West and on the Eastern coast of the Mediterranean, whereas the apsidal buttresses of Armenian domed churches without exception mark the four cardinal points. Here, as well as in Asia Minor, the long church was consistently orientated towards the East, and from these regions the practice was diffused in all directions. On the coast of Syria, and in Egypt and North Africa, the introduction of an Eastern apse opposite to the ancient Western apse produced the church with double choir, a type of which we seem to trace the influence on the early art of Western Europe. It is not impossible that the practice of orientation in the pioneer districts of Armenia was due to pre-Christian ideas, connected perhaps with the Mazdean sun-cult ; in this connexion we may recall the association of dawn clouds with the ideas of redemption and of the Last Judgement (p. 180).

On the other hand the later combination of church and assembly hall appears to have been due to the influence of classical temples, and to occur first in the church in which the main axis is longitudinal. My attitude is, throughout, that of an observer ; discerning theologians will find suggestion here without need of any lessons from me. Was the whole of the church treated as a place of worship, or was only a certain section of the large assembly hall set aside for this purpose ? In Armenia an altar-dais was introduced as a special feature in the Eastern portion of a building radially planned round a central bay with a high dome with vertical axis ; this altar was raised about three feet above the space left for the congregation, and approached by two lateral flights of steps. The unity of the building was thereby destroyed. One seems to see the origin of those later liturgical representations of the Last Supper, in which Christ appears as priest by the ciborium distributing bread on one side and wine on the other to the apostles approaching from right and left.

In the Mediterranean area the altar was placed at the end of the long nave. This arrangement had the merit of preserving artistic unity ; but it introduced a perpetual conflict between the upward view into the dome (even after its removal from its original central position) and the perspective view into the apse.

In the Mediterranean the only type accepted by the Church was the long assembly hall with the main axis longitudinal ; where we find the domed type of building, we must ascribe it to the interference of temporal power, which introduced it from the East in order to gratify its desire for effect. This is the most probable explanation of S. Lorenzo at Milan, and certainly of S. Vitale at Ravenna and the imperial chapel at Aix-la-Chapelle. The plan of the two latter buildings was not determined by the founder's tomb alone. The introduction of galleries suggests that they were also intended to serve as imperial assembly-halls. It was otherwise in Armenia ; there the dome originally prevailed to the exclusion of all other types ; Zwarthnotz was probably also intended by Nerses III to serve as a kind of imperial hall. But after the alliance of the Armenian Church, in the fifth century, with Nisibis, Edessa, and Byzantium, a tendency towards length of nave set in, and this type for a time prevailed, in accordance with Canon 182, though still in conjunction with the dome. It thus appears that the tendencies of East and West were in opposite directions. A compromise was first reached in the intermediate region, the dome being generally adopted by the Orthodox Church. In the West the influence of Iran secured its first triumph during the height of the Renaissance in the church of S. Peter, its second in the church in which Vignola crowned the attempts of Leonardo and Bramante by constructing his famous domed hall-church for the Jesuit order. In just such a way Armenian architects had succeeded centuries before.

A. *Non-representational Decoration.* The decoration, like the construction of churches, had originally a practical aim ; it had significance without any second purpose alien to the principle of art for its own sake. Its object was to heighten the effect of the exterior mass and the interior space of the building, and this was achieved by the use of light and colour, the starting-point being line and ornamented surface ; the human figure was excluded, as in the case of the nomadic and Northern races. This type of decoration seems to have been permeated with symbolism even in Mazdean times. Animal- and plant-motives, introduced as vehicles of Hvarenah, that is, the glory of God, imparted a religious atmosphere to the purely decorative wall-linings. This style was transmitted both to Christianity and Islam; the former developed its symbolism still further and combined it with representations of a purely objective character.

Sculpture and painting are usually called the representational arts in the narrower sense of the term; but this is incorrect. There are many artistic provinces which practised sculpture and painting, but did not represent; the religious art of ancient Iran was found to belong to this order, and also ancient Chinese and Teutonic art. Again, following the track of the nomadic races south-west of Iran, we came upon the same thing among the Jews and Arabs. Christian art, in its earliest period, belonged to this non-representational group of Northern races and pastoral nomads, who used ornament of wood, stucco, and stone, and painted in colours, but did not represent. I was compelled to take architecture as my starting-point, since Christian art did not originally, like late-Hellenistic, produce paintings or sculptures designed for near and intimate contemplation, but confined itself to the decoration of buildings and objects of personal use. When figures of Christ and the chief apostles were first produced in the fourth century, they caused general indignation even among the Greeks and Aramaeans, who later became the most determined agents in the diffusion of picture-worship; so great was the change wrought upon the spirit of Christianity in the course of time by Church, State, and general culture. Hellenism, with the patronage of Church and State, triumphed over popular non-representational art; the latter revived somewhat under the influence of the Middle Ages and the iconoclastic movement; the Renaissance once more accepted the sole dictatorship of Hellenism, while 'Baroque' made extravagant use of both styles. We are only just beginning to recognize the primordial nature of non-representational art, and many years must elapse before we can fully realize its fundamental significance.

The decoration of Christian churches was designed for mass effect and intended to be seen from a distance. The first Christian masters had no thought of figure sculpture such as that of Greek temple architecture, nor of painted representations like those found in the interiors of Pompeii or in the Catacombs. The nature of the wall was not destroyed ; it retained its character as a flat surface covered with a decorative lining. It is therefore futile to confine the treatment of early Christian art to a study of types, and this study itself to the region of sepulchral art. This is deliberately to ignore the crucial importance of church art, and to substitute false light for the true.

B. *Representational Decoration.* Like architecture and the decorative art associated with it, representational decoration differs in character according to its origin. The differences are in this case, however, not geographically conditioned, but by the will of authority and by racial factors. The East-Aryans and Armenians drop out, except for the fertilizing effect of Mazdean ideas which were translated by Southern art into representational form. Representational art derived its distinctive features from the West-Aryans and from the Semitic empires. The West-Aryans had a preference for symbolic representation until Greece and Rome adopted the policy of the old Semitic monarchies. The chief vehicle of this symbolism, as in all representational art, was the human figure. Originally the West-Aryans never depicted God as a human being endowed with power; this was an illusion practised by the Semites, though not by the Jews. Indian art, again, rigidly excluded the anthropomorphic treatment of God until the Hellenistic style was introduced into Gandhâra.

In place of architectural decoration, designed purely for artistic and symbolic effect, the Church about A. D. 400 introduced representation for didactic purposes, and with it Semitic traditions. Previous to this date the non-representational style of Iran and Armenia, as well as of Judaism, had prevailed, at least so far as church architecture was concerned. As this representational art flourished on the same soil from which the Buddhist art of Gandhâra derived, it probably grew up at a period during which intercourse between Asia Minor and India still existed In monumental art, however, symbolic representations of the idea of redemption had established themselves from the very first, as I have already explained. It is significant that no trace of this art was introduced into Church decoration—Achthamar, A.D. 915–921 is an exception—and that its development shows a sudden and abrupt transition from the decorative to the didactic style.

Generally speaking, the Semitic style very soon began to predominate in church representation ; this style was essentially realistic. Thus Christ appears as a Semite, generally as a judge enthroned with the Christian book of the law in his left hand, and his right hand raised ; the Virgin appears not as the simple Mother, or as interceding for mankind, but enthroned as the Mother of God. Both are surrounded by figures of angels and saints, who keep the Founder at a proper distance, and thus resemble the figures of the minor deities in a Gudea relief at Berlin. The hope of redemption is no longer depicted in parallel scenes from the Old and New Testaments, but is associated with the Apocalyptic conception of the Last Judgement. This is supplemented by didactic biblical scenes resembling in treatment those Semitic series of biographical subjects dictated by the ruler's insatiable desire to dazzle the people by personal display and to give weight and permanence even to the most trivial details of his life. Self-glorification and irresponsible autocracy determine in like manner these representations of the deity.

The stream of Semitic representation appears to have sprung from the intellectual centre in Northern Mesopotamia, though probably not before the severance of the old Hellenistic relations which had connected Asia Minor with India; the chief gate through which it communicated with the Mediterranean was Antioch, the secondary gates to North and South were Constantinople and Jerusalem. This was the style of church art which won permanent acceptance ; one of its aims was to depict God, or the Church, as the Judge and Teacher, another to instruct the illiterate, a third to make such dogmatic manifestoes as that on the triumphal arch of S. Maria Maggiore or in the choir of S. Vitale. It maintained these aims simultaneously throughout all periods. Artistically speaking it hardly ever rises above the subservient rôle assigned to it by the Church, and the artists were, naturally, never mentioned by name. Subsequently, in the sixth century, came the intrusive influence of the Byzantine Court. The cycles fixed by the Church were heightened to the point of dazzling effect by accentuating magnificence, and, in the representation of persons, by displaying Christ and Mary in all the bravery of court splendour. The climax in effect was reached when angel guards take the place of human witnesses. A decisive impetus seems to have been given to the cult of the Virgin by the imperial foundations at the Church of the Nativity at Bethlehem.

In the West the ideas transmitted from Nisibis by Cassiodorus flourished and grew up into a great system which clearly betrays the didactic basis, and the nature of that ecclesiastical philosophy which was only broken, in so far as it affected art, by the rise of lay craftsmen in the towns.

The idea of the subject as now understood was first introduced into Christian art by the theological schools of Nisibis; the idea, that is, of an event depicted for its own sake, and so in the present case, historically. Here we see the old Semitic spirit at work. The conception is inherent in a didactic and hieroglyphic style; the one aim is the clear rendering of the object. It is well illustrated in Byzantine art and, earlier, in the school of Gandhâra.

This ecclesiastical influence very soon turned to dogmatic illustration. Learned expositions of dogma were evolved like those on the triumphal arch of S. Maria Maggiore, in the church of S. Vitale, and other places; it is a tendency which permeates the whole of mediaeval art, attaining its due consummation in scholasticism and the works of Thomas Aquinas. Mere objective fact is emphasized to such a degree that all other elements recede into the background and form is, as far as possible, replaced by geometrical division. The student cannot be too clearly warned not to regard this changed view of the significant as the main factor in the development of mediaeval art, as has recently been done in a work entitled ' Idealism and Materialism in Gothic Sculpture and Painting '.

Appearance. It is true, as a general observation, that religious emotion creates forms, and that the Church stereotypes these into permanent shapes. Hence it comes about that only the first four centuries of our era were essentially creative. In this period arose, or were selected from the previously existing stock, those appearance-values which give to early Christian art its essential character and supply the materials upon which later artists worked, bringing them together in various ways to form fresh units, or subordinating them to new values conditioned by place, time, and cultural environment. In the West the movement began with the traditions of the Mediterranean area, those of the Semites and the East-Aryans. The great migrations led to fresh developments in this region, and to the adoption of new types differing from those of early Christian times. A logical development of Eastern values took place in the West, leading eventually in the North to the so-called ' Gothic ' style; this North-Aryan creative achievement was unhappily brought to a premature close by the ill-considered adoption of Italian Renaissance art. A few great masters now stood out in intellectual prominence ; but the general masses merely accommodated themselves to the demands of State, Church, and Humanism ; in this way there originated styles which spread throughout the whole of Western Europe. Eastern Europe, for the most part, remained faithful to the style established by the Orthodox Church.

The units of shape and form fall into two distinct groups : the first of these is characterized by its imitation of nature or of types derived from earlier art ; the second by its independent treatment of mass, space, light, and colour. We might say that the whole of Christian art, from its beginnings to A.D. 1600, lies between a world of nature-imitation in process of decay and another world in which that imitation was deliberately resumed. Had not the spirit of Nisibis won the day with its objective method of edification, carried into effect by Syro-Hellenistic types, the effort to attain form through the symbol might have remained the fundamental principle of Christian art. The Iranian East and the Teutonic North both, like the Hellas of earlier times, strove in this direction, though the means which they employed were different.

3. *Shape*. Christian Church architecture sprang from such diverse sources that we cannot say of any particular shape that it was typical, in the sense in which the classical temple was a type. This diversity embraced not only raw material and technique ; it extended also to the use of the building whether as founder's tomb, place of worship, baptistery, or assembly hall, as the case might be ; thus the artist's freedom was necessarily limited by the conditions under which he worked, even when authority permitted him to exercise his own choice in the matter of form, provided always that he produced something impressive and monumental in character. When he worked in the central seats of Church or State he adopted such outward forms as he found ready to hand. He created no new types of building, but merely heightened the effect by increasing the proportions of those already existing. In the matter of decoration he was equally un-inventive, contenting himself with introducing Eastern features into the West, just as, at an earlier date, Western features had been brought to the East through the medium of Hellenism ; such was the state of affairs until the North asserted its influence, to be followed almost immediately by the humanistic and classical revival in the South.

A. *Constructional Form*.   Historians of art have always shown a predilection for this in their works ; they have classified it into ' styles ', laying special stress upon similarities in ground-plan, elevation, and ornament.   In the sphere of early Christian architecture this was simple enough.   The basilica was taken as the type ; it consisted of a central nave between columned arcades and terminating in an apse ; on either side was an aisle closed on the outer side by a wall ; above was a clerestory. Domed buildings did not fit conveniently into this scheme ; but as they only occurred in isolated instances, they could be treated as belated survivals of classical architecture.

My books *Kleinasien* and *Amida*, published in 1903 and 1910, made us acquainted with the vaulted long churches in Cappadocia and Mesopotamia.   The facts were disturbing, and every effort was made to force the date of these churches into the mediaeval period.   There was much excitement in certain quarters ; accusations of dilettantism were made, and even of disingenuous procedure.   What will be said now that Iran and Armenia have come into the very foremost rank with their domed architecture ? An end has been made of the easy old classification by ' styles ', each with its distinguishing marks, counted on the fingers, and of its modern substitute, faith in the sole dominion of arbitrary laws in the historical explanation of style.   Three architectural types, each with its own wide area of distribution, existed side by side as early as the fourth century; these were : (1) the East-Aryan dome upon a square plan ; (2) the Semitic church with transverse nave, vaulted in Mesopotamia, and furnished in East Syria with the South-Arabian stone-roofed arches ; (3) the West-Aryan timber-roofed long building which was given a vaulted roof in the East. These three types maintained a separate existence, despite the aggression of the West-Aryan church.   The dome soon triumphed in the middle region at Constantinople ; the barrel-vault at a later period in the West, until here too the dome at last made its way with the Renaissance.   These types were not Hellenistic in origin.   Only the basilica was Greek in its three-aisled form and its clerestory ; its timbered roof was displaced by forms indigenous to the East.

Amid this surprising diversity of local forms which became distinctive types, it was not so easy for the Church entirely to check the diffusion of national forms by the different peoples. But accepting, as she did, only forms sanctioned by liturgical needs, she in fact succeeded in imposing the long-naved type of church. At Rome her success was complete, not so at the imperial capitals of Milan, Ravenna, and above all Constantinople. These seats of temporal power were, indeed, quick to recognize the single dome as a form of architectural expression ; its demand for the absolute subordination of all the parts to the whole agreed with their own principles, and they set it in effective opposition to the demands of the Church. While Roman church architecture was stagnating in the monotonous uniformity of the timber-roofed basilica, Armenian and other architectural forms forced an entry into the West, at first by way of the Eastern and Western imperial capitals, afterwards by routes that left them on one side. This partly explains the abrupt appearance of the single dome in the West. It was otherwise with the barrel-vaulted long-naved church, the diffusion of which from East to West was effected by gradual stages. The Roman Catholic, unlike the Byzantine Orthodox Church, was never in complete subjection to a Court ; it was thus able to hold out against the dome, though eventually succumbing to the barrel-vault.

B. *Decoration.* Much is explained by the fact that, in the matter of decoration, the long-naved church of the Mediterranean contented itself with marble columns and painted and gilded wooden ceiling, a limitation also observed by Constantine in the Church of the Holy Sepulchre at Jerusalem. All other kinds of decoration were later additions, and derived from the Eastern art of covering walls with sumptuous linings. As regards exterior decoration, a distinction was observed between the wooden-roofed churches which rejected it and the vaulted church which practised it from the very first. In the West, in the same manner, exterior decoration was exceptional until after the introduction of the vault.

In spite of the tenacity with which the church in the Mediterranean area clung to Hellenistic traditions in architecture, Eastern influence ultimately prevailed ; this is perhaps most clearly proved by the fact that it was not construction but the covering of walls with decoration which really influenced the builders. Northern (Gothic) art, with its traditional feeling for construction derived from its work in wood, was the first to reintroduce organic methods, though it started from the pier and the vault, not from the classical column. Down to Gothic times all Christian architecture, even the columned basilica, was really so much walling decoratively lined. Whether it was executed in the simple and popular style, as in Armenia, or received, as at Constantinople, the rich embellishment characteristic of work done in the sphere of Court influence makes no essential difference.

The change which took place in the capital is significant. The appearance of the acanthus in Greece and of other plant forms in the North marks the transition from pure construction to the imitation of natural forms. Such a development was impossible in the East, since the ideas of the simply articulated building and of realistic representation were entirely foreign to the Eastern mind. When in the Mediterranean area it actually came to making the decorated capital look like a basket, and by a still more audacious step, like a basket with beasts and birds upon its top, what we have before us is nothing more nor less than a frankly Hellenistic version of an Iranian idea.

The Church concerned herself exclusively with distinctive types, preferably with those upon which it has set its official seal; pure form was to her of minor importance. Every movement in the direction of artistic freedom was hampered, by regulations, by old tradition, and by the rules in Painters' Manuals; we must therefore draw a clear line of demarcation between ecclesiastical and real religious art. At the present time we take it absolutely for granted that religious feeling must express itself by means of the human figure. This is one of the chief causes which have almost deprived us of the capacity to distinguish between art and representation.

C. *Representation.* In the treatment of the human figure, the essential difference between Hellenistic and early Christian art lies in the fact that the representation of the one is taken direct from nature, that of the other is derived from ideas. The most impossible theories have been advanced in explanation of this fact. I need only mention the latest, according to which Neo-Platonism and, in formative art, illusionism are supposed to have substituted for the sensualism of classical art a spiritualism, regarded as the basis from which the structure of all mediaeval art was to rise. But quite apart from the connexion of Neo-Platonism with the East, through the Indian doctrine of Yoga (Conrady), the development of art in the transitional period from classical to mediaeval was not determined by the fashions and catch-phrases of large towns, as development is to-day. The creative energies of mankind, even within the limits of the then civilized world, were by no means exhausted. Later classical art indeed, whether 'immanent' or 'autonomous', had indeed lost all creative power ; it lay in its last throes at the mercy of the East-Aryan reaction which now broke out after centuries of repression, and succeeded in obtaining full recognition even in an unfamiliar domain, that of representational art. To East-Aryan influence was due that non-natural envisagement of figure subjects which was destined to prevail throughout the Middle Ages ; the new kind of vision implied an earlier state of non-representational art in which abstract form predominated. This change did not affect the catacomb paintings or the sarcophagus sculptures, the figures of which are in the direct line of classical tradition. It showed itself most markedly in figures on the monumental scale and, above all, in that of the vaulted apse, on which the eyes of the congregation were naturally focussed. Of course no anatomist would ever think of using the figures of early Christian art for the study of human anatomy ; even the mosaics of outstanding artistic excellence are synthetic compositions pieced together out of classical elements. This applies especially to the drapery, to which heads and hands are merely attached in their proper places, without any suggestion of a lifelike figure supporting them and giving them cohesion ; much less of that art, in which the Greek excelled, of bringing out the significance of limb and joint through the drapery that overlies them. The human figure was reduced to a symbol, and was used, in the scheme adopted by the church, just like the written letter. The figure-compositions, like the landscapes, were merely collections of such symbols. The types were used to represent Christ, the Virgin Mary, and the Apostles, and were absolutely fixed ; they were as obvious and as familiar as the letters of the alphabet. At this period art was even less identified than at other times with the treatment of the solid figure. The type, such as it was, was taken over from classical art, and only given naturalistic traits when portraiture was attempted. The treatment of landscape has been fully discussed in connexion with the subject of Hvarenah.

Thus the interaction of Hellenistic, Iranian, and Semitic influences produced a remarkable change in the classical treatment of solid figures. The three-dimensional rounding off of the body disappears, the figure is flattened, modelling persists only in a perfunctory way, lighting and shading to indicate depth are abandoned or survive in the most rudimentary form. Things continued after this fashion until the great period of North-Christian art revived a feeling for organic structure. How are we to interpret the change which took place at the end of the classical period?

Late classical art itself shows a very striking development from modelling in tone to the abrupt contrast of light and shadow, producing a similar effect to that of contrasting colour. The result was obtained by the use of the drill, the chosen instrument for the purpose. The process was marked at the beginning by virtuosity in the detachment of the figure from its background. The impulse to this change probably came, as in India, from the purely decorative art of wall covering in Northern Iran. The movement very soon produced a reaction; the surface-filling flat figure completed by colour came into its rights; the classical types appeared flattened, and all sense of three-dimensional space was eliminated. Only a meagre remnant of the antique style lingered on in the almost hieroglyphic representational art affected by the Semites, of which ancient models might still be seen in the old Mesopotamian palaces and reliefs on triumphal columns. The theological school of Nisibis then created the artistic 'Canon' which was to dominate the whole of mediaeval art. This still admitted some tendency towards realism especially in portraiture, as is evident from the 'Edessene' types of Christ, S. Peter, S. Paul, and others. The appearance of these types must be later than that of the Hellenistic types of Christ and Buddha created in Asia Minor and Gandhâra.

By the side of this broad stream of Semitic art certain classical reminiscences continued to survive here and there, both in the technique of painting and in the types presented.

The reaction from a conventional to a naturalistic art is first seen in the architectural church sculpture of the North, which introduced not only animal and plant figures into the ornament of its constructional members but also those of men, and so transmitted them to Italy. There the Humanistic movement, involving the study of classical forms, and, even more, the awakening demand for scientific knowledge, led to a predominance of observation at close range, and, as a result, to a more or less exact imitation of natural forms. Hence arose the common belief that correctness in delineation was the supreme object of art. The subjective treatment of form was at times almost forgotten.

4. *Design*. It is in the province of form that the contrast appears most marked between the Hellenistic and Christian classical art on the one hand, with their partly non-artistic methods, and the new East-Aryan stream on the other. In the catacombs

the walls are covered with representations with a lack of feeling for interior spatial effect as conspicuous as that shown by Buddhism. Only the Iranian East continued to treat interiors as a medium of artistic expression in themselves and dispensed with representation entirely. This comes out most clearly in the domed churches of Armenia, the nobility of which, like that of the earliest Doric and later Northern (early Gothic) buildings, lay in the purity of their architecture ; all decoration in the form of painting and sculpture was at first almost wholly rejected, and subsequently treated as altogether subordinate to the architectonic plan. In Armenian buildings exterior effect was produced by mass, the interior effect by space ; the decoration in both cases was held in restraint.

It is otherwise with Christian classical architecture in the Mediterranean area. There the exteriors are neglected, the interiors form an incongruous patchwork made up to suit the exigencies of the moment. The columns are brought together anyhow from older buildings, except in cases where the hand of authority intervened to produce uniformity. The interior decorations, executed with an especial object in Rome, Ravenna, Parenzo, and other places, are all borrowed from East-Aryan vaulted architecture and thence transferred to the long building now regularly demanded by the Church. This is the case with all the new forms of the capital brought from the quarries of the sea of Marmora, and to a large extent also with the surface linings of floors and walls, especially those in mosaic. Owing to the way in which they were constructed out of small cubes designed for curved surfaces, mosaics can only have reached their highest level of artistic excellence in the vaulted architecture of the East ; how high that level was can be seen from the earliest and best-known churches that have survived, so far as their mosaics are not mere imitations of paintings or even of miniatures transferred to the available space on wall and roof. A good criterion is afforded by the decoration of the apse. This was at first purely formal and non-representational in style, or consisted of a landscape with the cross; it is only about the beginning of the fifth century that human figures make their appearance which, in their disposition of mass, space, light, and colour, rival in importance the structure itself and its decoration.

A. *Mass*. The idea, derived from Graeco-Roman and Italian art, that buildings should have one particular side, the façade, designed to impress the spectator, has diverted the attention of art-historians from mass as such, from one of the essential values in formative art. If we look at an Armenian church, even one built after the combination of the long nave and the dome (Fig. 12, facing p. 72), we notice that it has no true façade, but is intended to impress the spectator by the totality of its structural mass from whatever side it is viewed. In the timber-roofed basilica on the other hand, as in the ancient temple, special importance is given to the gabled end. Thus in our impression of the exterior a single wall takes the place of the whole structure. Hildebrand's *Problem der Form* is a good illustration of the extent to which we have accustomed ourselves to the classical point of view. Naïvely assuming the self-evident nature of his views, an assumption only to be explained by a long and one-sided devotion to the study of classical and Renaissance art, he treats the question of relief as alone admissible in artistic appreciation, though it may be admitted that he is primarily thinking of sculpture. But if we recall the Armenian centralized church with niche-buttresses as it existed in the fourth century before the introduction of a long axis, a building not unlike the dome of the cathedral at Florence as it would appear without its nave, we must admit that this Christian type of structure was well fitted to introduce a wholly new ideal, opposed to that inspiring the antique temple, an ideal in which centralization and height, rather than concentration upon the façade, were the outstanding features. Only the influence of Hellenism and the Church, with their adherence to the classical plan with long major axis, prevented the development of the centralized church, which would otherwise have become the standard type in Northern (Gothic) architecture. The remarkable contest waged after the time of Leonardo and Bramante by certain of their successors, who favoured the execution of the original design for S. Peter's, had been anticipated in the East more than a thousand years earlier. The feeling for mass in architectural design clearly exerted an influence upon Eastern painting of the early Christian period.

The use of ornament to accentuate the effect of mass was at first naturally confined to the East. In Armenia blind arcading like an embroidery in delicate low relief after the Persian style forms a strong contrast with the massiveness of the whole building; in Mesopotamia the edges of the roofs with their alternating bands of light and shade, in Syria the mouldings of similar character round the windows, and, most important of all, the development of a regular church façade, derived in part from the Hittite Khilani, all served this common end. The last-named feature was the prototype of that later Western type of façade which consisted of a porch flanked by towers. On the other hand, door and portal in Christian architecture were derived from Armenia, and combined with Syrian traditions to form those magnificent Northern façades, which the Renaissance was unable to understand, because it misunderstood the character of antique columns, and utilized them not as working members but as mere decorative features.

In representational art the Semitic arrangement in zones prevents the fusion into a single mass-unit of different groups, which are sometimes massive in themselves. Only in the apse, as once in the gable, do we find a pronounced feeling for construction. At the apex of a pyramidal group, generally somewhat loosely compacted, rises the figure of Christ, which appears erect, although in reality it follows the curve of the surface.

In the North, at a later time, church art transformed mass into dynamic energy, which became a new source of quickened life. The close alliance with the builder's art exerted a wholesome restraint upon the rules of form ; in Italy this alliance was all too readily dissolved, thus paving the way for an inartistic realism at times pursued to a point at which it becomes positively repulsive. Humanism then proclaimed itself dispenser of classicism and of salvation.

One word more on the subject of line in its relation to mass. The mischievous use of the term ' Gothic ', begun by Vasari, shows how little we have yet learnt to appreciate the importance of the Goths as carriers of culture. We are here concerned primarily with the use of the line as a medium of expression. To the representational South the human figure was a puppet, its type selected, its attitudes, gestures, and features all arranged for a play-acting mistaken for true expression. But in the North, in Iran and Armenia, all effects are produced solely by means of abstract form, by the use of lines at rest or in movement, in harmony or in contrast ; the contribution of colour in enhancing the effect of line cannot for the moment be defined. As examples of linear expression we may quote the geometric devices of Islamic art, derived from Iran, and the figures of animals in motion which occur on early Northern bronze ornaments and on the panels of the wooden church of Urnäs (fig. 56, facing p. 153). In their use of line and colour the art of India and China are alike related to that of the region between the Oxus and the Altai.

At this point it is particularly important to recall how strongly the formal influence reacted upon the human figure as soon as it was adopted by Northern art. Examples earlier than 'Gothic' exist in the south of France as well as in Armenia.[1] The result is seen during the great period of Northern Christian art when the figure itself is neglected and the drapery becomes the real medium of expression. A change first occurred when the North learned on its own account to observe the human figure ; the movement was taken up and developed in Italy, where it led to the study of the nude and the reversion to classical models. Drapery in Egyptian art lies stiffly upon the body ; in Greek art it sometimes clings to the figure as if wet, after the Southern style, while at other times, as in the North, it develops into a system of folds which sweeps with ease and freedom across the body in the perfection of rhythmic line.

B. *Space*. The artistic value of space, in its narrower sense as a homogeneous interior, was first understood so far as Christian art is concerned by the East-Aryans ; it is first found actually developed in Armenia. The original function of an interior space as a place of assembly for the community was soon combined with that of a house of worship. Thus spiritual unity corresponded to the building standing free and compact, and might well have found satisfaction in a dome over a central altar, a plan possibly occurring in Armenia during the fourth century.

The building with lengthened nave first destroyed this unity ; the genius of the architect who created the domed hall-church, or that of a Vignola, was needed to restore it even in part. The horizontal view focussed on the apse, as opposed to the upward view into the dome, was at first the usual disposition in the Mediterranean area, where it was associated with the triple division of the nave by rows of columns. The provenance of the semi-circular apse and of orientation is still an open question ; they were certainly first definitely accepted in the interior of Asia Minor, and in Eastern Syria and Armenia. The whole of the North gradually fell under the influence of the triple-aisled type, and centralization was sacrificed to length. Centralization, proceeding from Armenia, only succeeded in making its way into Constantinople and the

[1] The reader is referred to my book on Armenia, ii. pp. 811 f., and advised to compare the portals of Moissac, Autun, and other examples.

architecture of the Orthodox Church ; here, by degrees, it entirely superseded the long nave, though the struggle between dome and apse continued.

Just as the façade destroyed the feeling for structural mass, so the long nave was fatal to the feeling for interior space as a compact unity. At first the basilica and the domed building existed independently side by side, the former directing the eye horizontally into distance, the latter upwards into height. Their amalgamation gave rise to a conflict between centre and dome on the one hand, and distance and altar on the other. In places like Armenia, where the dome formed the starting-point in the development of the communal church, its central position was retained. But where the basilica was the original type, the influence of the horizontal view forced the dome out of the centre in the direction of the apse. It was the theologians of Nisibis who succeeded in settling the conflict, at least so far as representational decoration was concerned ; they retained the cross in the apse as the symbol of sacrifice and redemption, and placed the figure of Christ Pantokrator in the cupola, thus giving representational expression to the meaning of the dome.

The Christian was the first religious art to utilize interior space for the expression of its constructional ideas. It is of course possible that it was anticipated in this by some form of domed temple in connexion with fire-worship or the cult of mysteries; nothing certain can yet be said on that point. But the function of the church as a place of assembly was sufficient to ensure the transference into religious architecture of an idea which had previously been confined to such secular buildings of general resort as halls, baths, and palaces. The idea has but rarely been carried to its simple and logical conclusion. The interiors of Armenian and Aquitanian[1] churches may be taken as models for the manner in which the simple grandeur of their spatial effect, unaided by richer ornamentation, inspires in the visitor, as he crosses the threshold, a sense of solemnity and awe, and awakens in him the devotional mood. The sole way to this end is to treat the interior space as a compact and homogeneous whole, and to heighten its effect by a bold use of light and shade. This can only be done by giving the architect control of the lighting of the interior ; but the condition was not fulfilled after the fourth century. The ecclesiastical movement very soon led to the closing up of the

[1] S. Front at Périgueux and its congeners.

old large windows, and to a preference for mysterious gloom in place of artistic effect. In the great period of Christian art in Northern Europe the walls were once more pierced in order to allow of the effective introduction of light and colour; this was, in truth, a return to the creative spirit of the first few centuries.

A particular form of representation, the landscape, which appears to have come from Iran together with the mosaic covering of wall surfaces, was also instrumental, unconsciously perhaps, in bringing into prominence the artistic value of space. The human figures in the foreground, it is true, are grouped in a single plane, and appear as if pressed against the front of the picture; but in the church of SS. Cosmas and Damian (Fig. 63, facing p. 180) the clouds descending from above, with the remoteness and elevation given to the figure of Christ, together give the illusion of infinite space. The effect of space suggested by the glitter of the gold background is probably accidental, since its true value was purely decorative; it was merely another substitute for real gold, like those so commonly used in India and Islam. In this particular mosaic the appearance of depth is probably subjective and due to habit. The idea of perspective in pictorial art was unknown to Iran; its landscape scenes are constructed by vertical projection without any attempt at giving the illusion of depth. The figures of the Four Evangelists in S. Vitale are good examples of this kind of treatment. The arrangement of zones in different colours used as a background in later wall-paintings and miniatures was probably derived from Hvarenah ideas.

Non-representational art was superseded by representation; nevertheless its artistic values remained. To its influence was due the change from the three-dimensional style of classical times to the opposite mediaeval style. Early Christian art began this important change by abandoning the illusion of space, and developing representation along formal lines in two dimensions. It almost seems as if the decorative impulse of the Northern and nomadic races were forcing the plastic figures of Greek and Semitic art forwards against the picture plane. The simultaneous tendency towards a dramatic effect calculated to impress the spectator finally stripped the human figure of all plastic suggestion, and thus prepared the way for the true mediaeval style of representation. The outstanding features of this style are the strict frontality of the figures and their direct gaze towards the spectator.[1] This does not mean that all feeling for nature and life has been paralysed or overwhelmed by the gold background ; it is simply the triumph of artistic form over imitation. The artistically important point is the disposition of line and colour upon a surface, not the use of subjects or figures for ecclesiastical advertisement.

The best evidence for the withdrawal of the human figure from nature lies in the rejection of even the limited perspective admitted by classical art in favour of significance in form. We see this in the disuse of true perspective, and the arbitrary treatment of lines indicating recession. Hence arose the so-called ' inverted perspective ', whereby figures in the middle distance were commonly depicted on a larger scale than those in the foreground. India and China did not originate this method, as one might feel inclined to suppose ; they could only accentuate it. Its true origin is to be sought in the Semitic point of view, according to which the figure of the ruler or hero, later that of the religious Founder, was regarded as transcending natural law. Buddhism indeed needed no impulse from Graeco-Semitic art ; in Sanchi and Barahat it was already following the same path. Representational art in the West also remained more or less under the influence of this style until the rise of scientific thought. Exactitude in representation is not required by an art producing its effect from a distance ; indeed they are mutually incompatible, a fact attested by numerous examples, including Raphael's ' Transfiguration '.

C. *Light*. In architecture lighting accords with the plan of the building. In the timber-roofed basilica the windows in the clerestory together unite with the aisle arcades to direct the eye towards the apse ; in the domed building the drum with its windows brings the lighting into harmony with the principle: ' Let the dome be central point and apex.' A peculiar method of lighting is illustrated by the single-aisled barrel-vaulted building and the hall church, which are lighted only from the sides. In the history of development these three methods are not always found alone ; sometimes we see a combination of two of them, more rarely all three, as in Vignola's Gesù. Usually, lighting from the sides is combined with one of the two types of lighting from above. I believe that unity of effect in mass, space, and

---

[1] This is a theme which I hope to elaborate further in vol. xvii of the publications of the *Kunsthistorisches Institut* connected with my chair.

light was attained by the earliest Armenian domed structures of the centralized type. Here the light from the drum windows spreads upwards into the hemisphere above and downwards into the apsidal niches, thus producing a tonal effect of perfect rhythmic balance. In the basilica with upper windows only, the intercolumniations produced a gentle gradation from the stronger light of the central nave to the dimness of the aisles ; by developing this feature in conjunction with the barrel vault, very remarkable solutions of lighting problems were achieved, especially in the West and the North. Windows are sometimes found in the west wall.

The use of light to relieve the monotony of mural surfaces was originally confined to the East. In Armenia the domed building was enlivened by means of a network of blind arcading, afterwards reinforced by the shadow and light effects of vertical triangular ' slits '. At first the Mediterranean made no use of such devices, but subsequently pilaster strips were introduced from Mesopotamia, supplemented, at times, by arch mouldings and later also by the true blind arcade. Finally Northern architecture (Gothic) wholly dissolved mass in tone values of free space. In Italy an attempt was made to enrich lined walls by tonal effects, using members of classical architecture ; but the impression produced is little better than that of joinery. The introduction of free-standing columns and genuine temple façades brought about a change ; but these organic members harmonize neither with the storeyed building nor with the dome.

Christian representational art, in so far as it models at all, follows classical precedents ; it does not use its own powers of observation, since in its representation it does not really perceive nature. Shading grows weak ; it is barely suggested, and that with timidity. It was left to Northern art to revive the free use of tone-values ; the folds of drapery in ' Gothic ' statues are hardly inferior to those of Greek sculpture, and sometimes even more significant as pure form. Italian art carries on the Northern tradition ; the gradual intrusion of the naturalistic figure is a mark of decadence.

D. *Colour*. Surviving buildings prove that colour as a predominant value in interiors was born anew in the ' lined ' architecture of the East. The end was achieved by the covering of walls with variegated slabs, and of floors and vaults with mosaic.

How far the effect of light was heightened by filtration through stained window-glass, we can only surmise in a tentative way from the evidence of Islam and the West.[1] In both of these provinces and especially in the North at a later period, the light on entering the building was transformed into colour by passing through richly coloured glass. The solid framework in which it was set can still be observed in West-Gothic churches in Spain ; it was derived from the similar stucco settings sporadically found in Christian churches in the Balkans and, in wider distribution, in the earlier mosques of the Mesopotamian type ; it would therefore appear to have originated in Persia.[2] The dim religious light suffused with colour which is thus created in Northern cathedrals does in cubic space what Rembrandt did on the picture plane. There can be no question that these combinations of colour were designed for definite effects. We know from historical records that the interiors of Nestorian churches in China were so brilliantly decorated ' that they resembled the plumage of a pheasant in flight ' ; some conception of what this means may be gained from the choir of S. Vitale, in which the dazzling splendour of the mosaics resembles the colours of a peacock's outspread tail.

5. *Content*. The basis of religion is a yearning of the spirit. It leaves the individual soul unfettered, until the Church binds it by her laws. The State exercises control in outward things ; the Church differs from it only in its attempt to control the inner life. It has perhaps been made clear that the spiritual content of the formative arts at the appearance of Christianity differs according to race and locality. The East-Aryan conceives a centralized building over a square plan in which the vertical axis dominates, the Semite a rectangular building in which the main axis is transverse, the West-Aryan one in which the main axis is longitudinal. It looks as though the latter merely adopted the Greek temple plan with the image of the god at one end which it replaced by a plain altar. The Hellenistic demand was satisfied, in the structural sense, by the symbol of the apse which made its appearance in Armenia, at first, it would seem, as nothing more than a supporting buttress. True, it is certainly striking that all Armenian churches without exception have their altars towards the east end, and that early regulations are unanimous

---

[1] In the excavation of S. Vitale, remains of stained window-glass were found, which may have been early Christian.

[2] The pictorial treatment of stained glass finally eliminated the earlier method.

in prescribing this direction. This may have been determined by previous conditions, as I have already pointed out.

Christianity was twice introduced in the North, once before and once after the great migrations ; on the first occasion it was adopted by the Gauls from the Hellenism of the Mediterranean area ; on the second, it reached the Franks from Rome. The Goths were intermediaries between these two movements. They brought the vaulted church from the Black Sea to the west of Europe. Introduced by them in the Dark Ages, it eventually triumphed over the types retained by Hellenism and Rome. The spiritual significance of this intrusion of Eastern influence between two successive periods of the timber-roofed basilica lay in its disturbing and quickening power, destined inevitably to bear fruit as soon as the religious feeling introduced into the North took on a national tinge, and in the several countries there arose personalities strong enough to pursue their own way and take their inspiration wherever it was to be found.

In establishing his relations with the external world, the early Christian sought to identify himself with the abnegation of the Founder, who renounced every thought of temporal power and possessions, an ideal only attainable far from the ordinary affairs of life, not in it. As soon as he fell under the spell of ordinary existence, succumbed to the desire for life, and conformed to the laws imposed on the community by Church and State, Christianity as its Founder understood it ceased to exist. To these changes correspond three successive motives influencing the course of art : first, the prayer for intercession uttered by the individual worshipper in the congregation ; second, the edification of the community by the local churches ; finally, the exaction of blind faith by the authority of the single state Church.

A. *Intercession.* The hope of redemption led to the production of many works of art, sometimes complete churches, sometimes parts of their decoration, which occasionally included representations of the donors. The spirit prompting this work was in harmony with that of Christ, but such work does not itself appear to have grown up in a Christian environment ; it originated in the religious thought of Iran, India, Greece, and Judaea. Purely symbolical art, and art inspired by Hvarenah, or by Jewish funeral and Paschal prayers, is confronted by representations of donors with their names beneath, sometimes in large buildings executed on such a scale as to be visible from a distance, in other cases set in places like Indian rock-cut chambers where they can scarcely be seen at all ; we even find pavement mosaics completed in sections contributed by many donors, and wall mosaics produced under the same conditions, like those in the spandrels of the first aisle in the church of S. Demetrius at Salonika. In this group a popular substratum seems to reach the surface, but both Church and Empire adopted and used it fully. The artist's freedom was hampered by the usage of the particular country in which he worked ; the conditions imposed both by patron and object interfered with the expression of his individuality. Nevertheless we see preserved by this Hvarenah tendency the spirit of those Aryan artistic influences which contributed to the formation of the early Christian style. Hellenistic and Mazdean art are alike symbolical in expression ; the former takes for its symbol the human figure ; the latter, animals, plants, and formal landscapes. As vehicles of spiritual content they are essentially distinct from the objective art of the Semites destined so soon to triumph over both. The peculiar charm of the earliest Christian church art during the predominance of the vault in the first four centuries, as well as of such remnants as survived into later times, consists in the fidelity with which it reflects the spirit of the Eastern and Western Aryan races.

B. *Instruction*. In a movement initiated by the Church for the definite purpose of instructing the faithful, and aiming therefore at clearness in representation, little free play was permitted to the artist. It is well known that types derived from pre-Christian art were widely used as symbols universally understood. They are given no new content ; the Church's sole demand was that its meaning should be expressed without ambiguity. For this purpose it issued rules and manuals for painters, which were probably more common than present evidence suggests. A late example has been preserved on Mt. Athos, but it has early prototypes.

C. *Use of Dazzling Effects*. National and popular art was submerged under ecclesiastical authority ; ultimately a single power prevailed in each half of the world, the Roman Church in the West, and the Byzantine court in the East. Even the early Christian state of Armenia could not permanently maintain its individuality in the face of powers like these. The long-naved building intruded upon the old domical type inherited from Iran; in like manner representation invaded the earlier formal art of ancient Mazdaism. In the sixth century all the provinces of the empire were at the disposal of the Court artists, who were enabled by the liberality of monarchs with a taste for architecture to override local taste and tradition. They created nothing new, but they did succeed in bringing out the latent possibilities of what they borrowed. Natives of Rome or Byzantium appear to have played only a subordinate part in this work; witness the church of S. Sophia and the artists who created it.

I am convinced that the nature of Eastern art was determined at first by the individual character of national groups, whose mentality was the joint product of environment and circumstances, and early traditions, especially those of a religious nature. These were the influences which prevailed in defiance of Church and State. Amid all this clash of forces, as between dome, barrel-vault, and wooden roof, square, broad and long building types, formal and representational art, and their exploitation by Church and Court, are we to take no account of the artist's individuality, which was the outcome of his birth, education, position, and personal ideals? Does he not intervene with decisive effect at the chief turning-points of development? Can we cite no names of great personalities who controlled the course of history in art?

D. *Artists*. The particular occasions in the history of art when names appear are in themselves significant; thus we hear of Zenobius, as the builder of Constantine's church of the Holy Sepulchre; of Anthemius of Tralles and Isidorus of Miletus as the architects of Justinian; and subsequently, in Armenia, of the reactionary monk Manuel, and the progressive Trdat in the service of the two Gagiks of Vaspurakan and Ani. All of these men were court architects, commissioned by their rulers to execute monuments of an exceptional kind. Are we to suppose that religious impulse played any part in their creative work? Or were they solely inspired by the desire to surpass in size and magnificence all previous efforts after monarchical advertisement? From the knowledge we have gained of East-Aryan art, and from an independent critical study of what Eusebius has to say upon the Church of the Holy Sepulchre, it is clear that none of these architects created anything which was not ultimately derived from the Iranian domed building on square plan. In all cases where they were controlled by autocratic power, the early Christian architects, like Leonardo and Bramante in later times, had recourse to the dome, which in Iran had characterized the dwelling-house, and in Armenia the church. Thus a form of building originally designed by a particular people for a particular purpose was converted into a symbol of arrogant domination. The artist no longer followed his own religious impulse, but obeyed the dictates of authority. How far the Sassanians acted as pioneers in this matter is a question into which I cannot now enter.

Or is it perhaps only the servile chronicler, seeking to find favour with the ' hero ' of his time, who has preserved the names of court favourites, and omitted all reference to the real innovators in art, the men who had a national message to deliver ? Is progress in religious art conceivable without personality, or personality without a national background ? The general disappearance of the vault which followed the rise of Christianity in the Roman and Hellenistic culture areas, and the substitution of the timber-roofed basilica, was perhaps due to the fact that officials and not artists controlled art amid the medley of peoples inhabiting the Mediterranean area in late Roman times. In the East, where down to the fifth century the different communities continued to go their own ways uninfluenced by Rome or Byzantium, individuality could still make its power felt. I have attempted, in a monograph on Armenia, to revive the memory of one such splendid period of growth and energy in that country under the Arsacid princes. Perhaps time will reveal an equally fascinating picture of creative rivalry in other parts of the East, such as Mesopotamia, Syria, Asia Minor, and especially the central region of Edessa and Nisibis. Wherever serious and intensive research has been undertaken in Western art, as in the case of Lombardy, France, and the Rhineland, a connected sequence of development in church architecture has been demonstrated, to say nothing of the logical development of Northern (Gothic) architecture from the work achieved by mighty pioneers in later times.

The chronological sequence in Christian art is somewhat as follows : first we find Iranian and Greek influences subsisting side by side ; a Semitic influence then sets in, and ultimately, radiating from Rome and Byzantium, sweeps all before it. The conflict of these forces began before the Christian era. Greece first took up the spiritual and intellectual contest with the Semitic East, flowered, and succumbed. Imperial Rome only triumphed by the aid of the Semitic elements which it derived through Hellenism. The second attempt to overpower the victor in the Mediterranean was begun by Christianity, aided by the spirit of

Northern Iran and the tradition of Praxitelean art. I believe myself to have attained a clear view of the development in formative art. Jewish Christians with their non-representational style found favour and support both among Mazdean Persians and Greeks, receiving from each of these peoples an attractive symbolical style. Greek and Persian might have joined forces. Vaulted architecture and its decoration might have combined with features of Hellenistic origin. But that would not have suited the plans of the Church either in Rome or Byzantium, nor would it have pleased the later courts which grew up in the North. The first national flowers of Christian art, both Iranian and Greek, were completely overwhelmed by Semitic influences from Edessa-Nisibis and Jerusalem, the didactic tendency of which soon surrendered in their turn to the interests of wealth and power. The stronghold of these influences was Christian Byzantium. The cheerful serenity of Hellenic art soon succumbed to the spirit of domination ; Christ was no longer depicted as the Shepherd and Spiritual Guide, but as the despot and the Judge. The forms of Iranian architecture and decoration passed wholly into the service of this anti-national movement. The path of the student is beset with difficulties ; he is met, at the outset, with almost pure Iranian art in Armenia, a similar Greek art in Asia Minor, and Semitic art in Edessa-Nisibis ; turning to the Roman mosaics and to Byzantium he perceives that intermingling of influences which the men of the West and the North, when they came South, marvelled at and copied before they had had time to bring their own energies into play. Northern love for interior space and decoration had already, through the Goths, come to terms with the Iranian style ; but the Semitically organized Church had at least as much power in spiritual matters as Byzantium possessed in the East. The long-naved church and the definite aim of representation were constant obstacles to the free development of Aryan art, until city life gave this art its chance, and from the surviving traditions of wooden architecture it produced that supreme creation of northern genius which is known as ' Gothic '. Italy eventually destroyed this art, which had degenerated by a too histrionic treatment of the human figure. She secured a triumph for the South, but this misfortune did not occur until after the Northern blood in her veins had produced a phase of representational art so brilliant that, in some of its features, it bears comparison with that of ancient

Greece. Nevertheless Leonardo, Michelangelo, and Giorgione were defeated, like Dürer and Rembrandt after them. Personality was almost entirely submerged in the conflict with a superficial element inspired by Southern feeling, and regarding art as a possession peculiarly its own.

I have already explained the plan of this attempt to investigate essential character (p. 193). I have numbered the divisions as follows: (1) Material and workmanship, (2) Subject, (3) Shape, (4) Form, (5) Content. This sequence is rarely observed in the actual history of development. It may be true that Christian art in Europe followed this order between the period of the great migrations and its climax in about A.D. 1500; certain it is that the ' early Christian ' art which preceded it reached its zenith almost immediately, and especially in the fourth century. Its spiritual content (5) flowed from the personality of Christ; this formed its starting-point and gave to all the subjects, figures and forms which it adopted their essentially Christian character. In the fifth and sixth centuries Church and Court enter the field; with them begins that exploitation (2) of the germinal forms which they found in existence, and that increase in size and magnificence which continued to the time of Justinian, and often makes correct appreciation difficult. Religious content (5) diminishes in proportion as the first four elements increase in importance; it only regains its full power with the rise of a racial art in the North.

Thus principles through a whole millennium obscured by the hot-house cultures of the South attained at last their full and logical expansion on their native soil. To attribute this splendid national movement to Southern influence or to scholasticism is both unseemly and unpatriotic. An honest history of development will be compelled to take account of the millennial persistence of Northern principles, although it must be admitted that in the end they were fully and brilliantly exploited by scholasticism.

In the foregoing chapters we have seen the North at work in the South fashioning mediaeval art. In Greece and India it yielded at first to the representational stream of the South; but in Parthia and Margiana, the ancient Sacian land, both situated to the South of and between the Caspian Sea and the Altai, it maintained its vital hold upon the people in spite of the appeal which Semitic and Hellenistic art naturally made to the material ambitions of the Achaemenian and Sassanian rulers.

The Arsacids carried Northern influence to Armenia.   It is important that the history of art should in future take account of that triangular area, the base of which is formed by a line drawn from the Caspian to the Altai, its apex by the mouth of the Indus. Within this region the Hindu-Kush mountains deflected the main stream of Indian culture towards Eastern Asia by way of the Pamir and Khotan.   This was the route followed by Buddhism, Kabul forming the central point of the ' Gandhâra movement', as did Ghasna that of Islam.   The centres of Northern culture were first Merv and Ferghana, later Bokhara and Samarkand, while Herat lay on the frontier of a region full of originative power. As a centre of intercommunication it is equally important for the student of art and the historian of religion.[1]

More important are the problems of origins connected with this region, to which I have made repeated allusion in this volume. Not only the West, but also India and Eastern Asia, received, as we have seen, streams of influence from this quarter ; but the art which made the heaviest drafts upon the valleys of the Oxus and Jaxartes is that which is generally named after its carrier, Islam. The origins of Islamic art, even more than those of Western mediaeval art, lie here.   This region actually anticipated the North as the source of a stream which in the course of a thousand years overran the world.   As regards the ecclesiastical provinces of Margiana and Bactriana, with their bishop's sees at Merv and Balkh respectively, and the more southerly centres of Herat and Sakastene, the student should consult Sachau's book on the expansion of Christianity in Asia ; he will then be as little surprised at the appearance of the Nestorians in China as at the flood of silver coinage from these regions in Northern Europe at the end of the first millennium.   The comparative study of art, with a view to tracing the history of its development, has only been rendered possible by the discovery of this Eurasian link connecting

---

[1] For the religious field, the reader may be referred to the attempt of W. Lüdtke to explain the Recognition myth and the Placidas legend, and to the writings of K. von Spiess on the Fountain of everlasting youth.   The researches of Nathan Söderblom into the origins of religion, published in 1915 under the title of *Das Werden des Gottesglaubens*, have shown how close is the bearing of essential character upon the history of development. It is to be hoped that his lead will soon be followed in the field of formative art ; the importance of this triangular region beyond the Oxus will then be amply vindicated as a point of junction for different cultures.   The works of Sir Aurel Stein have introduced us to a rich material from the Eastern side.

Altai-Iran with the Indus. We may, perhaps, be permitted to express the hope that the new world-order, which is even now emerging, may find ways and means to send out expeditions to excavate, and so acquire an accurate knowledge of this Asiatic centre, which is of such extreme importance to the history of civilization. For here Christianity and Buddhism met, the culture of East Asia and our European North had their common home.

IX

Hiberno-Saxon Art in the Time of Bede

IN the preceding chapters I attempted to cover the whole field of Early Christian and Mediaeval art ; in the present chapter, written for the English edition of this book, I propose to re-examine and supplement my work with special reference to the most westerly section of this wide field. Does England tend to confirm the view, which I have expressed with regard to Christian art in general, that its early development can only be properly understood if we enlarge our horizon, and learn to appreciate not only the differences between popular art and the art associated with Church and Court, but also national and local differences in the East in Early Christian times and the relations, in which formal and representational art stand to each other ? I shall consider the problems in a certain sequence, which seems to me to minimize the risk of overlooking points of importance. Admittedly the framing of questions will in most cases be the limit of my achievement ; my answers cannot be regarded as anything more than tentative suggestions.

I. *The Study of the Monuments*

In all the excellent English books on the subject of early Christian art in Ireland, Scotland, and England, concluding with Baldwin Brown's great work *The Arts in Early England*, the student invariably finds the same uncertainty in the critical appreciation of an art, which cannot be brought into connexion with Rome or explained in the usual way by reference to Roman monuments. No solution of the problem is possible so long as modern investigators limit their horizon (as I myself did before the publication of my *Mschatta* in 1902) to Syria and the great Hellenistic cities. Baldwin Brown, in the second and fifth volumes of his book, dealing with what I judge to be the most important period, has collected all the threads of evidence with indefatigable patience and care, and proved in a very convincing manner that Rome did not exercise the decisive influence. This, however, is merely a negative conclusion, for which I may be able to substitute something of a more positive character. By supplementing my work of the last few years, summed up in this volume, with the impressions formed on my journey through England in 1920, I am able to venture upon a definite answer to the question of the nature and origin of Christian art in England in the second half of the first millennium. But, admittedly, the first thing to do is to decide which monuments belong to the early period of Anglo-Saxon Christianity.

Curiously enough, I find it necessary to express the hope that the very existence of Anglo-Saxon monuments in England may first find recognition. It is astonishing to see that Dehio and Bezold's standard work on mediaeval art, *Die Kirchliche Baukunst des Abendlandes* (1892), omits the extant Anglo-Saxon buildings as of minor importance, and only uses Latin sources. Comprehensive study in this field of art is, in fact, a recent growth, and one for which we are indebted to Baldwin Brown. His *Ecclesiastical Architecture in England from the Conquest of the Saxons to the Norman Conquest* (1903) is so thorough a piece of research, supplemented as it is by a catalogue and a chart of Saxon churches, that such an omission as that of Dehio and Bezold is no longer conceivable. Future students of the development of Christian art will have to reckon with England as a distinct province, in the same sense as the provinces discovered by me in Asia Minor, Mesopotamia, and Armenia and, at an earlier date, by de Vogüé in Syria. That, however, is only a beginning. In order to establish research on a firm foundation we require the determinant of time as well as of place ; in this matter Anglo-Saxon buildings fare no better than those of Asia Minor, of which scarcely a single example can be dated with certainty. It was only by means of his strictly scientific and comparative method, in contradistinction to that of the philological historical school, that Baldwin Brown was able to determine the existence of a distinct group of English monuments in the seventh century at about the time of Bede.

In the province of sculpture we are scarcely more fortunate. It was difficult to prove the existence of a flourishing period of architecture in Anglo-Saxon times ; it is no less difficult to obtain recognition of the fact that those important sculptures preserved in the north of England, the Crosses of Bewcastle, Ruthwell, and Hexham, date from the time of Bede. Such recognition upsets the whole Roman scheme of chronology as it applies to England ; consequently repeated attempts have been made to cast doubt upon the view which attributes these exceptionally important monuments to the earliest period of Northern art.   But it is one of the main principles of honest scientific research that chronological sequences based upon local evidence cannot be bodily transferred from one area to another.   What struggles has it not cost to free the dating of Christian monuments in the East from the mechanical application of Roman standards![1]

When I visited the Bewcastle Cross in person I learned with some surprise, what the literature on the subject had never informed me, that there is external evidence for attributing to it a high antiquity ; this consists in the immediate proximity of an extensive Roman fort, which makes it highly probable that there was an early settlement in the neighbourhood.   When we hear from the philological side that there are no grounds for doubting the authenticity of the historical portion of the inscription, according to which the stone was cut in A.D. 670, we feel that we can fairly accept what we are told without subjecting the date to further special inquiry.

Nevertheless people might refuse to be convinced of the great antiquity of the three High Crosses if the claims of Early England were based on nothing more than these monuments and the remains of her ancient buildings.   But there is evidence of another kind which proves beyond a doubt that the time of Bede was a period of artistic achievement without parallel in the narrow zone between Ireland and Iona on the west and Northumberland and Lindisfarne on the east; in other words, in the very area to which the crosses belong.   I refer to Irish illuminated MSS. such as the Book of Kells and the Book of Durrow, and to Anglo-Saxon MSS. under Irish influence, such as the Lindisfarne Gospels.   Their antiquity as Early Christian monuments is fortunately beyond dispute, even for those who rely upon the unscientific philological-

---

[1] Roman theologians may be ignored, since they are not to be converted ; but it is worth while to recall what happened when Sir William Ramsay questioned my early dating of the churches of Central Asia Minor in the *Athenaeum*, 1903, p. 656, and then, converted by his own excavations, admitted the correctness of my view in both an article in *The Expositor* (vol. iv, 1907) and in his book *The Thousand and One Churches*.   Similar admissions will have to be made not only in the Christian East, but also at the extremity of the Christian West, in England.   If it is once clearly recognized that these crosses date back to the seventh and eighth centuries, it will be necessary to revise the existing history of art ; just as in the East, such a recognition will open up quite new possibilities in the history of development.

historical method. Every handbook of art history informs us that, to mention only the chief example, the Lindisfarne Gospels were written A.D. 698–721 by Bishop Eadfrith. To many students this is the first bedrock fact, from which scientific investigation into the whole archaeological group must begin. In reality the study of art must lay its own foundations firmly and independently by continual use of the comparative method. This is a point which I shall consider in greater detail.

II. *Investigation of Essential Character*

Whether I turn to the remains of Anglo-Saxon churches, to the crosses, or to the MSS. of the time of Bede, I feel in the presence of an art which differs from every other art in the world. Above all, I feel that we have here no mere pale reflection of Roman or Byzantine art, but an art which, in comparison with these, shows no less individuality than do the remains of buildings, sculptures, and paintings of Hither Asia which I have been able to identify as belonging to the Early Christian period. Any one who is familiar with the distant East—distant, that is, as seen from Rome—feels himself here in the far West in a closely related province. It will be our duty thoroughly to grasp the peculiar nature of this Western art, just as we have grasped that of the Christian East, and this can only be done by a systematic investigation of essential character on comparative lines. But it may not be out of place to warn the reader at the outset against the common fallacy of regarding imperial centres like Rome or Byzantium as starting-points; we found it more probable that such stages for the scenic effects devised by Court, Church, and Academic Culture do not create artistic values, but merely exploit them to advertise their power. Remote and self-sufficing regions are much more fitted to produce individuality in art than imperial centres, which, like sponges, absorb everything within their reach.

1. *Material and Work.* It is beyond all doubt that in the seventh and eighth centuries England contained a widely distributed series of architectural monuments. In these the timber buildings customary in the North would appear to have been superseded by stone structures which reveal traces of their wooden origin no less clear than those observed in Greek temples or in the railings of Indian stûpas. The character of the architecture that preceded the Persian period in Greece or Asoka in India can be inferred from later buildings in stone; and

so it is in the case of England.   Many of the towers so characteristic of Early English architecture show us the wooden prototype translated into stone.   The best example is Earls Barton (see Frontispiece); here the tower, when seen from a distance, has every appearance of being timber-built, but a closer inspection reveals the surprising fact that it really consists of rubble concrete faced with stone 'beams', in which the earlier wooden forms have been preserved with meticulous care.   Even if the tower only goes back to the later Anglo-Saxon period, it remains the most perfect and typical example illustrating the origin of indigenous church architecture in England.   This class of building also shows the decorative features characteristic of wooden construction in all periods : the cushion capital, the knob capital with its surface rounded by turning, and the baluster.   These features occur in Anglo-Saxon England no less than in Scandinavia, Georgia, Armenia, and Lombard Northern Italy.   In the building of enclosed rooms or halls the whole of the North must be pictured as still in the wooden stage at the commencement of the Christian era.   We can hardly be surprised at Bede's statement that building in the ' Scottish ' style meant building in wood.

Nevertheless timber cannot have been the only building material used by the Irish and Anglo-Saxons in Early Christian times.   In the crypts, which are the only extant portions of the Anglo-Saxon cathedrals of Hexham and Ripon, the cutting and the jointing of the stone are of such quality and so clearly the result of long practice, that stone must undoubtedly be considered as an alternative to wood in Early Christian architecture in England.   How otherwise can we account for the fact, not appreciated by Dehio and Bezold, that noteworthy Anglo-Saxon churches do not survive merely in Latin accounts with a Roman colouring, but in their original stone and mortar ?   Of wooden buildings nothing remains, for Greenstead must be attributed to a later period ;   only chance or methodical excavation can still bring to light remains like those discovered in Scandinavia at Hemse or Oseberg.   For the present we have to rely upon the stone buildings, which are not mere imitations of their wooden prototypes, but show clear traces of having developed peculiar features independently of Roman architectural tradition.

Christian architecture might be defined as the construction of interiors for the purposes of assembly and the ritual sacrifice. So long as the architect clung to the traditional wood, so long as he built only for his own generation with no thought of eternity, the old indigenous methods prevailed. But as soon as he began to build in stone, the vault made its appearance and with it the characteristic feeling for organic construction. That the art of vaulting was known in England in Bede's time is attested by the subterranean chambers of Hexham and Ripon. They both consist of a rectangular main chamber with barrel-vaulted roof, and an antechamber attached to the west end; in Ripon this is covered with a transverse quarter-vault. At Hexham the roof adjacent to the vault in front of the south staircase consists of stone slabs inclined so as to form a gable. These are very important facts and have never received the attention they deserve. The problem which here confronts us is the same as that which reappears in so perplexing a form in many of the Norman and 'Gothic' cathedrals of England : why was not the vault used to crown all that elaborate substructure of walls and buttresses ? are we really justified in ascribing such an eleventh-hour abandonment of plan to incompetence or timidity ? Is it not rather that Northern usage frustrated the transition from a wooden roof to the vault, and explains the delight obviously taken in heaping up huge masses of stone ? Even in Palermo the Normans retained the wooden roof; they could at any moment have drawn on the resources of Byzantine architecture.

It might equally well be said that there was no one in Bede's time competent to decorate manuscripts with representations of biblical scenes in the manner of Rome and Byzantium, later adopted in the European West under Charles the Great. Some of the Evangelist figures in the Lindisfarne Gospels are unquestionably derived from Greek prototypes ; other MSS. contain figures of Evangelists and biblical scenes of similar origin. All these figures are translated into the style of the calligrapher, who was obliged to modify his old native methods to suit the new material of parchment and the new craft of writing. The crosses show that the stone-mason was much quicker to adapt himself to the novelty of representing the human figure. It is an important point that here, no less than in the MSS., the workmanship was native, and not Roman as in the monuments of the preceding period. Art was now founded upon nationality ; that is the outstanding feature of the Christian movement. For the building of basilicas it had been necessary to import foreign artificers from Gaul and Italy. But Christianity in England, as in the East, evoked forces not in the service of a foreign power such as Rome ;

it tapped sources of national talent, hitherto exercised only in the ornamentation of objects for daily use, and later of houses, temples, or tombs. Here in the distant West the process was closely analogous to that which I have demonstrated in the East.

2. *Object or Purpose.* All that survives of the architecture, sculpture, and painting of the time of Bede was made for the service of the Christian faith. Unhappily the works of art wherewith the Roman Church in England sought to create an impressive display have perished in their entirety. But the remains of native origin give the impression of an art freely practised and independent of the dictates of ecclesiastical or any other kind of authority. There is nothing servile in this national art ; each new work proclaims Irish and Anglo-Saxon freedom from the influence of Rome. Culture in Bede's time had not been forced into the grooves of tradition ; otherwise art could not have displayed the freshness which distinguishes it. So far as architecture is concerned, the reason for this independence must be attributed to the failure of the Graeco-Roman triple-naved basilica to win acceptance as a national form of expression. Great as was the expenditure lavished upon these buildings by Roman missionaries in the chief missionary centres, and imposing as they may have been in outward appearance, they nevertheless occurred only as sporadic examples. Here, in the North, the main purpose of church buildings was from the very first a special one ; it was not the few large city churches which gave the keynote, but the numerous small buildings distributed all over the country, and designed to protect the community in times of sudden attack. Hence we find that even in wooden buildings all the customary provisions for defence were made, as is proved by accounts of the founding of the monastery at Lindisfarne. An indispensable feature of this type of church throughout the North was a massive tower, not built for height like the minaret or Italian campanile, but resembling rather the ancient Indian monasteries in having a number of inhabitable stories ; it often formed the central point of the whole structure, which radiated from it like the arms of a cross : excellent examples have survived both in England and Sweden. Occasionally we also find the tower placed in front of the long building. Another point of interest is the function of the earliest crypts ; I have only seen those at Hexham and Ripon, which have almost the appearance of habitable cells.

The customary interpretation of the crosses as gravestones

cannot be accepted without question. The character of the latter
is illustrated by the slabs of Hartlepool, those from Clonmacnois,
and others, which should be compared with examples from
Nestorian cemeteries in Central Asia. In addition to these,
examples occur, throughout the North, of memorial stones unconnected with the grave cult ; in Scandinavia they still continued
to be erected and engraved with runes as late as the eleventh
century ; I observed similar, if isolated, examples in Armenia.
A monument of this type, supposed to be dated A.D. 922, and consisting of two square shafts, is still standing erect at Odzun.[1]
Its Eastern face is covered with horizontal rows of figures, quite
contrary to Armenian custom, and its Northern face with ornamental designs ; it thus resembles the Ruthwell and Bewcastle
crosses. The biblical scenes, however, lack the modelling found
in certain ancient Georgian and Armenian churches ; they are
flat and treated in a manner quite different from the Southern style
so conspicuous in the figures of the English crosses. Here, too,
there is some doubt whether the monument is really a grave,[2] as
is generally assumed. The two obelisks have now been placed
next to the church underneath two arches approached by steps
(Fig. 65, facing p. 238). Possibly the two pilasters from Acre now
standing in front of S. Mark's at Venice (Fig. 68, facing p. 241)
belong to this group of stone monuments in pairs. I shall refer to
these again later.

The calligraphers were undoubtedly able to exercise freedom
of choice as between Roman and Eastern models. But it is not
unlikely that pressure was put upon them by Roman missionaries
to imitate the style of contemporary Graeco-Roman MSS., which,
whether in the form of the earlier papyrus rolls or of the later
vellum codex-pages, were illuminated with representational subjects
and never with abstract ornament in the true sense. Now one of the
distinguishing features of all Anglo-Saxon MSS. is the prevalence
of a homogeneous and purely artistic decoration. The placing
of the so-called Eusebian Canons at the beginning is significant.
The earliest dated example is to be seen in the Gospels of Rabula,
written in A.D. 586 in the monastery of S. John at Zagba in
Mesopotamia, and now preserved in the Laurentian Library at
Florence. The regular sequence of Evangelist's portrait and
initial is a matter of course in Armenian and Byzantine MSS.,
but not in Roman.

---

[1] *Baukunst der Armenier*, II. 695.   [2] Of Ashot II.

Particularly interesting is the so-called Franks casket in the British Museum ; here a border of runes encloses a number of carvings in low relief on whale's bone, the subjects being derived in part from Northern mythology and in part from biblical history, and that of Rome and Jerusalem. I expressed the opinion in 1904 that the latter or secular group probably goes back to the illustration of Chronicles recording the world's history, like the Alexandrian papyrus which I published in 1905. Bede does, in fact, allude to an artistic cosmographical codex, which was given to King Aldfrith by the Abbot Ceolfrith of Wearmouth and Yarrow (A.D. 690–716) in payment for newly acquired land.[1]

3. *Shape.* In order to make himself readily intelligible, the artist employs such shapes as are familiar both to himself and the spectator. Rome endeavoured to introduce the Hellenistic basilica, with its triple nave and wooden roof, into England as the regular church type. Did the indigenous Christianity of the British Isles accept this alien type without question ? Had it no other to offer in opposition ? In my book on Armenia I have attempted to show how, in the Ararat district, a constructional unit originally borrowed from Iran became by separate use and by enlargement the starting-point of a peculiar development in Christian times. The England of Bede had also its type distinct from the basilica. It has nothing to do with the Armenian domed type on a square plan, but appears to be descended from an earlier indigenous form, the single-naved long building with or without a tower. It is certainly a noteworthy fact that it existed in wide distribution in the seventh century. Other special features of this building are the rectangular choir and its separation from the public space by means of walls or supports projecting at right angles from the sides. The same features have been noted in the wooden churches of Sweden, and have been explained as survivals of ancient Northern temples. If that is really the case, and Christianity in the North Sea area originally adopted the shape of an earlier pagan temple, it should be possible to prove the existence of buildings directly descended from it, and independent of the Roman basilica. In Armenia also the type occurs as a religious building at the same period as in England ; subsequently in Provence and Aquitaine it became the starting-point of an important development in form. The

[1] The allusion is in the Anonymous Lives of the Abbots ; *see* Plummer, vol. i. p. 380, par. 15.

65   Odzun ; pillars from monument   See p. 237.

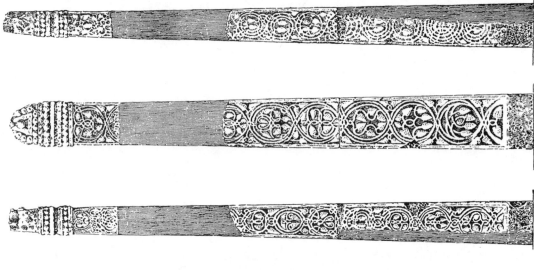

66   Acca Cross.   1–3, three views of the cross ; 4, enlargement of part of 1 ; 5, enlargement of part of 2.   See p. 239.

question is whether England was not the pioneer country for this type of building in the West, just as Armenia and Mesopotamia were in the East. The central tower may have led to the development of the cruciform plan as early as the time of Bede, although the existing examples are all later. In Eastern Christianity all these single-naved types were the source from which the art of vaulting sprang. Did not the same thing occur in England? Subterranean vaults existed in Bede's time; in Monkwearmouth we also find an example of barrel vaulting on the ground-floor of the tower. No definite conclusion is possible on this point at present; nor can we be certain whether its origin was indigenous or connected with Rome or the East.

The problem of the origin of types in Anglo-Saxon art recurs in an accentuated form in the case of the human figures and decorative motives. If, as Baldwin Brown has proved, these were not derived from Rome, what was their origin? Are they indigenous, or is a connexion with other provinces of art conceivable? We should naturally expect that the decorative motives were indigenous. It is beyond question that much of this rich fund of figures is Celtic-Irish and much also Teutonic and Anglo-Saxon in origin; it is unnecessary to refer once more to particular details. But there remains a considerable residue of motives as to which the problem arises whether they were borrowed as chance suggested from one or other of these sources, or whether they are all derived from some third common source. My investigation of this problem will be based upon the high crosses and the manuscripts; for the sake of brevity I shall ignore the decoration of buildings.

In the Acca cross of A.D. 740 (Fig. 66, opposite) three of the surfaces are ornamented with vine-scrolls, rising in a series of interlaced circles or pointed ovals, in which the natural form of the vine is wholly subordinated to the geometric design. The chief school for this type of ornament is, as I have shown, the Mshatta façade; there it is possible to trace its evolution in all its stages, varying from the realistic to the absolutely conventional. The 'rows of pellets', which appear at the upper end of the Acca cross, were also a favourite form of decoration in Altai-Iran and the East. In the Bewcastle cross (Fig. 67, facing p. 240) three of the surfaces have scroll designs, the construction of which is reminiscent of the Mshatta façade in that the stems spring directly from the corner or the centre of the base line without the intervention of a vase. The manner of their interlacing has features which reappear in a well-known monument from the region of Antiochene influence ; I refer to the pilasters from Acre now in Venice (Fig. 68, facing p. 241). Comparison does indeed reveal that the work of the Antiochene artist was further from the Eastern and nearer to the Graeco-Roman style than was that of the Anglo-Saxon. The reason for this is simple ; the Anglo-Saxon and the Iranian, in virtue of their Northern affinities and remoteness from Rome, are in closer agreement with each other than with the Aramaean of Palestine, who, in his advanced position on the Mediterranean coast, was led to vacillate between Iranian-Northern conventionalism and the naturalism of the Greeks and Semites.

In my *Altai-Iran* (p. 204 f.) under the heading ' multiple surface ' (*Mehrflächigkeit*) I brought together for comparison Afghan and Norwegian examples of wood and stucco ornament in angular relief ; I then considered pierced work ; both methods were treated as characteristic of nomadic and northern art. In introducing the ' Nigg Stone ', a slab with a cross in Ross-shire, I would first call attention to stelae, such as those of Armenia, sometimes of enormous dimensions, erected as memorials or grave-stones ; above all I would remark upon the angular relief given to the lines of the sculptured designs on both sides and the pierced bosses on one side of the plinth (Fig. 69, facing p. 242) ; here the cross stands out in the front plane above a sunk background, an effect reproduced in colour in the Lindisfarne Gospels. The ground is filled with scrolls, the negative residue of which, reserved in champlevé style in the stone, is fashioned into round or lozenge-shaped bosses covered themselves with interlacings presenting sharp contrasts of light and shadow. The reader should compare with this the stucco frieze at Deir es-Sûryani by the Natron Lakes in Lower Egypt, executed, as I believe, by Iranian workers in stucco for the Abbot Moses of Nisibis in the tenth century (Fig. 70, facing p. 243). Apart from the general resemblance in the feeling of the ornament, I would call special attention to the horizontal frieze below and the quartered bosses enclosed in the lower scrolls.

In the purely decorative pages of the Irish-Anglo-Saxon manuscripts one peculiarity is particularly striking. I refer to the ornamental projections—the humanist would explain them as *Akroteria*—which appear in the four angles and still oftener in the middle of the sides (Fig. 71, facing p. 244) ; these have attracted even less attention, so far as I am aware, than the existence of

67 Ruthwell and Bewcastle Crosses. See p. 239.

68   Pillars from Acre in Venice.   See pp. 237, 240.

the ornamental pages themselves. Can slab-crosses like the Nigg Stone have furnished the model for these? Or indeed for the whole idea of a framed surface completely filled with ornament? The reader may compare with these the bordered panels of the Kairwan Mimbar, which I believe to be derived from Iran (Fig. 35, facing p. 117). Such works of art, inspired by the inmost feelings of the nomadic and northern races and executed in a definite material with a definite technique, furnished the prototypes from which, in some as yet unknown region of Hither Asia, was born the new style of ornamenting parchment; for the purpose of reconstructing this style the manuscripts of early England are no less important than Armenian and Byzantine illuminated books of later date. It originated in another region than the Merovingian fish-and-bird initials, which never travelled as far as England. This is a significant fact, since it is clear proof that the Anglo-Saxon province of art was independent of the Frankish. Where then was the home of the decorative art enriching Anglo-Saxon manuscripts in the time of Bede? At home, or in the East?

I believe that the clue to the problem is to be found in those peculiar salient motives, introduced as an ornamental feature in the angles and on the sides of those ' frames ', which are a general and independent product of the Northern spirit, quite distinct from the architectural panel borders of the Southern culture-area. These projecting motives appear in the East in conjunction with the ⊓-shaped moulding described in my books on Altai-Iran and Armenia. The Armenian miniature (Fig. 40, facing p. 123) shows that we have here to do with a form of art which resembles the Middle Byzantine in its insistence on this feature. The reader is referred to my remarks on this subject in *Kleinarmenische Miniaturenmalerei.*

It is very striking to find on the Bewcastle and Ruthwell crosses not only scroll ornament, but also representations of human figures; these occur on one side of the former, and on two sides of the latter cross. Though they have no connexion with Rome, they strongly suggest the sarcophagi of Ravenna, and show the closest agreement, as I pointed out in my book on Armenia (ii. 720), with those ancient flat reliefs, which we sometimes find no less surprising on Armenian and Georgian churches than in Anglo-Saxon England. Possibly we have here a branch spreading westwards, as another had spread eastwards, from the same Antiochene stem formed by the convergence of Hellenistic Asia Minor and Semitic Mesopotamia. We are only just beginning to observe these relationships ; hitherto all eyes have been blinded by the Roman obsession. In spite of the necessity for being brief, I should like to recommend a comparison between the figure of Christ in the cruciform church at Mzchet (Fig. 72, facing p. 245) in Georgia with the two figures of Christ on the Bewcastle and Ruthwell crosses, so frequently illustrated together. It is as though the same hand had been at work, not only in the posture, bearing, and features, but also in the schematic treatment, a subject to which I shall refer again later. The figure would be the more striking if, as Baldwin Brown remarks, it had been depicted without the full beard and with the moustache only. The reader is advised to read my comment on this subject in *Altai-Iran* (p. 262 f.). He should also compare these figures with the Gandhâra type of Buddha.

It has often been observed that the introduction of the falconer in the Bewcastle cross points to a direct influence from the East. Perhaps we should also include the figure of the archer, which appears on the terminal cross of the Ruthwell stone and corresponds to the four figures of the Evangelists which must have existed on the back. The archer occupying the lower limb of the cross, we may perhaps supply on the others the unicorn, the mountain, and a bird, somewhat as we find them in a landscape of Iranian style in the MS. roll of Ku-K'ai-Chi in the British Museum, where the archer kneels over against the landscape. What is here represented is the struggle between good and evil, a Mazdean motive which started in Iran and during the Middle Ages is found everywhere between China in the East and England in the West.

4. *Form.* In demonstrating that a variety of influences and prototypes may have determined the course of an artistic movement, I am preparing the way at the end of which their independent action will become intelligible. What, now, is the peculiar factor determining form in Anglo-Saxon art ? The bulk of the surviving monuments reveals an unpretentious treatment of interior space in architecture, and in sculpture and painting a preference for pure decoration. Representation in formative art and the use of the vault in building are both of secondary importance.

On buildings there is apparently no trace of the excessive ornament employed in Norman work. The churches are almost

69 'Nigg-stone.' See p. 240.

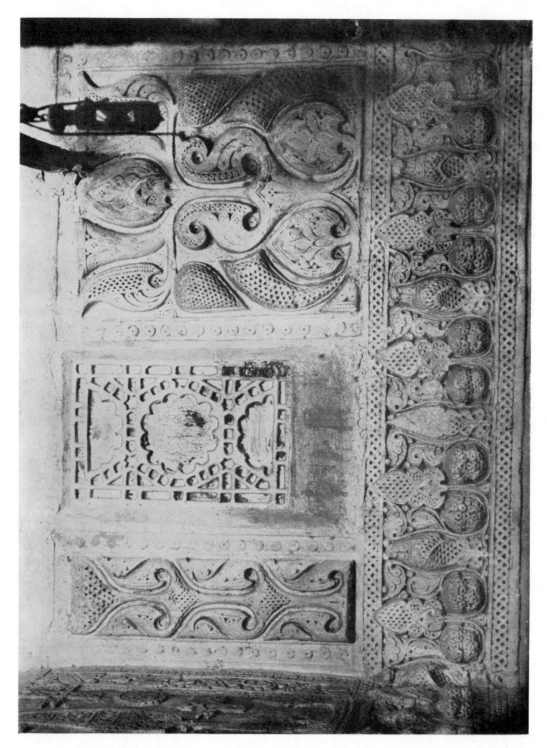

70   Stucco ornaments from the Deir es-Sûryani.   See p. 240.

entirely undecorated, as they were in Syria and Armenia, where in
like manner the earliest builders were intent on construction pure
and simple. The national stone architecture of the earlier
Christian centuries in Armenia eschewed elaborate ornament.
The exterior produces its effect by the lines of its compact and
massive structure ; the interior space in the one-aisled indigenous
churches is unique in its proportions. In what has preceded, I
have not emphasized the problem of origin ; in the present place
I must make it clear that a type perhaps derived from the pagan
temple may have developed into a fertile form in the hands of
Christian builders as early as the time of Bede. It is significant
that at so early a period England should have possessed a type
peculiar to herself : in the other parts of Europe, Dehio and
Bezold have established the existence of the one-aisled type only
after A.D. 1000. In England, as in Armenia, the type stands at the
beginning of the whole development, and, if a Georgian reviewer
of my work on Armenia is correct,[1] it was also the primitive plan
in Georgia, though here there was a groined vault over the middle.

In England this single-aisled church has proportions which at
once arrest the attention (Fig. 73, facing p. 246). The interior space
looks as if it had been heightened to accord with the adjoining
tower. At any rate the height is so remarkable in comparison
with the breadth that we are reminded of the proportions in
Gothic cathedrals, where the breadth is to the height as 1 to $3\frac{1}{2}$.

A tendency to vaulting is intrinsic to the single-aisled building ;
I cannot believe that it was resisted by Anglo-Saxon architects.
The impulse towards vaulting is plainly expressed in the design
of the later Norman churches, though even in the case of three-
aisled buildings this vaulting was not finally carried out. But
it is remarkable that here there should have been a feeling for
organic development which was wholly lacking in the case of the
basilica. The point of departure for this development is always
the vault, for which due supports have to be provided. In the
North other influences led up to it, derived from wooden construction ; this style of building was perhaps more fitted than that
of the Graeco-Roman basilica to combine the feeling for organic
construction with the three-aisled plan. In this connexion I throw
out the following conjectures.

I assume the existence in early England of wooden churches
in addition to those built of stone. Arguing from a parallel case in

[1] *Tschubinaschwili*, 1921.

Norway, I infer that side by side with the simple stone churches
there arose a wooden type, in plan and elevation closely related to
the basilica, I mean the so-called ' mast churches '. In these the
nave is raised on tall masts above the level of the aisle-roofs, thus
enabling windows to be placed in the upper walls and admitting
direct light to the whole middle part of the church. It has
generally been supposed that this treatment of walls is later than
the vaulted Romanesque churches, and that it is to be explained as
an imitation in wood of a basilican type in stone. As a matter of
fact, as I have already pointed out (Figs. 14–17, facing p. 80),
the wooden churches of the North have little to do with
Romanesque, so little that they probably introduced the development of Gothic themselves. Among other things I may point to
their decisive influence in originating the triforium, a member which
people have usually associated with the Southern and Byzantine
gallery. Viewed in this connexion, the triforium would represent
the first effort to break the monotony of the nave walls, raised to an
excessive height through a custom which had become traditional,
as we have seen, in single-naved churches built of stone. A glance
at Fig. 18 shows the sequence : at a given height the rows of tall
masts required strutting. Even in wooden construction the
requirement was in part fulfilled by means of arcading. In stone
churches, and as an enrichment of upper walls, this arcading
remained as a decorative feature when its practical function
had ceased.

Anglo-Saxon art of about A.D. 700, from whatever point we
view it, is not antique but mediaeval in its forms, so purely
' mediaeval ' that in pre-Carolingian times we can only find its
like in two quarters : in the North in so far as it was uncontaminated by southern influence ; and in the Asiatic East,
though here only in the so-called period of antiquity. It is a consequence of this that while in architecture pure space was the aim,
in the other arts all idea of depth is lacking, and likewise all idea
of the effect to be produced by light and shade. The only features
that tell are surface line and colour. If figures enter into the plan
they look exactly as if thrust forward from behind against the
picture plane ; ornamental motives have no definite direction ;
everywhere there is a preference for the repeat-pattern. These
distinguishing marks are at least as characteristic of Anglo-Saxon
as of any other art of the North or East. All centres in ornament.
If in the time of Bede reliefs appear (or are we to say reappear ?),

71 Page of the Lindisfarne Gospels, fol. 26ᵛ; British Museum. See p. 240.

72   Mzchet; the Christ outside the apse.   See pp. 242, 245.

they submit to the constraint of the design in every case where they are free of southern influence.

The reliefs upon stone crosses show certain peculiarities also shared by monuments in a Greek style contrasting with that of late-Roman sarcophagi, with their undercutting and its effects of light and shadow ; the monuments to which I refer are found on Islands of the Aegean, and in isolated instances in Georgia and Armenia. I take as an example the figure of the founder in the church of Mzchet (Fig. 72, opposite). Compare the Christ of the Bewcastle Cross. The ground is cut away from the border, as in champlevé work, and Christ in his rigidly frontal pose reserved in such a manner that the ridges of the complicated folds in the drapery are kept uniformly at the level of the border.

The above-mentioned sequence of the full-page illuminations in books of the Gospels is worthy of especial remark. First comes a page of pure ornament, then the portrait of the Evangelist, finally the beginning of the text in large initials. Single pages with crosses occur in all oriental manuscripts, whether Syriac, Coptic, Armenian, or Byzantine : under Islam, these decorative pages, though of course without the cross, are especially frequent in the oldest MSS. of the Koran. But the usual sequence at the beginning of the book, whether Irish or Anglo-Saxon, appears to represent a native development actuated by Eastern suggestions. In the play of line in these ornamental pages and in the initials we note a quite exceptional delight in personal invention. Tame indeed is the ornament of Byzantine MSS. in comparison, where the decorative page is generally contracted to a mere head-piece, as seen in an illustration from a Paris MS. of Gregory of Nazianzus (Fig. 74, facing p. 247). All this joy in decorative design must have come from the *scriptoria* of Hither Asia.

Turning the pages of Anglo-Saxon MSS. I am again and again struck by the recurrence of the colour-combination of red and yellow. For me this in itself is enough to establish the close connexion of the group with Coptic illumination, though the Coptic work is infinitely cruder. Wherever you have to deal with the art of nomadic or northern peoples you find these two colours dominant ; there are certain classes of objects, notably carpets and embroideries, in which the colour scheme never goes beyond this point. At present I am unable to follow this clue further for lack of published monographs on the subject bringing together sufficient material to justify general conclusions. It may be that in illumination the colours are connected with the material, parchment, to which they are applied.

5. *Content.* The spiritual content of any art is the first of its values to be considered, even though its development is known. We may say at once of Anglo-Saxon works of art that they create an impression of spontaneity and freshness as enduring as that produced by works of early Greek or early Gothic art. In the values employed at the time and in the country of Bede, and in their combined effect, there is the attraction of youthfulness and frank simplicity, qualities which may be regarded as more original than those of the Roman art which preceded them or the Norman art which came after. Since the impression created by different works is not the same, the crosses and the MSS. should be considered as separate groups; the determining factor lies not merely in the culture represented, but even more in the national individuality evinced. This is the feature in which the art of earlier and later times was more or less deficient. The individuality of the Anglo-Saxons, like that of the Franks and Lombards, was somewhat repressed through contact with southern culture and through the effect of their conversion to Christianity upon their purely northern style. At the time of Bede we clearly mark the transition from a decorative to a didactic and representational art; the luxuriant design of the MSS. belongs to the days before theology; the northern joy in linear dexterity persists by the side of the foreign intrusive elements.

We should observe the extraordinary difference in temperament between the artists who executed the decoration in the Book of Kells and the Lindisfarne Gospel. We might take the one for a Celt, the other for a German.

III. *History of Development*

We can put the matter in a few words by saying that Anglo-Saxon Christian art developed no less independently of Rome than did that of the various countries of Hither Asia. Native elements were naturally preferred, but it need excite no surprise that oriental motives were welcomed in England by virtue of their analogy to those of northern art.

Professor Baldwin Brown's work, *The Arts in Early England*, so admirable in its methodical treatment of Anglo-Saxon buildings, so thorough in its investigation of their character and evolution, reveals the necessity for testing the current myth as to the course

73 Bradford-on-Avon Church ; interior. See p. 243.

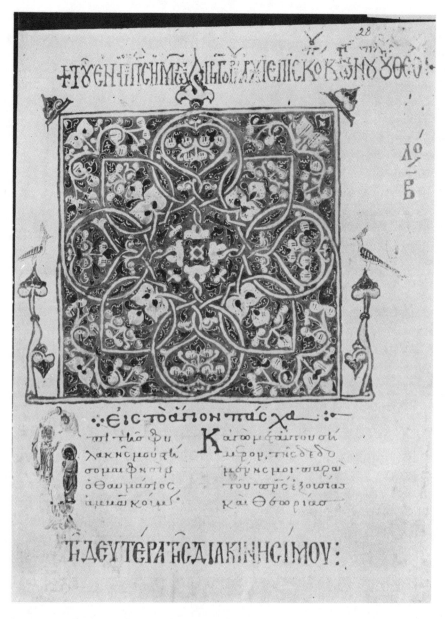

74   Heading of MS. Paris Bibl. Nat. 543, fol. 28ᵛ.   See p. 245.

followed by development in the field of early Christian architecture as a whole. This myth came into existence because points of small evolutionary significance, or even of no significance at all, were put into the foreground ; in the demarcation of the antique and the mediaeval periods, and, again, in relation to Vasari's division between Gothic and Renaissance art, points were treated as cardinal which were in fact of secondary importance.

Baldwin Brown rightly perceives that the basilica ' is strangely lacking in principles of growth ', and that the mediaeval movement could no more have started from basilican building than from Italy and Rome. He finds in Gaul, and later in the North, from the sixth to the ninth century, new social forces at work to re-design the long-naved church in combination with the centralized type. In England this attempt may be traced in the employment of both these constructional forms at Hexham. Professor Brown finds in the description of the Hexham churches analogies with the Octagon built by Constantine at Antioch, as it is described by Eusebius.[1]

The essential point is to be found in the negative admission that the timber-roofed basilica contained no principle of growth ; it lacked the power of organic development. I may add a supplementary argument of a more positive kind. This power of development existed in Hither Asia ; it was bound to make itself felt as soon as the step from wooden building to stone construction was taken in the North : this is a point which Professor Baldwin Brown has overlooked. The first effects ensued in the country churches. The large cathedrals of Anglo-Saxon episcopal cities and the great monastic churches are all unfortunately lost ; but though they freely used columns in the Hellenistic manner, it may be assumed that they also made tentative efforts towards true organic construction, because there were regions in which pioneer construction of this kind had already appeared.

Similar observations may be made in the case of high crosses. These do not connect with the Roman tradition interrupted about A.D. 450; if they did, the connexion would be unmistakable, however rough the work. As, however, despite the interval of two hundred years, these crosses rank with the best work produced during a period of half a millennium, we may perhaps infer not only the creative vitality of the local element, but also the importation into the island of some vigorous foreign influence

[1] *The Arts in Early England*, ii, pp. 320 ff.

such as that which I believe to have been exerted in Gaul
and the Frankish dominions by the Visigoths and their retinue
of Anatolian and Armenian craftsmen. The parallel examples
from the Orient which I was able to adduce do in fact suggest
that the general trend of influence in those times from the East
westwards was decisively felt in England. We have here merely
to inquire how such a penetration became possible.

For the sake of brevity, I have hitherto said nothing of the
earlier art which flourished on English soil. We discern its
character in the linear designs on the bronze ornaments of the La
Tène period, slant-cut and thus heightening the effect by a play
of light and shadow over the bright metal ; [1] we discern it too
in intrusive Teutonic features with their analogy to Scandinavian
art, and the motives which the Lombards and Franks brought with
them into Italy and Gaul. For the entry of oriental influences into
England two routes were available, the one by land, the other by
sea. More than once we have found traces suggesting a connexion
with Antioch. I refer especially to monastic types reaching
Ireland from the East Mediterranean by the usual maritime routes
followed by trade and colonization. These types were developing
in Ireland during the decisive years when the Anglo-Saxons were
conquering England and were preserved by a national Church
throughout the two centuries when Teutonic paganism established itself in that country. Does any other hypothesis explain
the fact that the Roman mission of Augustine and his successors
was promptly confronted with a formidable resistance, formidable
because it was offered not by paganism, but by an advanced
culture of East-Christian origin ? Does any other hypothesis
explain the appearance on the Continent of Irish monks as teachers
of Greek in the reign of Charles the Great ? How, if we reject it,
are we to account for the Gospels of Lindisfarne produced on that
English Iona half a century after the foundation of its monastery
in A.D. 632 ? For the luxuriant illumination of this book reveals
no single trace of Roman influence, but incontrovertible proofs
of all those germinative forces, native and oriental, the character
of which I have attempted to demonstrate in these pages. The
discovery in Northumberland of a Greek inscription relating to
a Syrian from Commagene suggests to me a confirmation, external
and material if you will, of influence from the theological centre

[1] For the origin of such methods *see* in *Zeitschrift für bildende Kunst*, 1921.
my *Altai-Iran*, and compare my paper

of Nisibis transmitted through Antioch. The oriental origin of Archbishop Theodore, a native of Tarsus, points in the same direction; so, finally, does the manner in which Cassiodorus adopted the theological system of Nisibis in his monastery of Vivarium, setting an example for all later monastic foundations and for the whole mediaeval culture of the West.

The second route, that by land, ran from the Black Sea across Russia to Scandinavia. It is characteristic that recent research ignores its very existence.[1] The reluctance of scholars used to the old ways to give it serious consideration is intelligible enough; an understanding of its significance throws too clear a light on the consecrated myth that all development comes from Rome; the debility of the whole tradition is too sharply exposed.

When Mazdaism had forced back Semitism and taken control of Hellenism, the North entered upon a period of independent development. What we call Gothic is the third art of northern origin which rose to greatness by its own merits. The Greek genius grew great in the South, the Iranian in the borderland between North and South, the Germanic in the North itself. In these pages we are concerned with the transition between the first and second of these achievements, during which, in so far as Christian art is concerned, I have shown Armenia to have been a main creative centre; the almost contemporary expansion of Islam on Iranian soil I here leave out of account. Throughout the centuries before the rise of Gothic art it was the function of Western Europe to act as a kind of mirror for all movements coming from the East; as early as the La Tène period, and more obviously yet after the Anglo-Saxon invasion, we find the characteristic signs of the exercise of this function. The North Sea area, previously far behind that of the Baltic, which was of decisive importance for the earlier Indo-Germanic migrations, now took the lead : interlaced bands, beast-ornament, the curious diagonal repeat-pattern treated by English stonemasons and illuminators in the same way as polygonal designs at a later time in Mohammedan art, finally initials in MSS.—these all travelled to and fro by land from one end of the North to the other. At present the source of the initials which dominate the ornament of manuscripts is not certainly known. I incline towards one connected with Iran, possibly the Manichaeans.

[1] Compare my *Altai-Iran*, and Arne's writings.

We cannot as yet definitely trace the course of the strong Antiochene and Armenian influences apparent in Anglo-Saxon art; enough that they exist. Their recognition will quicken the activities of research and heighten the satisfaction in the study of our own Northern art. One piece of evidence strikes me as deserving of attention. In the *Libellus Islandorum* there occur in a list of Icelandic bishops the names of three Armenians, Peter, Abraham, and Stephen.[1] The MS. in which this list occurs dates from the middle of the twelfth century; it was probably first written in Latin and later translated into Anglo-Saxon; the Armenian bishops probably belong to the eleventh century, and must certainly be placed before 1125. How did they reach Iceland? By the northern or by the southern route? And are these orientals only found in the North Sea area, or had they predecessors, perhaps as far back as the time of Bede?

IV. *The Subjective Side*

With regard to one aspect of artistic inquiry I have left the student to read between the lines; I refer to the aspect affecting the spectator himself, as opposed to the objective side of the monuments, their artistic character, and the evolutional forces which find utterance through them. I have said nothing of the attitude of aesthetic criticism towards Early Christian art, though from the outset I opposed the usual standpoint of scholars who assign the leading place to Rome and to a Christian classical art. Perhaps I may be permitted, in conclusion, to say a few words as to the manner in which this error has affected research in the field of Anglo-Saxon art.

In the second volume of his *Lombardic Art* Rivoira gave a classical exposition of the Roman theory. If, he asks, Britain and Ireland had not been devoid of native artists, would Benedict Biscop and Wilfrid have introduced foreign craftsmen? The North, needless to say, is regarded as incapable of developing unaided such an art as that which flourished in the time of Bede. Facts count for nothing against sophisticated Latin sources, or against that tissue of imagination spun by Church, Court, and Humanism together during the last few centuries, and undisturbed in its traditional academic supremacy by any illumination from geographical, historical, or economic sources. In the case of

---

[1] Communicated by Charles Singer. Cf. G. Vigfusson and F. York Powell, *Origines Islandicae*, i, Oxford, 1905, p. 299, note 2.

Rivoira, who was my highly respected friend, we have also to reckon with the influence of patriotic feeling for Italy, and above all for Rome, which inevitably warped his judgements.

We are now beginning to write the history of art-history; the one chance of improvement lies in a knowledge of the path already traversed. As long as we believe in the myth still repeated in the handbooks, there can be no prospect of freeing research from the dross of a fixed tradition. Who can say whether he has really stepped clear of antiquated beliefs and stands now upon firm ground ? The present book has only been concerned with a short period of two centuries in the first Christian millennium. Our study can only attain its definitive form by rising to a survey of the whole field in which its aims and activities are displayed. But no one nowadays has the leisure, whatever the ripeness of his supposed knowledge, to accomplish a task so immense as this.

When, a good many years ago, I defined my position with regard to the proverb ' all roads lead to Rome ', people chose to see in my action a political movement in favour of emancipation from Rome. To-day I am suspected of raising the ' battle-cry of the new aesthetic ' the moment I confront representational Southern art with a purely decorative art of the North. With the problems of beauty my line of inquiry has for the time being nothing to do. The present volume is absolutely unconcerned with them ; it is occupied with questions of essential character and of development without pretending in any way to pass judgements from the emotional or individual standpoint of the spectator. It is natural enough that there should be people who prefer the Acca Cross to the crosses at Ruthwell and Bewcastle, because its sculpture is composed of pure ornament without any admixture of edification in the form of Christian figure-subjects. For us the one important thing is to point out that in the time of Bede there actually existed monumental crosses which on no less than three of their sides renounced representation in favour of vine-scrolls geometrically planned.

There can be no doubt that artistically the British Isles belong not to Rome but to the North, and, their eastern part more especially, to the North Sea area. In the second half of the first millennium their relations with the North were closer than with the Continent immediately opposite their shores, whence the Roman mission under Augustine came. Ireland, with Scotland and Northumbria, felt both the northern influences coming from

Eurasia by the land route and the southern influences arriving by sea. The former resulted from the movement discussed in my *Altai-Iran und Völkerwanderung*,[1] the latter from the development which formed the subject of *Die Baukunst der Armenier und Europa*. Both together contributed to the remarkable Northumbrian art of Bede's time, which seems to be even more important than the pagan art of the North in Scandinavia, and beyond, as far as the seed-bed of Islamic art between Altai and Iran. We have to envisage the whole of this vast region as a single unit. We shall then be able to understand the immensity of the blunder made by a contemporary northern scholar whose eyes are for ever fixed on Rome, whether it be the imperial city of the first half-millennium after Christ, or the papal city of the second. Through this error he denies his own country, and her part in a northern artistic province in its degree at least as worthy of attention as the southern province in Hellenistic times, or the Armenian province on the borderland between South and North. Science has nothing to do with this or that artistic preference, this or that conception ; it demands of us one thing and one only, that we renounce our predilections, that we become the faithful instruments of facts, and that we leave the facts to speak for themselves. Only if we so act shall we cease to move round and round the old circles of the theorists ; only so shall we find the solid support of a development discovered by comparative research, and of a history based on a specialized and scientific knowledge. The first pre-requisites of this reform are a horizon which, theoretically at least, embraces all the world, and a point of view which does not suffer the obtrusion of particulars to obscure the vision of the whole.

[1] The reviewer of the German edition of the present book in the 'Literary Supplement' of *The Times* (June 16th, 1921) seems to have overlooked *Altai-Iran*. Otherwise he could hardly have suggested that I had paid too little attention to the work of Rostovtzeff.

BIBLIOGRAPHY

THE following list of works, arranged in chronological order, forms a continuation to my *Orient oder Rom*, 1901, *Kleinasien, ein Neuland*, 1903, *Koptische Kunst*, 1904, and the last section in vol. iii of *Byzantinische Denkmäler*, 1903, p. 119 f. (cf. periodical reports in the *Byzantinische Zeitschrift*). This list only includes such of my publications as bear upon the subject-matter of this volume.

1903. *Seidenstoffe aus Ägypten im Kaiser-Friedrich-Museum. Wechselwirkung zwischen China, Persien und Syrien in spätantiker Zeit.* (Jahrbuch der preussischen Kunstsammlungen, xxiv, 1903, pp. 147–78, with 19 illustrations in the text.)

1903. *Antinoë-Bawit und die deutsche Wissenschaft.* (Supplement, Allgemeine Zeitung, 12. September 1903, no. 206, pp. 493–5.)

1903. *Der Ursprung der 'romanischen' Kunst.* (Zeitschrift für bildende Kunst, N.F. xiv, pp. 295–8 ; 3 illustrations.)

1903. *Der angebliche Stillstand der Architekturentwicklung von Konstantin bis auf Karl den Grossen.* (Zeitschrift für Bauwesen, liii, 1903, pp. 629–34.)

1903. *Der Pinienzapfen als Wasserspeier.* (Mitteilungen des deutschen archäologischen Instituts in Rom, xviii, 1903, pp. 185–206, with 13 illustrations.)

1904. *Der Dom zu Aachen und seine Entstellung. Ein Protest.* Leipzig. Hinrichs. 1904.

1904. *Mschatta, Kunstwissenschaftliche Untersuchung.* (Jahrbuch der preussischen Kunstsammlungen, xxv, 1904, pp. 225–373 ; 4 plates and 104 illustrations in the text.)

1905. *Die Schicksale des Hellenismus in der bildenden Kunst.* (Neue Jahrbücher für das klassische Altertum, Geschichte und deutsche Literatur, xv, 1905, pp. 19–33, with 1 plate and 4 illustrations in the text.)

1905. *Die christliche Kunst in einigen Museen des Balkans.* (Österreichische Rundschau, iii, 1905, Part 30, pp. 158–65.)

1905. *Eine alexandrinische Weltchronik ; Text und Miniaturen eines griechischen Papyrus der Sammlung W. Goleniščev.* Adolf Bauer und Josef Strzygowski. (Denkschrift der Akademie der Wissenschaften in Wien, philosophisch-historische Klasse, li, 1905.)

1906. *Die Miniaturen des serbischen Psalters der königlichen Hof- und Staatsbibliothek in München. Nach einer Belgrader Kopie ergänzt und im Zusammenhange mit der syrischen Bilderredaktion des Psalters untersucht.* With an introduction by V. Jagić.

254   BIBLIOGRAPHY

(Denkschrift der Akademie der Wissenschaften in Wien, philosophisch-historische Klasse, lii, 1906.)

1906. *Spalato, ein Markstein der romanischen Kunst bei ihrem Übergange
vom Oriente nach dem Abendlande.* (Studien aus Kunst und
Geschichte, Friedrich Schneider gewidmet von seinen Freunden
und Verehrern. Freiburg i. Br., Herder, 1906, pp. 325–36;
6 plates and 10 illustrations.)

1906. Review of Walter Altmann's *Die römischen Grabaltäre der Kaiser-
zeit.* (Göttingische gel. Anzeigen, 1906, no. 11, pp. 908–14.)

1907. *Kleinarmenische Miniaturenmalerei. Die Miniaturen des Tübinger
Evangeliars MA. XIII, 1 vom Jahre 1113 bezw. 893 nach Christi
Geburt.* (Veröffentlichungen der königlichen Universitätsbiblio-
thek zu Tübingen, ii, 1907; 4 plates and 11 illustrations in the
text.)

1907. *A Sarcophagus of the Sidamara type.* (Journ. Hell. Stud. xxvii,
1907, p. 99 f.)

1907. *Christliche Antike.* (Supplement to the Münchener Allgemeine
Zeitung, 1907, no. 64, pp. 505–6.)

1907. *Bildende Kunst und Orientalistik.* (Memnon, i, 1907, pp. 9–18.)

1907. *Zum Christustypus.* (Der Türmer, ix, 1907, part 10, pp. 505–9.)

1907. *Der Kiosk von Konia.* (Zeitschrift für Geschichte der Architektur,
i, 1907, pp. 3–9.)

1907. *Amra als Bauwerk.* (Zeitschrift für Geschichte der Architektur,
i, 1907, pp. 57–64, with 3 illustrations.)

1907. *Amra und seine Malereien.* (Zeitschrift für bildende Kunst, N.F.
xxviii, 1907, pp. 213 ff., with 6 illustrations.)

1908. *Das orientalische Italien.* (Monatshefte für Kunstwissenschaft,
i, 1908, pp. 6–34, with 12 illustrations.)

1908. *Zur frühgermanischen Baukunst.* (Zeitschrift für Geschichte der
Architektur, i, part 10, 1908, pp. 247–50; 1 illustration.)

1908. *Muhammadan Art.* (Hastings' Encyclopaedia of Religion and
Ethics, i, pp. 874–81.)

1908. *Altchristliche Kunst.* (Die Religion in Geschichte und Gegenwart,
i, pp. 381–97.)

1908. *Oriental Carpets.* (Burlington Magazine, lxvii, 1907, pp. 25–8.)

1908. *Neuentdeckte Mosaiken von Salonik.* (Monatshefte für Kunstwissenschaft, i, 1908, pp. 1019–22; 2 illustrations.)

1909. *Die Geburtsstunde des christlichen Kirchenbaues.* (Supplement,
Münchener Allgemeine Zeitung, 1909, no. 51, pp. 417–19.)

1909. *Der signalförmige Tisch und der älteste Typus des Refektoriums.*
(' Wörter und Sachen ', i, 1909, pp. 70–80; 10 illustrations.)

1909. *Antike, Islam und Okzident.* (Neue Jahrbücher für das klassische
Altertum, 1909–10, xxiii, part 5, pp. 354–72; 19 illustrations.)

1909. *Die persische Trompenkuppel.* (Zeitschrift für Geschichte der
Architektur, iii, 1909, pp. 1–15; 13 illustrations.)

1910. *Wilperts Kritik meiner alexandrinischen Weltchronik.* (Römische Quartalschrift, xxiv, 1910, pp. 172–5.)

1910. *Der Eintritt Mesopotamiens in die Geschichte der christlichen Kunst.* (Monatshefte für Kunstwissenschaft, iii, 1910, pp. 1–4; with 5 illustrations.)

1910. *Die nachklassische Kunst auf dem Balkan.* (Jahrbuch des freien deutschen Hochstiftes zu Frankfurt am Main, 1910, pp. 30–43.)

1910. *Amida. Matériaux pour l'épigraphie et l'histoire musulmanes du Diyar-Bekr par Max van Berchem.* Beiträge zur Kunstgeschichte des Mittelalters von Nord-Mesopotamien, Hellas und dem Abendlande. With a supplement, 'The Churches and Monasteries of the Tur Abdin' by Gertrude L. Bell. (23 plates and 330 illustrations. Heidelberg. 1910. Karl Winter.)

1911. *Orientalische Kunst in Dalmatien.* (Brückner, 'Dalmatien und das Österreichische Küstenland'. Lectures delivered in March 1910, on the occasion of the first expedition of Vienna University. Vienna and Leipzig. Deuticke. 1911.)

1911. *Felsendom und Aksamoschee.* (Der Islam, ii, 1911, pp. 79–97; with 5 plates.)

1911. *Kunsthistorisches in H. Grothe,* 'Meine Vorderasienexpedition 1906–7', 1910, pp. ccxii–ccxxviii; with 15 illustrations in the text and one map.

1911. *Kara-Amid.* (Orientalisches Archiv, i, 1911, pp. 5–7; with 2 plates and 1 illustration in the text.)

1911. *Ornamente altarabischer Grabsteine in Kairo.* (Der Islam, ii, pp. 305–36; with 38 illustrations in the text.)

1911. *Das Problem der persischen Kunst.* (Orientalistische Literaturzeitung, xiv, 1911, col. 505–12.)

1911. *Ein zweites Etschmiadzin-Evangeliar.* (Huschardzan, Festschrift aus Anlass des 100-jährigen Bestandes der Mechitaristenkongregation in Wien, pp. 345–52, 1911; with 5 illustrations in the text and 2 plates.)

1912. *Der grosse hellenistische Kunstkreis im Innern Asiens.* (Zeitschrift für Assyriologie, xxvii, 1912, pp. 139–46, with 1 plate.)

1913. *Alhambra.* (Enzyklopädie des Islams, i, 1913, pp. 292–4.)

1913. *Ein Werk der Volkskunst im Lichte der Kunstforschung.* (Werke der Volkskunst, i, 1913, p. 12 f.; with 1 plate and 5 illustrations in the text.)

1913. *Ostasien im Rahmen vergleichender Kunstforschung.* (Ostasiatische Zeitschrift, ii, 1913, pp. 1–15.)

1914. *Erworbene Rechte der österreichischen Kunstforschung im nahen Orient.* (Österreichische Monatsschrift für den Orient, xl, 1914, pp. 1–14; with 9 illustrations.)

1914. *Zentralasien als Forschungsgebiet.* (Österreichische Monatsschrift für den Orient, xl, 1914, pp. 68–82; with 18 illustrations.)

1915. *Die Entstehung der Kreuzkuppelkirche.* (Zeitschrift für Geschichte der Architektur, vi, 1913, pp. 51–77 ; with 26 illustrations.)

1915. *Das Mausoleum König Karols von Rumänien.* (Österreichische Monatsschrift für den Orient, xli, 1915, pp. 46–8 ; 1 illustration.)

1915. *Die sasanidische Kirche und ihre Ausstattung.* (Monatshefte für Kunstwissenschaft, viii, 1915, pp. 349–65 ; with 5 illustrations in the text and 17 figures on 8 plates.)

1916. *Der Ursprung des trikonchen Kirchenbaues.* (Zeitschrift für christliche Kunst, xxviii, 1916, pp. 181–90 ; 1 plate and 10 illustrations.)

1916. *Ravenna als Vorort aramäischer Kunst.* (Oriens christianus, N.F. v, 1915, pp. 83–110 ; with 1 plate and 8 illustrations.)

1916. *Ornamentet hos de altaiska och iranska folken.* (Konsthistoriska Sällskapets publikation, Stockholm, 1916, pp. 5–18 ; with 11 illustrations.)

1916. *Die bildende Kunst des Ostens. Ein Überblick über die für Europa bedeutungsvollen Hauptströmungen.* 28 illustrations. Leipzig. Werner Klinkhardt. 1916. (Bibliothek des Ostens, ed. Kosch, vol. iii.)

1916. *Religion och personlighet i den bildande konsten.* (Ord och Bild, xxv, 1916, pp. 625 ff. ; with 12 illustrations.)

1917. *Altai-Iran und Völkerwanderung. Ziergeschichtliche Untersuchungen über den Eintritt der Wander- und Nordvölker in die Treibhäuser geistigen Lebens. Anknüpfend an einen Schatzfund in Albanien.* 229 illustrations and 10 plates. Leipzig. Hinrichs. 1917.

1917. Discussion of P. Frankl : *Die Entwicklungsphasen der neueren Baukunst,* and A. Schmarsow : *Kompositionsgesetze in der Kunst des Mittelalters.* (Theologische Literaturzeitung, 41, 1916, col. 61–4, and 513–16.)

1918. *Die bildende Kunst der Arier.* (Deutsche Warschauer Zeitung, nos. 59 and 60–1, 28 Feb. and 1 and 3 March 1918.)

1918. *Vergleichende Kunstforschung auf geographischer Grundlage.* (Mitteilungen der Geographischen Gesellschaft in Wien, lxi, 1918, pp. 20–48 and 153–8.)

1918. *Die Baukunst der Armenier und Europa. Ergebnisse einer vom Kunsthistorischen Institute der Universität Wien 1913 durchgeführten Forschungsreise, planmässig bearbeitet.* 2 vols. Vienna. A. Schroll & Co. 1918.

1918. *Persischer Hellenismus in christlicher Zierkunst.* (Repertorium für Kunstwissenschaft, xli, 1918, pp. 125–48 ; with 10 illustrations.)

1918. *Leonardo-Bramante-Vignola im Rahmen vergleichender Kunstforschung.* (Mitteilungen des Kunsthistorischen Instituts, Florence, iv, 1918, pp. 1–37 ; with 12 illustrations.)

1919. *Probleme der nordischen Kunst.* A lecture delivered to the 'Kunsthistorische Gesellschaft' at Stockholm. (Konsthistoriska Sällskapets publikation, 1919.)

1919. *Süden und Mittelalter.* (Monatshefte für Kunstwissenschaft, xii, 1919, pp. 313–23.)

1919. *Norden und Renaissance.* (Zeitschrift für bildende Kunst, xxxi, 1920, Jan.)

1920. *Neue Bahnen der Kunstforschung.* (Österreichische Rundschau, lxii, 1920, pp. 33–8.)

1920. *Ein Christusrelief und altchristliche Kapitelle in Bulgarien.* (Byzantinisch-neugriechische Jahrbücher, ed. by Nikos A. Bees I.)

1920. *Orpheus- und verwandte iranische Bilder.* (Contribution to Otto Kern: *Orpheus, eine religionsgeschichtliche Untersuchung.*)

WORKS OF COLLABORATORS

ERNST DIEZ:

1906. *Die Funde von Krungl und Hohenberg.* (Jahrbuch der k. k. Zentralkommission für Denkmalpflege, iv, 1906, pp. 202–27; 2 plates.)

1910. *Bemalte Elfenbeinkästen und Pyxiden der islamischen Kunst.* (Jahrbuch der preussischen Kunstsammlungen, xxxi, 1910, pp. 231–44; 1 plate and 4 illustrations.)

1914. *Isfahan.* (Zeitschrift für bildende Kunst, xxvi, 1914–15, pp. 90–104 and 113–28; 34 illustrations.)

1915. *Die Kunst der islamischen Völker.* (Akademische Verlagsgesellschaft Athenäum. Berlin-Neubabelsberg. 1915. 5 plates and 288 illustrations.)

1916. *Burgen in Vorderasien.* (Der Burgwart, 1916, pp. 90–101; 10 illustrations.)

1918. *Churasanische Baudenkmäler.* Vol. i. (Berlin. Dietrich Reimer, 1918. 5 colour and 36 other plates, and 40 illustrations.) Vol. vii of the works of the 'Kunsthistorisches Institut' of Vienna University (Lehrkanzel Strzygowski).

L. POTPESCHNIGG:

1912. *Aus der Kindheit bildender Kunst.* Leipzig. B. G. Teubner. (Saemannschriften für Erziehung und Unterricht. Part 2.)

1915. *Einführung in die Betrachtung von Werken der bildenden Kunst.* Wien. Schulbücherverlag. 1915. Works of the 'Institut'. Vol. ii.

1917. *Planmässige Wesensforschung in der Dichtkunst.* (Neue Jahrbücher für das klass. Altertum. Leipzig, 1917, vol. xl, part 2, pp. 209–34.)

RICHARD KURT DONIN:

1915. *Romanische Portale in Niederösterreich.* (Jahrbuch des Kunsthistorischen Instituts der Zentralkommission für Denkmalpflege.) Works of the 'Institut'. Vol. iv. Vienna. Anton
Schroll & Co. 1915.

HEINRICH GLÜCK:

1916. *Ein islamisches Heiligtum auf dem Ölberg. Beitrag zur Geschichte
des islamischen Raumbaues.* (Der Islam, iv, part 4, p. 328.)

1916. *Der Breit- und Langhausbau in Syrien, auf kulturgeographischer
Grundlage bearbeitet.* With 49 illustrations and 4 plates. (Zeit-
schrift für Geschichte der Architektur, Beiheft 14. Heidelberg.
C. Winter. 1916.) Works of the 'Institut', vol. vi.

1917. *Die beiden 'Sasanidischen' Drachenreliefs, Grundlagen zur seld-
schukischen Skulptur.* With 5 plates. (Publications of the
Musée Impérial Ottoman, part 4. Constantinople. Ahmed
Ihsan & Co., 1917.)

1917. *Türkische Kunst.* Lecture delivered at the session of the Hungarian
Institute of Science at Constantinople, 5 May 1917. (Mitteilungen des ungarischen wissenschaftlichen Institutes in Konstan-
tinopel. 1917. Part 1. With 26 illustrations. Budapest–
Constantinople.)

1920. *Das Hebdomon und seine Reste in Makriköi.* Contributions to the
comparative study of art, published by the 'Kunsthistorisches
Institut' of Vienna University (Lehrkanzel Strzygowski).
Part 1.

1920. *Die Bäder Konstantinopels und ihre Stellung in der Baugeschichte
des Morgen- und Abendlandes.* (Vienna, 1921.) Works of the
'Institut', vol. xii.

ARTUR WACHSBERGER:

1916. *Stilkritische Studien zur Wandmalerei Chinesisch-Turkestans.* (Ostasiatische Zeitschrift. Special publications, no. 2. Berlin.
Osterheld & Co., 1916.) Works of the 'Institut', vol. iii.

KARL WITH:

1919. *Buddhistische Plastik in Japan bis zum Beginne des 8. Jahrhunderts.
Ergebnisse einer 1913–14 vom Kunsthistorischen Institute der
Wiener Universität (Lehrkanzel Strzygowski) nach Ostasien unter-
nommenen Forschungsreise.* Kunstverlag Anton Schroll & Co.,
1919. Works of the 'Institut', vol. xi.

The following works of the *Kunsthistorisches Institut* of the University of Vienna (Lehrkanzel Strzygowski) have been published since 1920:

Vol. iii. K. Ginhardt: *Das christliche Kapitell zwischen Antike und Spätgotik*. Vienna, 1923.

Vol. iv. J. Strzygowski: *Kunde, Wesen, Entwicklung*. Mit Beiträgen von E. Diez, K. Ginhardt, H. Glück, T. Plutzar, M. Stiassny, E. Wellesz. Vienna, 1922.

Vol. xiv. M. Dimand: *Die Verzierung der koptischen Wollwirkereien. Strömungen des Weltverkehres im Kreise der Mittelmeerkunst*. Leipzig, Hinrichs, 1921.

Vol. xvii. H. Berstl: *Das Raumproblem in der altchristlichen Malerei*. (Lüthgen's 'Forschungen zur Formgeschichte der Kunst'.) 1920.

Vol. xviii. S. Kramrisch: *Wesen der altindischen Kunst*. (This will probably appear in Lüthgen's 'Forschungen zur Formgeschichte der Kunst'.)

Vol. xx. J. Strzygowski: *Die Krisis der Geisteswissenschaften*. Vienna, 1923.

Vol. xxii. C. Petranu: *Inhaltsproblem und Kunstgeschichte*. Vienna, 1921.

Vol. xxiii. E. Diez: *Persien, Islamische Baukunst in Churasan*. 1923.

Vol. xxv. Josef Strzygowski: *Die indischen Miniaturen im Schlosse Schönbrunn*. Vienna, 1923.

Studien zur Kunst des Ostens, Josef Strzygowski zum sechzigsten Geburtstage von seinen Freunden und Schülern. Edited by Heinrich Glück. Vienna and Hellerau, 1923.

INDEX